Baedeker

Copenhagen

Hints for using the Guide

Following the tradition established by Karl Baedeker in 1844, important buildings and works of art, places of natural beauty and sights of particular interest, as well as hotels and restaurants of especially high quality, are distinguished by one ★ or two ★★.

To make it easier to locate the various places listed in the "A to Z" section of the Guide, their co-ordinates are shown in red at the head of each entry: e.g., Tivoli G/H 7.

Coloured lines down the right-hand side of the page are an aid to finding the main heading in the Guide: blue stands for the Introduction (Nature, Culture, History, etc.), red for the "A to Z" section, and yellow indicates Practical Information.

Only a selection of hotels, restaurants and shops can be given; no reflection is implied therefore on establishments not included.

In a time of rapid change it is difficult to ensure that all the information given is entirely accurate and up-to-date, and the possibility of error can never be entirely eliminated.

Although the publishers can accept no responsibility for inaccuracies and omissions, they are constantly endeavouring to improve the quality of their Guides and are therefore always grateful for criticisms, corrections and suggestions for improvement.

Preface

This pocket guide to Copenhagen is one of the new generation of Baedeker guides.

Baedeker pocket guides, illustrated throughout in colour, are designed to meet the needs of the modern traveller. They are quick and easy to consult, with the principal features of interest described in alphabetical order and practical details about location, opening times, etc. normally shown in the margin.

Although this particular volume has Copenhagen as its subject, a number of places of interest in Zealand (Seeland) are also described. With its traditional establishments mingling happily with more modern cultural centres and events of all kinds, Denmark's capital is truly a cheerful and lively city with a special charm all of its own.

This city guide is divided into three parts. The first part gives a general account of Copenhagen, its citizens, the Danish Parliament, culture, transport, economy, Danish design, famous people and history. A brief selection of quotations leads

The Frilandsmuseet (Open Air Museum) in Lyngby, to the north of Copenhagen, documents traditional living and working conditions in rural Denmark, while the National Historical Museum housed in Frederiksborg Palace portrays the history of the Danish monarchy.

into the second part where the principal places of interest in Copenhagen and Zealand are described. The third part contains a variety of practical information designed to help visitors to find their way about and make the most of their stay. Both "Copenhagen from A to Z" and the Practical Information section are given in alphabetical order.

Baedeker pocket guides, which are regularly updated, are noted for their concentration on essentials and their "user-friendly" style. They contain many coloured illustrations and specially drawn plans, and at the back of the book will be found a large plan of the city. Each main entry in the A to Z section gives the co-ordinates of the square on the plan in which the particular feature can be located. Users of this guide, therefore, should have no difficulty in finding what they want to see.

Contents

Baedeker Specials

Wonderful

Copenhagen is not a vast metropolis like Paris or London – you can easily walk through the city centre in an hour or so – but nevertheless Denmark's capital possesses a wonderful variety of places of interest and cultural activities. The lively cultural scene embraces many famous events, famous virtuosos perform at the annual jazz festival, and the traditional ballet performances by the Royal Theatre Company have been world-famous for many years. Probably the most popular attraction is the daily Changing of the Guard outside Amalienborg Palace – with luck you may even see Her Majesty Queen Margrethe II. Old Copenhagen, picturesque Nyhavn, the very heart of the city, is at the same time cosmopolitan, lively and intimate. Its lovingly restored house fronts look down on old three-masted sailing ships lying at anchor in the "museum harbour". The Danes describe Nyhavn as "hyggelig", which means more or less "very friendly" but furthermore conveys the charming atmosphere of this colourful harbourside street. From here stroll to the island of Slotsholmen, where the Danish Parliament sits in Christiansborg Palace, and then on to Strøget, Denmark's longest street and a veritable shoppers' paradise. Browse in antique shops or avant-garde boutiques and treat yourself to an example of Danish design – blue-painted porcelain, Jensen silver or perhaps a piece of Holmegaard glass. If you fancy something to eat there is a wide choice of excellent restaurants, friendly pubs and pretty cafés. Those on a culinary journey of discovery simply must try the delicious varieties of the legendary *smørrebrød* with a beer fresh from the keg – Carlsberg

Børsen

The tails of four dragons are intertwined around the tower of the old Stock Exchange.

Ny Carlsberg Glyptotek

– with its Mediterranean Winter Garden

Christiania

The drop-out society of the "Free State of Christiania"

Copenhagen

and Tuborg are among the local breweries. The city's most famous symbol is the "Little Mermaid", based on the story by Hans Christian Andersen. The sight of the bronze mermaid gazing longingly out to sea may well awaken memories of fairy-tales read during childhood. At night the lights of the Tivoli, Copenhagen's most popular amusement park and culture centre for all ages, make it appear like a fairy-tale from "A Thousand and One Nights". In Rosenborg Palace the Danish crown jewels can be seen, in Louis J. Tussaud's Wax Museum visitors can "meet" many illustrious people, while in the Statens Museum for Kunst (State Art Museum) there is a representative sample of

European art covering seven centuries. The pictures exhibited in the Louisana Art Museum are regarded by the art world as unique examples of 20th c. works. Or perhaps you are more interested in ancient treasures and Danish sculpture? Both are there to be admired in the Ny Carlsberg Glyptotek which was enlarged in 1996, while Northern Europe's largest museum, the recently extended National Museum, displays collections illustrating Danish culture from the Stone Age to the present day. Those who explore the greener northern parts of Copenhagen can experience rural life of days gone by in the Frilandsmuseet (Open Air Museum), follow in the literary footsteps of Karen Blixen in Rundstedlund or wander through the world's oldest amusement park, the Bakken. In Zealand a visit to a castle or palace is almost obligatory – Frederiksborg Slot is Denmark's most beautiful Renaissance palace, Kronborg Slot the stage for the Hamlet tragedy – and, of course, do not forget to spend a long sunny day on the beach!

Tussaud's Wax Museum

The famous figures include Hans Christian Andersen with some of his fairy-tale characters

Facts and Figures

General

Denmark as holiday destination

Denmark is considered by many visitors as the embodiment of holidays, pure summer sensation and pleasant tranquillity. Here you can take your time – everything is a little bit more pleasant and cosier than elsewhere. When you think of Denmark you think of fresh sea air, warm days on the beach and a whole host of fun for children, a cultural scene of world class quality, LEGO, beer and porcelain, green meadows, throbbing city life and idyllic seaside homes.

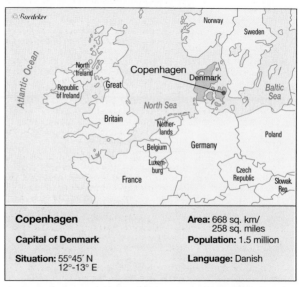

Copenhagen	**Area:** 668 sq. km/ 258 sq. miles
Capital of Denmark	**Population:** 1.5 million
Situation: 55°45′ N 12°-13° E	**Language:** Danish

Kingdom of Denmark

Like a bridge or "bird migration line" between central Europe and Scandinavia is the Kingdom of Denmark, which consists of the peninsula of Jutland and 474 islands, barely 100 of which are inhabited. It has a short land frontier of only 68km/42 miles with Schleswig-Holstein, as opposed to a total coastline of some 7300km/4560 miles, including about 5000km/3125 miles of bathing beaches. What is more, nowhere within Denmark is more than 52km/32 miles away from the sea. Holidaymakers can choose between the gentle dunes of the Baltic beaches and the rougher waves of the North Sea coast. The adjoining seas, known as the Kattegat and the Skagerrak, mark the transition between the Baltic and the North Sea. The Faroe Islands and Greenland are overseas territories belonging to Denmark.

Danish Capital Copenhagen

Copenhagen is the capital of the oldest European monarchy. It is a charming modern metropolis, which proves that cosmopolitan flair

◀ *View of the Christiansborg Palace*

has nothing to do with the size of a city, especially not one which, since 1966, has been the cultural capital of Europe. Copenhagen stretches out partly on the eastern shore of Zealand, the largest Danish island (area 7525sq.km/2905sq.miles), and partly on the island of Amager in the Øresund.

It is the seat of Parliament (Folketing) and the country's government, and the royal family have resided here in the Amalienborg Palace since 1794. First mention of the Danish capital is made in a document of 1043 under the name "Havn". In 1167 Bishop Absalon had a fortress built near the fisherman's harbour, and nearby a lively trading centre quickly developed with the name "Købmændes Havn" (Merchant's Harbour).

As regards size and number of inhabitants, Copenhagen is rather small compared to other capital cities. The actual area of the city of Copenhagen comprises the community of Copenhagen with 88sq.km/34sq.miles and the community of Frederiksberg with 9sq.km/3½sq.miles. The population is approximately 580,000. In addition, there is the "department" of Copenhagen in which eighteen communities are merged. This enlarged district has a total area of 571sq.km/220sq.miles and a population of almost 623,000. Greater Copenhagen, called in Danish "hovedstadsområdet" (capital and surroundings), is therefore made up of the two communities of Copenhagen and Frederiksberg together with 26 other communities. The area of the capital is thus 668sq.km/258sq.miles and the total population 1.5 million. This makes Copenhagen the largest city in Scandinavia – more than one quarter of the country's population lives in the capital and its surroundings. Its development into a city of more than one million inhabitants is not primarily due to population growth. It resulted principally from the expansion of the city area and the incorporation of adjoining communities. Indeed, at present, the city is losing about 15,000 inhabitants a year.

About 94% of the population belong to the Evangelical-Lutheran national church, whose nominal head is the Queen.

Area and population

One unusual thing about Copenhagen is that within the city area lies the community of Frederiksberg, an independent authority with its own mayor, town council, town hall and administration, and yet otherwise integrated into the economic structure and transport system of Copenhagen. The following communities with their own administration belong to the department of Copenhagen: Albertslund, Ballerup, Brøndby, Dragør, Gentofte, Gladsaxe, Glostrup, Herlev, Hvidovre, Hoje-Tåstrup, Ishøj, Ledøje-Smørum, Lyngby-Tårbæk, Rødovre, Søllerød, Tårnby, Vallensbæk and Værlose.

Copenhagen, in the narrower sense, is governed by a council of 55 citizens, determined by municipal elections. These appoint from among their number a Chief Burgomaster (Mayor) and six assistant burgomasters who, as full-time local government officials, form the city executive. These elected representatives have the same voting rights as all other council members.

Since the individual communities of Copenhagen enact their own independent legislation (particularly in the fiscal area), there is a certain tendency for people to move into communities with more favourable tax laws.

Administration

The Danish Parliament

Under the 1953 Constitution, Denmark is a democratic parliamentary monarchy. The throne is hereditary, and under the 1953 Act of Succession the right of succession for females was restored.

Constitution

According to the constitution the monarch, that is the Danish head of state, has "supreme authority in all the affairs of the kingdom and exercises this through his ministers". Accordingly, sole responsibility

Monarch

lies with the relevant ministers. The monarch's most important political tasks are: to represent the kingdom of Denmark abroad; to initiate and pass laws; to frame laws temporarily whenever Parliament (Folketing) cannot assemble, so long as such laws conform to the constitution; to call a general election (though only at the instigation of the Prime Minister) and to appoint the Prime Minister and the Cabinet. The Queen of Denmark is Margarethe II (of the House of Glücksburg, Schleswig-Holstein–Sonderburg–Glücksburg line). In 1997 she celebrated the 25th anniversary of her accession to the throne.

Council of State and Council of Ministers

In the Council of State (consisting of monarch and ministers) all laws and important government measures are dealt with. The Cabinet is known as the Council of Ministers. Each individual minister, as head of a department, is responsible to Parliament and can be forced out of office by a no-confidence vote. Furthermore, any minister can, in the State Court and at the instigation of the monarch or of Parliament, be charged with maladministration.

Prime Minister

The Prime Minister is not elected by Parliament, he is appointed by the Queen after consultation with party representatives. If he risks being voted out on a no-confidence motion, he can counter by calling for a general election. These two provisions allow even minority governments in Denmark to continue in office for prolonged periods.

Folketing

Since the abolition of the first chamber (Landsting) in 1953, the Parliament (Folketing) has been the sole representative and legislative body. Its 179 members – including two each from the Faroes and Greenland – are elected for a four-year term on the basis of universal suffrage. All men and women of eighteen and above have the right to vote. The dissolution of Parliament is mandatory whenever any change in the constitution is made.

Commerce and Industry

Commercial centre

Copenhagen is the centre of Danish commerce and industry (which are entirely in private hands) and the headquarters of numerous banks and industrial firms. More than two thirds of Danish industrial products are exported and half of these go to EU countries.

Branches of industry

Premium beer is among Denmark's leading products. It is made by the two breweries Tuborg and Carlsberg (now amalgamated) and exported world-wide. Danish design (see pp. 18–22) is a part of Danish culture and enjoys international fame. The functional design of basic household commodities, which characterise and brighten up house, home and office, represents productive innovation and a special feel for design and colour. This applies not only to furniture, silver, glass and porcelain but also to ship and bridge construction, electronics and architecture.

Transport

Port

The freight and passenger traffic using the port of Copenhagen (area approximately 450 hectares/1110 acres), which for centuries made the Danish capital one of the leading industrial centres in the Baltic area has, since the Second World War, been in sharp decline. When, in the post-war period, many ocean-going vessels were no longer able to put into harbour because of its shallow depth (10m/33ft), the importance of Copenhagen diminished in favour of other ports such as Rotterdam, Gothenburg and Hamburg – Rotterdam harbour has, by comparison, a depth of 22m/72ft. Furthermore, as in other cities,

The Folketing: the sole representative body of the Danish Parliament

An artist decorating the typical blue painted ware of the Royal Porcelain Manufactory

Shopping arcade at the Airport

a large volume of goods traffic moved over to lorry and train. As a result, the significance of the port is nowadays confined essentially to the Copenhagen area. In recent years, however, increasingly frequent efforts have been made to revive the harbour area, and these efforts have already produced the first increases in the volume of parcel freight, not forgetting the numerous cruise ships which drop anchor by the beautiful harbour front of Langelinie. The port is divided into three different areas according to use:

Yderhavnen and Nordhavnen: container ports for freight transport, shipyards.

Frihavn: principally warehouses.

Inderhavnen: passenger port with Customs office, administration blocks and converted former harbour buildings, now housing hotel accommodation, service industries and flats.

Sydhavnen: industrial port with industrial firms, office-blocks, owner-occupied flats and hotels.

Passenger shipping services

A regular ferry service operates from Copenhagen to Sweden (Tuborg Havn–Landskrona: Dragør/Amager–Limhamn), to Norway (Dragør/Amager–Oslo) and within Denmark to Bornholm (Dragør/Amager–Rønne). No direct ferry link exists between Copenhagen's harbours and Germany. Denmark's capital can be reached by boat via the car ferry from Sweden (Landskrona, Limhamn) and Norway (Oslo). The car and train ferry from Puttgarden to Rødbyhavn takes one hour, from Rostock to Gedser two hours, but by rapid ferry only 70 minutes. Passenger ships sail from Copenhagen to Helsingør and hydrofoils provide an additional connection between Copenhagen and Sweden (Malmö, Hven).

Airport

Copenhagen's Kastrup airport is today among the busiest in Europe. It lies on the island of Amager, some 10km/6 miles south of the city centre. Kastrup is currently the sixth largest airport in Europe, and by the year 2000 its passenger capacity is set to rise to fifteen or sixteen million. The terminals and waiting-rooms have already been enlarged, but the principal attraction is the modern departure lounge in the main building, with a shopping centre in the style of Copenhagen's pedestrian precinct ("Strøget"), which offers space to more than 20 shops. The airport's duty-free arcade – in contrast to normal price levels in Denmark – offers some of the best value for money in the whole of Europe.

Zealand and Copenhagen have been linked to the mainland since 1997 by train, and since 1998 also by car, by means of two colossal bridges (toll-paying) and a twin tunnel – an achievement of architectural, technological and logistical brilliance. In October 1994 the breakthrough stage was reached of a 7.7km/4¾ mile long rail tunnel. This is a twin-tunnel crossing running beneath the east channel of the Great Belt between Halskov and the small island of Sprogø, and since 1997 it has enabled passenger and freight trains to reduce by one hour the current ferry time between Fünen (Fyn) and Seeland (Zealand). Since 1998 motorists have also been able to drive straight through from Flensburg to Copenhagen and cross the Great Belt without a ferry in 15 minutes (hitherto it took 90 minutes). From Knudshoved (on the island of Fyn) cars and trains initially travel side by side across the 6.6km/4 mile long West Bridge (which rests on 62 flat concrete piers) to the artificially widened and dyke-protected sandy island of Sprogo. From here trains go through the aforementioned rail tunnel to Halskov on Zealand, whereas cars and lorries will continue their journey across the 6.8km/4 mile long four-lane East Bridge, which spans the busy shipping route of the Great Belt at a maximum height of 65m/213ft. Environmental problems connected with this giant project (construction costs about three million pounds sterling) are coming to light because of the expansion of the island of Sprogø (by sand deposition) to almost four times its original area, and also because of the bridge piers (weighing up to 6000 tonnes), which have been sunk into the seabed and which will bring about changes in the currents of the Great Belt. Even the oxygen supply of the already badly affected Baltic sea is being impaired, but a deepening of the Belt should counteract this development.

Bridge across the Great Belt

Since 1995 work has been going on to create a road and rail link across the Øresund to the neighbouring country of Sweden. The 17km/10 mile long bridge and tunnel combination, resting on 51 piers and two pylons, is due for completion by the year 2000. With its massive twin-deck bridge carrier (the lower level will carry trains whilst the upper level is reserved for lorries) and its pylons approximately 200m/656ft high, this construction will become a landmark visible from a great distance. While conservationists are concerned about the consequences for bird protection areas and fish stocks, supporters of the project are hoping that this new arterial system will invigorate the entire Øresund region from Copenhagen to Malmö in Sweden. Then, at the beginning of the next millennium, the proposed crossing of the Fehmarn Belt between Puttgarden and Rodby/Lolland is set finally to realise the age-old dream of achieving the "bird migration line" – no matter how eider ducks and cod fish react.

Bridge across the Øresund

Some motorways reach the outskirts; others extend right into the city itself. Main routes from and to Germany:
The E47 to Koge and Rødbyhavn, then by ferry to Puttgarden: exit Nykøbing, then on to Gedser, and finally by ferry to Rostock (E55);
The E20 to Korsor, and then over the new bridge to Nyborg (on the island of Fyn): thence across Jutland to the Danish/German border at Flensburg; The E47 also runs north to Helsingør.
    One trunk road which is important to domestic Danish transport is the expressway (21/23), which runs from Copenhagen westward via Roskilde to Kalundborg (from where there is a ferry to Jutland).
    A well-developed suburban rail system (see map at back of guide) connects Copenhagen city centre with the suburbs, supplemented by an extensive bus network.

Motorways and local public transport

Art and Culture

Cultural Scene

City of culture
and flair

Nowhere else in the country can one gain the same access to Danish culture as in Copenhagen. The busy capital offers an endless variety of sights and experiences for every taste: famous museums and fabulous entertainment at Tivoli and Co.; idyllic summer days to be spent in the tranquillity of the parks at Nyhavn and in the beautiful restaurant courtyards – a veritable paradise for shoppers frequenting Europe's longest pedestrian precinct, "Strøget"; an intense musical and theatrical life – not forgetting, of course, Danish cuisine to tempt the palate, as well as a lively café culture.

Utopia for
museum-goers

In the city centre alone 50 museums of varied sizes inform the visitor about high quality art and antique toys, eroticism and world records, the crown jewels, Danish design and a great deal more. In 1996, Copenhagen rightly carried the official title of "Cultural Capital of Europe". In order to create the appropriate setting, substantial renovations and new building works were carried out, including extensions to the Ny Carlsberg Glyptotek, the State Art Museum and the Royal Library, as well as the construction of a new Museum of Modern Art called "The Ark", situated some 20km/12 miles south of the city in Ishøj.

Ballet legends
and hot jazz

The Royal Theatre, with its performances of drama, opera and especially ballet, enjoys worldwide renown. Linked with the Royal Danish Ballet are the names of illustrious dancers and choreographers such as Landé, who in 1726 staged the first danced intermezzi in Copenhagen, August Bournonville, the predominant ballet master of the 19th century, John Cranko, Neumeier, Lærkesen and Lander, as well as the legendary dancing stars Erik Bruhn and Peter Schaufuss. For visitors without a good command of Danish, a visit to the Royal Theatre's ballet performances is strongly recommended – above all the Bournonville ballet "Et Folkesagn" – today with the stage set of Margarethe II. A typical form of Danish entertainment are the "Revyen", a blend of music, dance, cabaret and satire, which are performed in the amusement parks of Bakken and Tivoli. Also worth a mention are the numerous street musicians, the "Vise-sangere" and live musical events in the bars and variety theatres of the old town, as well as the wide range on offer for cinema-goers, particularly in the modern cinema complex on the Axeltorv. High points in the calendar are the Copenhagen Summer Festival, with a varied programme of events and numerous open-air activities, as well as the much-praised Jazz Festival which, for ten days in July, stages jam sessions of international quality throughout the whole city.

Royal shopping

In Copenhagen a shopping expedition can turn into a pleasurable relaxation. Everything the heart desires can be reached on foot: from the avant-garde in Larsbyørnstræde to designer clothes in Gønnegade, books in Fiolstræde, stores and exclusive shops on the 1.8km/1 mile long Strøget (shopping precinct), as well as Strædet, Nyhavn and Farvergade, all of which constitute the undisputed European Mecca for antiques across the whole price range.

City of Jazz

Copenhagen has earned its reputation as a city of jazz mainly through the Jazz Festival which has been held here every year since 1979 and is without doubt one of the highlights of the Danish musical scene. Jazz enthusiasts come to Copenhagen at all times of the year in order to enjoy their favourite music, but the real "fireworks" occur during the programme of events held from the first Friday to the second Sunday in July, when the streets, squares and parks of the Danish capital provide the arena for some excellent jazz concerts. Fans of "swing" met up in Copenhagen back in the late 1950s, and in the mid-1960s such famous soloists as the tenor saxophonists Stan Getz, Dexter Gordon and Ben Webster made guest appearances in the legendary Café Montmartre in Store Regnegade. In 1976 the Jazzhus

Montmartre in Nørregade was re-opened and soon became a popular meeting-place for international artistes as well as innovative Danish ensembles. Traditional jazz is also played in many bars and cafés, including the famous De Tre Musketerer on Nikolaj Plads, while the Montmartre and the Copenhagen Jazz House, opened in 1991, concentrate mainly on modern jazz. In addition to the above mentioned highlights, there are of course some spontaneous jam sessions at the annual festival, when such illustrious jazz musicians as the trumpeter Wynton Marsalis or the bass player Nils-Henning Ørsted Petersen may join in with unknown amateurs – a wonderfully casual and relaxed atmosphere which makes an unforgettable impression on the whole audience, whether jazz enthusiasts or not.

The "Blue in Green" group at the Copenhagen Jazz Festival

Danish Design

Visitors to Denmark are constantly fascinated by the charming inter-action of colours and shapes, and also by the beautiful and func-tional design that is evident in so many different areas of the Danes' daily life. Tastefully decorated window-ledges, delightful still-life fig-ures in simple ceramic pots, coffee-pots by Bodum or the Royal Porcelain Manufactory, antique Jensen silver and modern PH lamps, children's highchairs and garden furniture from trip-trap or hi-fi equipment from Bang & Olufsen – all gems of the art of Danish design. The hallmarks of Danish design were, and still are, its out-standing craftsmanship and later the industrial quality of its prod-ucts, the artistic design (numerous designers were formerly eminent artists of their time) and the value of "functionality" (demonstrated by Kaare Klint), following the principle that "the form of an object fol-lows its function". Anyone wishing to gain an overall view of the whole subject of Danish design should visit the Museum of Art in Industry in Bredgade.

Royal Copenhagen

One of the most important amalgamations in the evolution of Copenhagen design took place in 1985, when the Royal Porcelain Manufactory merged with Georg Jensen's silverworks and the Holmegaard glassworks to form "Royal Copenhagen". The famous porcelain, silver and glass products can be obtained at Amagertorv 6.

Ceramics

The history of Danish ceramics is closely connected with the two famous Copenhagen porcelain factories, the Royal Porcelain Manufactory and the Bing & Grondahl porcelain factory.

Royal Porcelain Manufactory

The Royal Porcelain Manufactory, founded by the apothecary Frantz Heinrich Müller on May 1st 1775 (at the instigation of the dowager queen Juliane Marie) was for a long time in the possession of the royal family. The firm chose as its porcelain mark three wavy lines, symbolising the three Danish sea channels, the Øresund, the Great Belt and the Little Belt. The Royal Porcelain Manufactory achieved its reputation above all through its superb tableware and its artistic underglaze decoration. The oldest service, the so-called "Mussel-malet" (Blue Painted), with decoration based on Meissen models has, apart from a few modifications, been produced ever since the year of foundation. The first large-scale order received – a 2600-piece table service – was the "Flora Danica", designed in 1789, and com-missioned by the Danish crown prince Frederik as a gift for the Russian tsarina, Katharina II, but she died before its completion. The tableware, which is still produced up to the present day, was then named after the botanical reference work of the same title, which deals with the flora of Denmark. The decorative technique of under-glaze painting, in which, before the application of the feldspar glaze, a design is put on using paint akin to watercolours, for technical reasons allows the use of only a few colours. Hence the derivation of the name "Blue Copenhagen Porcelain".

The Royal Porcelain Manufactory enjoyed its heyday under the management of Arnold Krog towards the end of the 19th century. Characteristic of this period are the many Danish landscape motifs. The fairly recent development of the Functional and Discrete was given significant impetus by the ceramicist Gertrud Vasegaard with

The peak of Danish design – decorative porcelain to grace a festive table ▶

her "Gemma" and "Gemina" tableware (designed in 1960), as well as by the architect Grethe Meyer with her faïence ware "Blue Border" (1962) and "Red Pot" (1981). Less functionality is to be seen in the works of the goldsmith Arje Griegst who, amongst other things, introduced in 1978 his "Konkylie" service.

Bing & Grøndahl
porcelain factory

In the porcelain factory of Bing & Grøndahl (established 1853) the painter Pietro Krohn introduced the technique of underglazing. His "Heron" service, designed in 1888, was developed with the collaboration of Effie Hergermann-Lindencrone and of Fanny Garde, who in 1901 created the famous "Seagull" service. The factory's "Blue Painted" service – with its three-part design, contrasting with the four-part design of the Royal Porcelain Manufactory – was conceived by the painter F. A. Hallin (who in 1895 also created the first "Christmas Plate", called "Behind the Frosty Window-pane"). Representatives of modern Functionalism in the 1930s were the silversmith Kay Bojsen and the artist Ebbe Sadolin with her white tableware, who managed her designs without coloured decoration. The sculptor Henning Koppel initially also produced pure white services, but later worked in addition with coloured compositions (e.g. "Comet", 1978). Even more practically orientated work was introduced by the ceramic artist Erik Magnussen, whose everyday tableware "Hank" (1972) is used by the Danish National Railway.

Silver

Georg Jensen
silverworks

In the early years of the silverworks established by Georg Jensen in 1904, Jensen himself, together with the painter Johan Rohde, created the designs that were to point the way ahead. From the outset the firm produced cutlery, dishes, bowls and jewellery. The skilled goldsmith and sculptor Georg Jensen, who may be regarded as among the leading silver designers of his time, created the highly praised silver cutlery "Antiquity" (1906). Other acknowledged names associated with the silverworks were Harald Nielsen, Sigvard Bernadotte, Magnus Stephensen, Søren Georg Jensen and Henning Koppel, renowned for his ceramic designs (see above) and his bowls and dishes. Jensen, in producing countless functional objects, transformed the silver into new forms of expression (e.g. "Fish Platter", 1954). As silver prices rose, the craftsmen turned their attention in part towards new materials (including steel). The firm's leading jewellery designers include Nanna Ditzel, Torun Bülow-Hübe, Arje Griegst, Anette Kræn and Ole Bent-Petersen. Numerous Danish cutlery designers used as a model Kay Bojsen's silver service "Grand Prix" (1938) which was produced in steel in 1951. Flowing shapes were evident in Arne Jakobsen's "A J-Cutlery" (1960). Kay Bojsen's reputation was enhanced by his wooden toy designs.

Glass

Holmegaard
glassworks

After a gap of almost 200 years, in which no glassware was produced in the whole of Denmark, there was a renaissance in the craft of Danish glassmaking instigated by Count Christian Danneskiold-Samsoe in the town of Holmegaard, 7km/4 miles north of Næstved (southern Zealand). Peat from the moors provided an important fuel, the glassmakers which Denmark itself lacked were recruited in Norway, and eventually the first glass kiln began operating in 1825. At first only green bottles ("bouteilles") were produced, followed in 1835 by plate glass, manufactured by master craftsmen also imported from south Germany and Bohemia. It is thus no surprise that some terms associated with glass production are of German origin. Later, various refinement processes were added, together with grinding, etching and decoration. With the advent of mechanisation and the use of stencils, mass-produced industrial glass became as important as the hand-produced variety. The principal product is still plate glass. In recent years the manufacture of semi-crystal glass ("ringing glass") has also been established.

The present-day craft of glassmaking in Denmark is characterised by two different, though not always distinguishable, lines of development. On the one hand, shapes evolve virtually by themselves, appropriate to the material and bound by tradition; on the other hand, the glass-blowers derive their inspiration for creative design from the artistic directions currently followed by painting, graphic design and sculpture.

Furniture and Lighting

The art of Danish furniture design emerged at international level in the course of the fifties. The way for its success was paved by the architect Kaare Klint, who worked as a teacher of furniture design in Copenhagen's School of Architecture. With his study of human proportions Klint initiated a new systematic working method which made the comfort and functionality of furniture a priority. On this basis he made use of pre-existing suitable types of furniture, which he then developed further (amongst other things he simplified English Chippendale). In so doing he created a new appreciation of furniture design. Since then many Danish artists have derived inspiration from the furniture of other countries, which they have then so greatly improved that the end-product appears quintessentially Danish. Among the best known representatives of the younger generation is the chair designer Hans J. Wegner, whose work "The Chair" (designed 1949) became a byword in furniture design – this "Chair of Chairs" is said to have been the only one on which John F. Kennedy could really sit.

Furniture design

The best known designer of Danish lighting appliances is Poul Henningsen, whose technical work in the field began in 1925, when he won a competition for the lighting of the Danish stand at the Paris World Fair. Poul Henningsen, however, whom the Danes call PH for short, not only designed lamps, but also supplied the theoretical basis which serves so many lighting designers today. "Chuck away your artist's floppy hat and put on your working gear – only ever produce objects which are useful." These were Henningsen's challenging words in the magazine "Critical Review". PH's lighting installations characteristically have several shades, which help to correct the colour of the light. Henningsen's "PH-5" lamp, introduced in 1958, can nowadays be found in countless Danish households, as can the "PH-Plate", originally designed for the Copenhagen restaurant "Langelinie Pavillionen".

Lighting design

Architectural Design

|In the field of Danish design many outstanding results have been achieved by completing functional tasks in connection with the construction of new buildings. So, for example, the architect Arne Jacobsen designed in 1960 not only the building for the SAS Royal Hotel in Copenhagen, but also applied himself to the furniture design and even to the restaurant glass and cutlery. Architectural student Søren Robert Lund was just 25 years old when, in 1988, with his design of a deconstructivist concrete sculpture, he won the competition for the construction of Copenhagen's new Museum of Modern Art, "The Ark", opened in 1996.

Industrial Design

The task of modern industrial designers is less the use of a particular material than the design of products which have the power to communicate. Well-known examples of a conscious design policy are the unmistakable coffee-pots produced by Bodum and the T.V. and Hi-Fi equipment of Bang & Olufsen, a firm which has received several awards for its products. This company is increasingly trying to make technically complicated equipment look less forbidding and more elegant. In pursuit of this goal, they adhere to the maxim "Form follows function" and, by dint of simple design, try to make it absolutely clear for what purpose and in what way each piece of equipment should be used.

Through Time and Space with Galoshes of Fortune

"**I**t was a peculiar trunk. As soon as you pressed the lock, it could fly. High up, over the clouds, far far away". Unrestrained wanderlust poetically expressed, countries and times alternating in a flash in the story "Galoshes of Fortune". Despite all the exertions of travelling in the 19th century, he "jetsetted" around by stage-coach, train and Shanks's pony – Denmark's most celebrated storyteller would undoubtedly have felt at home in our modern age of travel mania. "I wish I could ride through the universe on a cannonball" wrote Hans Christian Andersen, who himself made more than 30 tours of Europe, visited London and Paris, Berlin, Weimar and Constantinople. In his travel books, novels and letters he assumed the rôle of historical reporter for an entire continent, reflecting the cultural blossoming of the "Golden Age" – that period between about 1800 and 1850, with which so many eminent names are associated, among them Oehlenschläger, Kierkegaard and Thorvaldsen (the last of whom was a close friend of the author). At the beginning of September 1918 when he was only 14 years old Andersen came to Copenhagen on his own initiative, in order to become an actor or singer – from the outset a rather unfortunate passion of his. With scarcely imaginable genius and artistic energy this shoemaker's son from Odense (on the island of Fyn) only a few years later wrote over 150 fairytales and stories, although only about a dozen of them have been preserved. Parts of his work exhibit autobiographical features. Thus, for example, in "The Little Match-Girl" he was recalling his beloved mother as a poor child, whereas the tale of the Chinese nightingale reminds us of Andersen's unhappy love for the singer Jenny Lind. Probably the best-known fairytale figure is his "Little Mermaid" who gazes longingly out to sea from the Langelinie shore. She presumably reflects his affection for Edvard Collins, whose family had taken in the young Andersen and subsequently provided for his education. His highly imaginative fairytales quickly made him a sought-after guest among the European aristocracy, and the works of this gifted linguistic artist were translated the world over. On the 4th August 1875 Andersen died in Copenhagen, where he was buried in Assistens Kirkegård (the city's largest cemetery). Among the many addresses in Copenhagen where this tireless traveller took temporary lodgings whenever he returned from his extensive travels, are three houses at Nyhavn: numbers 20 and 67 and, during the last four years of his life, number 18. This last address was Andersen's favourite home, with its view of the lively hustle and bustle of harbour life, the sailors, traders and travellers.

Famous People

The following alphabetical list consists of a series of well-known figures who, because they either were born, lived, worked or died there, are connected with Copenhagen, but have achieved national or international fame.

Absalon
(c. 1128–21.3.1201)

The Danish statesman Absalon may be regarded as the founder of the city of Copenhagen. In 1901, the 700th anniversary of his death, the town erected a memorial to him on the Højbro Plads. The grandson of the powerful Skjalm Hvide, who had ruled over Zealand during the reign of Sven Estridsen, was born in the family seat of Fjenneslev near Sorø. After he had supported the men of King Waldemar I in the struggle for the throne in 1157, Absalon was appointed Bishop of Roskilde in the following year. As a further reward from the king, he was granted rights to the district of "Havn" where, some ten years later, on the island of Strandholm (now called Slotsholm), he had a fortress built as a protection against Wendish pirates. The rapidly expanding settlement around the castle acquired the name "Købmændenes Havn" (Merchant's Port).

In 1177 the office of Archbishop of Lund was conferred on him. Furthermore, he became one of the most influential advisers of Waldemar I and Knut VI; he strengthened the position of the Danish church and extended its sphere of influence as far as Rügen and Pomerania. In the spring of 1201 Absalon died in Sorø, where he was buried in the monastery church.

Hans Christian Andersen
(2.4.1805–4.8.1875)

Hans Christian Andersen, born the son of a shoemaker in Odense on the island of Funen (Fyn), lived from 1819 onwards in Copenhagen. There he trained for the theatre and worked as chorus member and supernumerary until his voice broke.

Andersen was blessed with an immense and natural literary talent. As a result of his early publications – including "The Improviser" (1835), a novel showing the development of a character – he received from 1838 onwards an allowance from the King. Between 1831 and 1871 the writer made numerous trips abroad, in particular to Germany, where his autobiography "The Fairy Tale of My Life" was also published in 1845/46 (in Danish in 1855). But Andersen achieved world fame with his fairy tale collection called the "Eventyr" (1835–1872). Among the best known are "The Emperor's New Clothes", "The Princess on the Pea", "The Ugly Duckling", "The Swineherd", "The Steadfast Tin Soldier" and "The Mermaid". In these stories, using an apparently naïve style, he creates a world which bears touches of humour, irony and resignation. Since these tales often have a deeper meaning, they are also directed at adults ("The mermaid has no immortal soul, nor ever can possess one, unless she wins the love of a human being!"). Andersen had the ability to derive unexpected perspectives from even the smallest of things.

With his less well-known novels Andersen laid the foundations of modern realistic prose writing in Denmark. His work also includes poetry, diaries and letters.

He died in Copenhagen in 1875, where he is buried in the Assistens Kirkegård – the city's largest cemetery.

Martin Andersen Nexø
(25.6.1869–1.6.1954)

Martin Andersen Nexø, who came from Copenhagen, spent most of his youth as shepherd-boy and cobbler's apprentice on the island of Bornholm. After attending various evening classes, he worked as a teacher, then writer. Having embraced Communism after the First World War, he lived in Dresden from 1951 up until his death in 1954.

Hans Christian Andersen

Martin Andersen Nexø

Karen Blixen

The main themes of his artistic works are, on the one hand, social criticism and on the other, sympathy for the poor and the outcast. In his novel "Pelle The Conqueror" (1906–10; four vols.), which has auto-biographical traits, he describes the life of farmers, fishermen and labourers. Over and above that, he describes the aims of the Workers' Movement around 1900. His second novel cycle, "Ditte. Daughter of Man" (1917–21; 5 vols.), written in a more pessimistic tone, has as its subject the life of a woman from the lower classes, who fails to break out of her unsatisfactory environment.

Andersen Nexø has also emerged as an author of novellas, travel books and memoirs.

The Danish writer Karen Blixen was born in Rungstedlund near Copenhagen, the daughter of the captain and author W. Dinesen. Her study of painting at the Danish Academy of Art was followed by trips to England, France and Italy. At the age of 28 she married the Swedish baron Bror von Blixen-Finecke, with whom she went to Kenya, where she managed a coffee plantation till 1931. During this time she met Denys Finch Hatton – the real love of her life – who died when his plane crashed in 1931. As a result of the economic crisis of the same year, she had to return to Denmark and then lived as a freelance writer on her father's estate in Rungstedlund where, in 1991, the manor house was turned into a museum. Karen Blixen, whose full name was actually Baroness Karen Christence Blixen-Finecke, published her works (written in Danish and English) under the pseudonyms Tanja Blixen, Isak Dinesen, Tania Blixen and Pierre Andrézel. Her highly imaginative stories and novellas, frequently characterised by the theme of fate, were developed outside of contemporary literary trends. Distinctive features of her writing are her rich storytelling skill, her frivolously ironic sense of humour, her sensitivity and the cryptic nature of her subject matter. With great empathy she portrayed in her books about Kenya the natural life of East Africa and the life of the natives. Among her best known works are: "Africa, Dark Alluring World", which in 1985 was made into an Oscar-winning film starring Meryl Streep and Robert Redford, entitled "Out of Africa"; "Winter's Tales", 1942; "Shadows on the Grass" ("Skygger på græsset", 1960) and the story "Babette's Feast" (first published 1950) from "Anecdotes of Destiny", 1960, the 1988 film version of which by Gabriel Axel won the Oscar for Best Foreign Film.

Karen Blixen
(17.4.1885–
7.9.1962)

Denmark's greatest physicist, Niels Bohr, was born in Copenhagen and became Professor of Theoretical Physics there in 1916. He definitively redeveloped Ernest Rutherford's atomic model into the Bohr atomic

Niels Bohr
(7.10.1885–
18.11.1962)

Famous People

Niels Bohr

Tycho Brahe

Christian IV

model (1913) and discovered the principle of correspondence between classical physics and quantum physics. In recognition of his research work, he was awarded the 1922 Nobel Prize for Physics. At the beginning of 1943, during the German occupation of Denmark, Bohr was smuggled out of the country, disguised as a fisherman. From here he found his way via Sweden and England to the U.S.A., where he collaborated on the development of the atomic bomb, despite fearing its repercussions. After the war he returned to Copenhagen and continued his work at his institute of theoretical physics (directed since his death by his son). In 1947 he received Denmark's highest honour, the Order of the Elephant.

Tycho Brahe
(14.12.1546–
24.10.1601)

Tycho Brahe, born in 1546 in Knudstrup (southern Sweden), initially studied law and then turned to astronomy. In 1572 he discovered in Cassiopeia (a northern constellation) a new star, the Nova Cassiopeia. After a trip to Europe, Brahe gave lectures in Copenhagen and, on the island of Ven in the Sund (lent to him in 1576 by the Danish king Friedrich II), he built the Uranienborg observatory, where he carried out his research. After the death of Friedrich II in 1588, he found increasingly less support and, at the beginning of 1597, he left Denmark and two years later went to Prague, where he took up the post of Imperial Astronomer in the service of Rudolf II. He died there in October 1601. His memorial tablet in the Teyn church (fourth pillar from the right) is always adorned with the Danebrog.

Brahe was the leading observational astronomer before the invention of the telescope. Through his observations of planetary bodies, in particular of Mars, he prepared the way for Kepler's work on planetary orbits. Brahe developed the so-called "Tychonic System", named after him. According to this, sun and moon circle the earth which is situated at the centre of the world, while the remaining planets circle the sun. In addition, he proved that the comets cannot simply be phenomena in the earth's atmosphere, as Aristotle had assumed. In memory of the great astronomer, Copenhagen's planetarium, opened in 1989, was named after him.

King Christian IV
(12.4.1577–
28.2.1648)

Christian IV, Denmark's most popular king, was responsible for some of the finest buildings in Copenhagen. He brought the Renaissance style to Denmark – a style evident in such buildings as the Copenhagen Stock Exchange, the Rosenborg Palace, the Round Tower and Frederiksborg Castle. This royal building commissioner, however, did not confine his activities to magnificent palaces and public buildings. For his seamen he built housing in the Nybodn district, and the district of Christianshavn was also developed on his initiative. In addition, he left his mark on towns in Sweden (Christiansstad), Germany (Glückstadt) and Norway (Oslo, Kongsberg).

In the field of politics Christian, who was crowned in 1596, had little success. He was unable to compel Sweden to join a league of northern states under Danish leadership, and moreover, in the Thirty Years' War, he was forced to accept heavy defeats. The king, who was popular with his subjects principally for his informality, finally died in 1648 in Copenhagen, an unhappy and disappointed man.

Carl Th. Dreyer, who was born in Copenhagen, is Denmark's most celebrated film director (especially in the realm of silent films). He made a crucial contribution to the development of film as an art form. His films "Joan of Arc" (1926–27), which made consistent use of close-ups, and "Vampire" (1928–29), achieved worldwide success, but his later films failed to make a similar impression.

Carl Th. Dreyer
(3.2.1889–
20.3.1968)

Grundtvig, after whom one of the most unusual modern churches in Europe (the Grundtvig Church in Copenhagen) is named, was the founder of the adult education movement and is the spiritual father of its systematic development. In 1844 he established the first such centre in Europe at Rødding (Jutland). After the incorporation of northern Schleswig in Prussia in 1864, the school had to be moved to Askov (also in Jutland).

Grundtvig, who was a pastor in Copenhagen from 1839 and who became bishop in 1861, also translated old Norse sagas and wrote over 400 hymns.

Nikolai Frederik
Severin Grundtvig
(8.9.1783–
2.9.1872)

The singer Max Hansen, born in Mannheim (Germany), achieved his first successes in Copenhagen's Apollo Theatre in 1919. He became an international star in the 1920's in the Metropol Theatre in Berlin, where he appeared in numerous operettas and revues – one of his most notable roles was that of the waiter Leopold in "White Horse Inn". After performing as a guest star in Copenhagen, he became manager of the Tivoli Theatre in 1956, retaining the post until his death.

Max Hansen
(22.2.1897–
12.11.1961)

Ludvig Baron von Holberg, born in Bergen (Norway), was the creator of the modern Danish theatre. He studied theology in Copenhagen and then worked as a domestic tutor in Holland, Germany, England, France and Italy, before becoming, at Copenhagen, professor of Metaphysics in 1718 and later of Rhetoric and History in 1720. In addition to his work as professor, historian and university treasurer, Holberg wrote comedies of social criticism and letters on the most varied subjects. After the foundation of the Copenhagen theatre in 1722 he wrote more than 33 comedies (including "The Alehouse Politician", 1723; "Jean de France", 1723; "Ulysses of Ithaca" and "Erasmus Montanus", 1731), in which he combines earthy realism with the ideas of the Enlightenment. His work at the university led him also to write historical and moral works in the spirit of the Enlightenment. He lived in Copenhagen from 1708 to 1740, and died there in 1754. This great dramatist is commemorated today by a statue outside the Royal Theatre.

Ludvig Holberg
(3.12.1684–
28.1.1754)

Jensen, born in Farsø on Jutland, is one of Denmark's leading writers. He initially studied medicine, but then moved to the United States in 1896, where he lived for some time. Later he made several trips to France, Spain and East Asia as newspaper correspondent. For his masterly novels and stories he was, in 1944, awarded the Nobel Prize for Literature. He spent his last years in Copenhagen, where he died in 1950.

Jensen's work reflects his attachment to his native land and a strong love of Danish tradition. One of his prime works, the six-part novel cycle "Den lange rejse" ("The Long Journey") depicts the history of Nordic man from the beginnings up to the discovery of America by

Johannes Vilhelm
Jensen
(20.1.1873–
25.11.1950)

Søren Kierkegaard *Friedrich Gottlieb Klopstock* *Bertel Thorvaldsen*

Columbus. The same devotion to homeland is evident in his "Himmer-landhistorier" ("Stories of the Homeland"), 1898–1910, a volume of fairy tales, sagas and stories.

Søren Kierkegaard
(5.5.1813–
11.11.1855)

The Danish philosopher Søren Kierkegaard was born the seventh child of a prosperous wool dealer in Copenhagen and studied theology and philosophy from 1830 to 1841 at Copenhagen university. In September 1840 he became engaged to the seventeen-year old Regine Olsen, but broke up with her a year later. Thereafter he lived on his inheritance, working as a freelance writer.

Most of his books were published under pseudonyms. Following the practice of Socrates, his chosen form of writing was frequently dialogue. In his writings the concepts of "angst" and "existence" occupy a central position, together with the related notions of "freedom" and "decision". His thinking leads to the realisation that the conquest of angst and despair is possible only through God's grace. Since Kierg-kegaard, as a religious thinker, adopted an emphatically subjective stance, he came into conflict with the Danish Lutheran Church of his time (a church which professed to possess a unified system of objective truth) – and finally rejected it completely. His works on the philosophy of religion have greatly influenced many 20th c. thinkers: the ideas expressed in these works to a great extent form the basis of dialectical theology and existential philosophy.

Among his important works are "Either-Or" (1843), "Fear and Trembling" (1843), "The Concept of Dread" (1844), "The Sickness unto Death" (1849) and "Training in Christianity" (1850).

Kierkegaard died in Copenhagen in 1855, where he was buried in the Assistens Kirkegård cemetery.

Friedrich Gottlieb
Klopstock
(2.7.1724–
14.3.1803)

Born in Quedlinburg (Germany), Klopstock studied theology at Jena and while there began his three-part biblical verse cycle "The Messiah" (1748–73), the first twenty cantos of which were enthusiastically received. This brought him an invitation to Copenhagen from the Danish minister Bernstorff in 1751, together with the offer of a good salary. Freed from material want, he lived in Copenhagen as a poet till 1754, then returned to Germany for ten years before coming back again to Copenhagen in 1763. After Bernstorff's overthrow and replacement by Struensee, he left Copenhagen in 1770 as Danish counsellor of legation (and with the right to a pension), and thereafter lived mainly in Hamburg.

Among Klopstock's principal works, apart from "The Messiah", are the odes (published individually in 1748 and in one volume in 1771). These poems, influenced by the bible and the verse of Horace, Pindar,

J. Milton and E. Young, deal with lofty themes such as love, friendship and the experience of nature. Best known are "Spring Celebration", "Lake Zurich" and "To My Friends", which were partly written also while he was in Copenhagen.

Poulsen's name is decisively linked with the development of wireless telegraphy and telephony, fields in which he held numerous important patents. This Copenhagen-born physicist constructed as early as 1898 the first workable electromagnetic sound recorder, and in 1904 he developed the "singing arc" (for the generation of radio waves), which influenced wireless transmission for years to come.

Valdemar Poulsen
(23.11.1869–
6.8.1942)

Qualifying as a doctor at the early age of twenty, Struensee became personal physician to King Christian VII of Denmark in 1769 and went to Copenhagen with the king, a degenerate and feeble-minded character. Before long he began a love-affair with Queen Caroline Mathilde and with her support he not only acquired influence over the king, but in the summer 1771 was also made a count and appointed minister in the inner cabinet. For almost sixteen months he held sway over the Danish court and country. The liberal reforms he introduced during this period anticipated the developments of the following century.

Johann Friedrich,
Count von
Struensee
(5.8.1737–
28.4.1772)

When Struensee's high-handedness became uncontrolled and his affair with the queen could no longer be concealed, a court clique opposed to him obtained a warrant for his arrest. He was arrested on Jan. 17th 1772 and executed on Jan. 28th of the same year, in accordance with the provisions of the law: his right hand was cut off while he was still alive and then his head, his body was quartered and the separate parts displayed publicly, but his head and hand were stuck on a pole. About 3000 citizens of Copenhagen witnessed this gruesome spectacle. The English-born queen was expelled from the country.

Thorvaldsen was Denmark's greatest sculptor, for whom his native city of Copenhagen established a special museum. While still a student at the Academy of Art, he distinguished himself by winning the academy's Great Gold Medal. With the help of a travelling scholarship from the academy he was able to go to Rome in 1797. There he settled down and began to create sculpture in marble, which brought him a reputation throughout Europe and ensured that his work was much in demand. After living in Rome for 40 years he returned to Copenhagen in 1838 and was received in triumph. Between 1839 and 1848, under the direction of Gottlieb Bindesbøll, a museum was built on the Porthusgade to house the works which he had bequeathed to the city.

Bertel Thorvaldsen
(19.11.1768–
24.3.1844)

Bjørn Wiinblad, a native of Copenhagen, studied painting and illustration at the Royal Academy of Art. In addition to book illustrations, he designed posters, stage sets and costumes for the theatre. Soon, however, he became interested in different materials and techniques and started to produce tapestries, wallpaper and ceramic pieces.

Bjørn Wiinblad
(born 20.9.1919)

He enjoyed his first great success when his ceramic work was exhibited in Copenhagen, Sweden and Norway. In 1954 he held an exhibition in New York. Among all Wiinblad's diverse creations, ceramic materials remained his preferred medium. His shapes and his decorative style create a bright, attractive effect.

As a designer, Wiinblad makes designs for table services and glassware, as well as for vases and wall plates. Sometimes he designs both shape and decoration, but sometimes either one or the other. His surfaces are covered with decoration or painted figures, or embellished with scenes from fairy tales ("1001 Nights"). As well as objects in black and white, he creates others decorated with bright colours. Wiinblad has for many years been working for the firm of Rosenthal – famous for its porcelain and ceramic ware – which has its headquarters in Selb (Bavaria).

History

Prehistory

Like the rest of Denmark, the Copenhagen area was originally occupied by Indo-European hunting tribes. Evidence of their culture (tools, weapons, jewellery) can be seen in the museums of Copenhagen. Especially notable are their unusual bronze trumpets, known as "lurs" (as seen in the monument outside the town hall).

From 800

The northern Germanic Danes, known as Vikings – warriors, seamen, peasants – surge into Denmark from southern Sweden. Their kings established the first Danish state (rune-stone of Jelling in Jutland).

1167

Valdemar I, the Great, presents a fishing village called Havn to Archbishop Absalon. Ten years later Absalon fortifies the village harbour by building a castle on the site now occupied by Christiansborg Palace on Slotsholmen. The settlement which grows up around the castle acquires the name "Købmændenes Havn" ("Merchant's Harbour").

1254

First charter of municipal rights.

1397

Union of Kalmar: Denmark, Norway and Sweden are united under the rule of Erik VII of Pomerania.

1417

Erik VII grants Copenhagen royal trading privileges. The town becomes an important trading centre in the Baltic area.

Siege of Copenhagen by the Swedes in 1658

Christoffer II (of Bavaria) makes Copenhagen his capital and confirms the rights of the municipality. The town has a population of some 10,000. — 1445

Coronation of Christian I – the first royal coronation in Copenhagen. — 1449

Christian I founds the University. Copenhagen becomes the country's cultural centre. — 1479

The Reformation reaches Denmark. King Christian III makes himself head of the Danish (Lutheran) national church. — 1536

During the reign of Christian IV building of the new district of Christianshavn, the housing area of Nyboder and numerous Renaissance-style buildings. — 1588–1648

Unsuccessful siege of the town by the Swedes. — 1658–60

As a reward for its successful defence against the Swedish siege, Copenhagen becomes a free city and the citizens enjoy equal rights with the nobility.
   Introduction of an absolute hereditary monarchy, which lasts until 1848. — 1660

Construction of the Citadel. — 1662

Copenhagen has a population of 60,000. — 1700

During the plague almost a third of the population perishes. — 1711–12

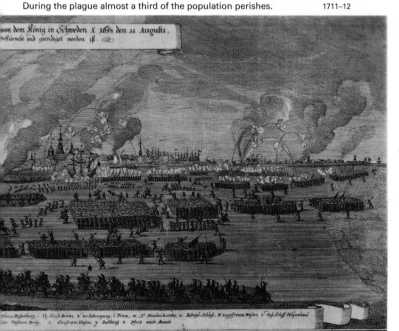

1728
A devastating fire destroys the town. Over 1670 houses are reduced to ashes.

1795
The second great fire of Copenhagen, with loss of more than 1000 houses.

1801
Copenhagen is attacked by the British fleet, in reprisal for Denmark's support of Napoleon I's continental blockade of England.

1807
Three-day bombardment of Copenhagen by the British, causing considerable destruction in the town centre.

1848
The bourgeois revolution brings the end of absolute rule. Denmark is granted a liberal constitution.
   Copenhagen grows out beyond its defensive walls.

1867
Demolition of the town's fortifications.

1894
The establishment of a free port gives a crucial new impetus to Copenhagen's economy.

1924
Opening of the major airport of Kastrup.

1940–45
Neutral Denmark is occupied by the German Army. There is passive resistance, in which King Christian X takes part, and the country's Jews are evacuated to Sweden.

May 4th 1945
Liberation of Copenhagen from German occuption.

1962
The pedestrian precinct "Strøget" becomes one of the first traffic-free shopping streets in Europe.

1984
A multi-phase building programme begins, designed to rebuild and extend Kastrup airport and make it (by the year 2000) one of the most modern in Europe.

1985
Re-opening of the "Gamle Scene" for ballet performances.

1989
Opening (beginning of November) of the Tycho Brahe Planetarium on the Gammel Kongevej.

1991
In September the full democratic assembly of Christiania gives its assent to the legal recognition of the "Free State" of Copenhagen (established in 1971).

1996
Copenhagen is the twelfth European city to be nominated "Cultural Capital of Europe", a title it holds for one year.

1997
On the 15th January Queen Margarethe II celebrates the 25th anniversary of her accession to the throne.

1997/1998
Completion of a combined bridge and tunnel link between Halskov (Zealand) and Nyborg (Fyn). With this spanning of the Great Belt, Copenhagen will in future be directly accessible by train and car.

Quotations

Fynes Moryson
c. 1566–1617

Elsinore and Cronenburg Castle

This is a poore village, but much frequented by sea-faring men, by reason of the straight sea, called the Sownd; where the King of Denmark hath laid so great imposition upon ships and goods comming out of the Balticke sea, or brought into the same, as this sole profit passeth all the revenues of his Kingdome. . . . In respect of the Danes scrupulous and jealous nature, I did with great difficulty (putting on a Merchants habite, and giving a greater reward then the favour deserved,) obtaine to enter Croneburg Castle, which was built foure square, and hath only one gate on the East side, where it lies upon the straight. Above this gate is a chamber in which the King useth to eat, and two chambers wherin the King and Queen lie apart. Under the fortification of the Castle round about, are stables for horses, and some roomes for like purposes. On the South-side towards the Baltich sea, is the largest roade for ships. And upon this side is the prison, and above it a short gallery. On the West side towards the village is the Church of the Castle, & above it a very faire gallery, in which the King useth to feast at solemne times. On the North side is the prospect partly upon the Iland, and partly upon the Narrow sea, which reacheth twenty foure miles to the German Ocean. And because great store of ships passe this way in great Fleets, of a hundred more or lesse together: this prospect is most pleasant to all men, but most of all to the King, seeing so many shippes, whereof not one shall passe, without adding somewhat to his treasure.
"Itinerary" 1617

Copenhagen is the best-built city of the north; for although St Petersburg excels it in superb edifices, yet as it contains no wooden houses, it does not display that striking contrast of meanness and magnificence, but in general exhibits a more equable and uniform appearance. The town is surrounded towards the land with regular ramparts and bastions, a broad ditch full of water, and a few outworks: its circumference measures between four and five miles. The streets are well-paved, with a foot-way on each side, but too narrow and inconvenient for general use. The greatest part of the buildings are of brick; and a few of free-stone brought from Germany. The houses of the nobility are in general splendid, and constructed in the Italian style of architecture. The royal palace is a magnificent pile of building of hewn stone, the wings and stable of brick stuccoed. . . .

The busy spirit of commerce is visible in Copenhagen. The haven is always crowded with merchant-ships; and the streets are intersected by broad canals, which bring the merchandize close to the warehouses that line the quays. The city owes its principal beauty to a dreadful fire in 1728, that destroyed five churches and sixty-seven streets, which have since been rebuilt in the modern style. The new part of the town, raised by the late king Frederic V, is extremely beautiful: it consists of an octagon, containing four uniform and elegant buildings of hewn stone, and of four broad streets leading to it in opposite directions.
"Travels into Poland, Russia, Sweden, etc." 1792

I see here nothing but heaps of ruins and only converse with people immersed in trade and sensuality
"Letter to Gilbert Imlay" 6 September 1795

Quotations

Baedeker's
Sweden and
Norway

Copenhagen is the focal point of all Danish trade. The trading port lies on the Zealand side and is separated from the naval port by a system of piles which bisects the Kallebostrand from north to south. The quaysides are always bustling with life. There are warehouses and storerooms on both sides of the harbour. The naval port (Orlogshavn) is close to the little islands of Nyholm, Frederiksholm, Arsenalø and Kristiansholm, which are a part of Amager and on which the Royal marine establishments are to be found. The town's fortifications on the landward side have been dismantled since 1870 – only those on the seaward side, in the citadel of Frederikshavn, the protruding batteries of Trekoner and Lynetten, together with the Sextus and Quintus batteries on Amager, are still capable of offering any defence.

From: Baedeker's Sweden and Norway together with the most important routes through Denmark.
Handbook for travellers, 1885, page 17.

Edward Daniel
Clark
1769–1822

Our French companions complained of the bad taste by which everything in Copenhagen is characterized. To our eyes, it seemed, indeed, that journey from London to Copenhagen might exhibit the retrogression of a century; every thing being found, in the latter city, as it existed in the former a hundred years before....
"Travels" 1810–22

Hans Christian
Andersen
1844–75

On Monday morning, 5th September 1819, I saw Copenhagen for the first time from the Frederiksberg Hill. I rose and with my little bundle of clothes walked through the park, the long path and the suburb into the town.... and put up at a small inn.

Sarah Bernhardt
1844–1923

Then I went on to Copenhagen where I was to give five performances at the Court Theatre.

On our arrival, which had undoubtedly been looked forward to with great excitement, I was seized with stage-fright. When my train stopped more than two thousand people shouted "Hurrah!" so loudly that I did not know what was going on. When Monsieur de Fallesen, the director of the Court Theatre and the First Royal Chamberlain, entered my compartment I was asked to appear at the window, to pacify the understandable friendly curiosity of the public. The frightful "Hurrah!" rang out once more, and I understood.

Yet a crazy anxiety came over me. Never, no never, would I be able to fulfil the great expectations which they had of me, however much I wanted to. My tiny stature will arouse sympathy among all these fine men and these magnificent radiant women. I alighted from the train and in comparison with them was so much smaller that I had the impression of being nothing but a breath of wind. On the orders of the police the crowd split into two dense rows, leaving a broad path for my carriage. I drove through this friendly double file at a gentle trot, with the gentlemen doffing their hats respectfully while kisses and flowers were showered upon me.

In my long career as an artist I have since had my triumphs, receptions and ovations, but the welcome I received from the Danes remains one of the most memorable.
Performance of "Adrienne Lecouvreur", mid August 1880 in the Court Theatre.

Sightseeing

The following recommendations should serve as a guideline for travellers visiting Copenhagen for the first time and have only limited time available, by helping to make their stay in the city as interesting as possible. The sights, places and squares printed in **bold** type refer to the descriptions to be found in the "Sightseeing from A to Z" section in the main part of this guide.

Note

Visitors who are staying only a few hours in Denmark's capital, yet still wish to see the most important sights, are recommended to go on one of the tours of the city (by bus or boat), or to join a guided walking-tour. Even on foot the tour will last only about two hours (thanks to the short distances involved in Copenhagen).

Flying visits

City Walks

Starting-point is the magnificent ★★**Rådhus**, whose tower provides the best panoramic view of Copenhagen. At the northern end of Town Hall Square begins the approximately 2km/1 mile long ★★**Strøget**, Denmark's most famous shopping street, with its elegant fashion boutiques and famed department stores, colourful souvenir shops and cosy, intimate cafés. About half way along this lively pedestrian precinct is the ★**Amagertorv**, on which the celebrated Royal Copenhagen Porcelain House and the Illums Bolighus furniture store are to be found. At this point, anyone interested in antiques can include a detour along adjoining Læderstræde and its westerly continuation, Kompagniestræde, and rummage through at least one of the numerous antique shops. Then proceed south via the ★**Hojbro Plads** to the island of Slotsholmen where in 1167 Absalon, the city founder, began the construction of the ★★**Christiansborg Slot**. Today it is a sumptuous three-storey palace which since 1918 has served as seat of the Danish parliament. On the northern canal side the monumental ★★**Thorvaldsens Museum** rises up in dedication to one of the most important Danish sculptors, whilst the eastern side of Slotsholmen is graced by the delicate Renaissance architecture of the ★**Børsen** (Old Stock Exchange). Opposite lies the ★★**Holmens Kirke**, where in 1967 Queen Margarethe II and Prince Hendrik were married. The Holmens canal leads into ★**Kongens Nytorv**, Copenhagen's largest square, on which the Royal Theatre and Scandinavia's oldest store, the "Magasin du Nord", are to be found. A mere stone's throw away it is possible to see in the picturesque harbour ageing museum ships bobbing up and down on the pleasant waters of the ★★**Nyhavn** canal. This is also a starting-point for boat trips which include such sights as Andersen's ★**lille Havfrue** (Little Mermaid) and ★**Christianshavn**. From the New Royal Market follow elegant Østergade (part of ★★**Strøget**) back to the Heiligåndskirken, before continuing to stroll through the ★**Universitet** district (Latin quarter) to the ★**Axeltorv** with its colourful Palad cinema complex. Evenings should be devoted solely to the ★★**Tivoli**, where thousands of lights transform the amusement park into a brightly-coloured fairytale world.

Walk 1

Starting-point for the second walk is ★**Kongens Nytorv** close to enchanting ★★**Nyhavn**. From here follow Bredgade as far as Frederiksgade where on the left it is possible to glimpse the massive dome of the ★**Marmorkirken** and on the right the royal residence of

Walk 2

The charming atmosphere of Nyhaven – a favourite meeting place in the heart of the Danish capital

★★**Amalienborg Slot**. It is definitely advisable to arrive here before noon in order to witness the changing of the guard in front of the palace, which takes place on the stroke of midday. Then go past the **Alexander Newski Kirke** and the ★**Kunstindustrimuseet**, and about 500m/550yds further north is the extensive parkland surrounding the ★**Kastellet**. At its southern edge stands the **Frihedsmuseet**, which documents the history of Denmark between 1940 and 1945. Nearby the massive ★**Gefion Springvandet** pours forth its waters on the Langelinie shore, where Andersen's ★**lille Havfrue** gazes longingly out to sea. On the way back you pass the Anglican **Saint Alban's Church**, before turning off into Gernersgade and walking towards the ★★**Statens Museum for Kunst**. In good weather a trip to the ★**Botanisk Have**, or a rest in the park of ★★**Rosenborg Slot** can be enjoyed before paying a more detailed visit to the picture-book palace. Among the treasures to be found in the nearby ★**Musikhistorisk Museum**, (Åbenrå 30), are precious historical musical instruments, such as the harmonium belonging to King Christian VIII. To end the walk climb the ★**Rundetårn**, or simply saunter along ★**Købmagergade** and Østergade (part of ★★**Strøget**), with a view to buying some attractive souvenirs and at least one piece of Danish design.

Walk 3

The third walk begins at the ★★**Rådhus**, which has the country's highest tower, as well as Jens Olsens' spectacular world clock, on which this meticulous craftsman worked for 27 years. Only a few steps separate the Town Hall from the ★★**Nationalmuseet**, Denmark's most important museum of cultural history. (Tip for children: the lovingly arranged toy collection.) On the south side of the Dantes Plads look at the famous ★★**Ny Carlsberg Glyptotek** and then enjoy the relaxing and Mediterranean-like atmosphere of the Winter

Garden. Next cross the Langebro Bridge to ★**Christianshavn**. Visitors who enjoy panoramic vistas will be drawn to the tower of ★**Vor Freisers Kirke** with a breathtaking view over Copenhagen. For many years the epitome of alternative life-styles has been the free state of ★**Christiania**, created in 1971 by the occupation of former military ground and legalised in 1991. Here a coffee-break can be taken in the fully-glazed café of the Gammel Dok architecture centre with a view of the passing ships, before returning to the town centre via the Knippelsbro Bridge and bringing the tour to a pleasant close at ★★**Nyhavn**. A good way to spend the evening is to meet friends for a drink or sample in full the delights of Danish cuisine – from bright rusages, through countless varieties of fish and game dishes, to the obligatory red fruit pudding with cream ("rødgrød med fløde").

Recommendations for a Longer Stay

In addition to seeing the principal sights in the city and visiting some of the museums, a somewhat longer stay will also allow time for excursions to the surrounding area and a tour of Zealand. Anyone with an interest in the history of Copenhagen should certainly visit the ★★**Københavns Bymuseum** with its excellent Kierkegaard collection, whilst Danish design is probably nowhere more vividly represented than in the ★**Kunstindustriemuseet**. The name of ★**Carlsberg** stands for Danish architecture. Modern "hands-on" technology is displayed in the ★**Experimentarium** in the former bottling hall of the Tuborg Brewery. A whole host of fun is to be had by young and old at the ★★**Zoologisk Have** and the ★★**Zoologisk Museum**. A walk around the ★**Assistens Kirkegård** (cemetery) is also worthwhile. Here many famous Danes have found their last resting-place. To the south, in the suburb of Ishoj, the futuristic ★**Arken** museum exhibits the work of high-ranking modern-day artists; about 8km/5 miles north of the capital in the ★★**Frilandsmuseet**, thatched peasant cottages, ancient windmill towers and traditional fishermen's huts from the 17th–19th centuries can be seen. About 10km/6 miles north of the town centre, more than 120 different amusement rides for the whole family are available in the ★**Bakken** amusement park – a popular version of the Tivoli. Those who have seen Robert Redford and Meryl Streep in the documentary-style film "Out of Africa" must, of course, visit the ★**Karen Blixen Museet** in Rungstedlund, the family estate of the Danish writer. Lovers of modern art and meet 35km/22 miles north of Copenhagen in the renowned ★★**Louisiana** artistic and cultural centre in Humblebæk. Finally, however, the absolute highlight of any trip to Zealand must be ★★**Frederiksborg Slot**, Denmark's most beautiful Renaissance palace, not far from Hillerød and the so-called "Hamlet Castle", ★★**Kronborg Slot**, at Helsingor. About 30km/19 miles west of Copenhagen lies ★★**Roskilde** which is well worth a visit. Its cathedral church and Viking Ship Museum deserve to have a whole afternoon devoted to them. And finally, amidst all this artistic pleasure, do not forget to enjoy at least one endless day's sunbathing on the beach!

Plan of the City
with sightseeing
walks

▬▬▬ Walk 1

▬▬▬ Walk 2

▬▬▬ Walk 3

Hillerød
※※ Stet Museum

Lyngby, Helsingør
※Grundtvig Kirke

Fredriks gade

Panum
Instituttet

København

500 m

Nørre Allé

Møllegade

Blegdamsvej

Ryesgade

NØRREBRO

Mosaik
Kirkegård

St.
Johannes

Skt. Hans
Torv

Ravnsborggade

Dosseringen

※Assistens
Kirkegård

Fælledvej

Sortedams Sø

Hans Tavsens Gade

Griffenfelds Gade

Nørrebrogade

St. Daniel

Sortedams

Dronning
Louises Bro

Gothersg

Rantzausgade

Blågårds
Plads

Blågårdsgade

Dosseringen

Frederiks-

Ågade Åboulevard

Korsgade

Peblinge Sø

Venders

Ågade Åboulevard

Griffenfelds Gade

Betlehems-
kirke

Peblinge

Nørre Søgade

Nansensgade

Rosenørns Allé

Radio-
huset

Herm.
Triers
Plads

Søpavillonen

Farimags

FREDERIKS-
BERG

Forum

Rosenørns Allé

Gyldenløvesgade

Nansensgade

Ørsteds
Parken

Nørre

Skt. Markus Allé

Nyropsvej

Jarmers
Plads

Skt. Pe

H.-C.-Andersens Boulevard

H. C. Ørsteds Vej

Forchhammersvej

Skt. Jørgens Sø

Vester Søgade

Vester

Voldg

Danasvej

Hammerichsgade

Studie

Niels Ebbesens

Danasvej

Kampmannsgade

Cirkus-
bygningen

Lykkesholms

Skt. Knuds

Vej

Forhåbningsholms Allé

Tullinsgade

Skt. Jørgens Sø

Vester Søgade

Nyropsgade

Vester Farimagsgade

Rådh
Plad

H.-C.-Anders
Sch
(Tivoli-Museu

St. Immanuel

Synnøgen

Vesterport

ℹ️※※
Tivoli

Gammel Kongevej

Tycho Brahe
Planetarium

Tussa
Kabin

Frederiksberg
Allé

Ny
Teater

Gammel Kongevej

Vesterbrogade

Reventlowsgade

Haupt-
bahnhof

Bernston

VESTERBRO

Vesterbrogade

Københavns
Bymuseum

St. Maria

Gasværksvej

Saxo-
parken

Skyde-
bane-

Dannebrogsgade

Istedgade

Eskildsgade

Halmtorvet

Tietgens

haven

Matthæusgade

Istedgade

Absalonsgade

Halmtorvet

Ingerslevsgade

©Baedeker

※Legetøjsmuseet

Ringsted, Køge

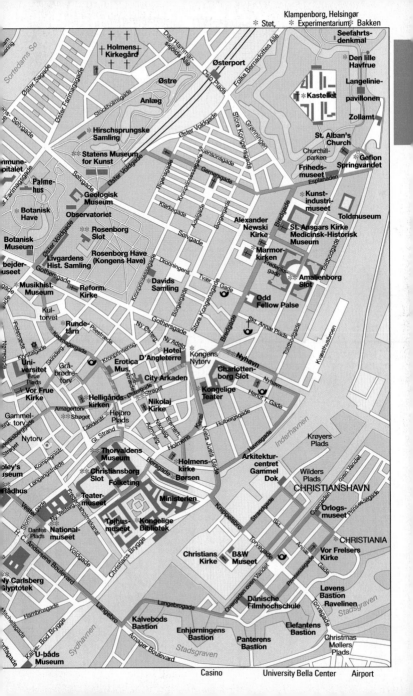

Sights
from A to Z

Note

Suggestions for devising a programme for a short trip to Copenhagen can be found under the heading "Sightseeing" in the Introduction Section. A plan of the inner city can be found on pp. 38/39.

★Akvarium (Aquarium; Danmarks Akvarium) H1

Location
Strandvejen
Charlottenlund

S-bane
Charlottenlund

Bus
6

The Aquarium, one of the most popular museums in Copenhagen, was opened in 1939 and considerably enlarged in 1974. It is situated roughly 5km/3 miles north of the city centre just off Strandvejen in the grounds of Charlottenlund Palace and in its 90 tanks it offers a comprehensive view of freshwater and sea fish from all over the world. (Captions given only in Danish.) Its wide-ranging contents include luminous fish, sharks, electric eels, and exotic species from Asia and South America including the notorious piranhas or pirayas, huge swarms of which can reduce even fully-grown cattle to skeletons in a matter of minutes. There are about 3000 varieties of fish on view. (Open: mid-Feb.–Oct.: daily 10am–6pm; Nov.–mid-Feb.: Mon.–Fri. 10am–4pm, Sat., Sun. 10am–5pm).

Alexander Newski Kirke (Church) J6

Location
Bredgade 53

Buses
1, 6, 9

Alexander Nevski Church, with its three golden onion-shaped domes, was built for the Russian Orthodox community between 1881 and 1883. At the request of the Empress Dagmar, daughter of Christian IX, Tsar Alexander III personally made a contribution to the building costs. The design for the sacred building was supplied by the Russian architect David Ivanovich Grimm of the St Petersburg Academy of Arts, while its execution was carried out by Albert Nielsen under the supervision of F. Meldahl. Its consecration in 1883 was attended by representatives of the Russian and Greek royal families as well as the Danish. The church reflects the Moscovian style of architecture of the 17th c. Whereas the façade is built of red and grey brick, the ornamental decorations are made of sandstone. Enthroned over the bells is the Prince of Novgorod, Alexander Nevski, who in the middle of the 13th c. defeated a Swedish army by the banks of the River Neva and later fought against the German order of knights in Russia. He is patron saint of the church. Inside the church a marble staircase leads to the upper floor where the hall of worship is situated. This contains an elaborate iconostasis with three doors, while the ceiling is adorned with Russian and Byzantine paintings. The icons show the influence of the "Romantic style", as it was interpreted in Russia at the end of the last century. Especially noteworthy is P. Bogolyobov's depiction of "Christ walking on the Sea of Galilee", where the colours cause the light not only to lend the work a compositional significance, but also a symbolic one.

★Amager (Island) H–K7/8

Location
in the Øresund

Buses
30, 33, 73E

The island of Amager, which lies to the east of the city centre of Copenhagen, is connected to it by a large bridge which can be raised and lowered in a short space of time to allow a ship through. On the island, besides Copenhagen's Kastrup Airport, there is the exhibition and conference centre, the Bella Center, with a covered area of some 85,000 sq.m/21 acres, making it the largest in Scandinavia. More than 40 fairs are held here annually.

Close by the stretch of rail which will link Copenhagen with the Swedish town of Malmo from the year 2000, a new area of the city, Ørestad, is now developing. Covering 310ha/765 acres, it will provide

◀ *Floodlit Tivoli – a fantasy for all age groups*

living accommodation and workplaces for more than 70,000 people. The town-planners have also obtained authority to begin work on the Copenhagen Riviera, a large leisure park with a marina and open-air arena. In addition, Amager boasts a series of excellent beaches for bathing.

There are ferry services between Dragør and the Swedish town of Limhamn.

Dragør

Dragør, on the east side of Amager, is a picturesque little 18th c. town which has preserved its original character as a village of farmers and fishermen. By virtue of the herring fisheries in the sound, Dragør gained a position of considerable economic importance in the Middle Ages, and in 1370 was granted trading privileges and the right to salt herrings. With the eclipse of the herring fisheries Dragør declined in importance until the middle of the 16th c. when boat piloting in the sound provided a new source of income.

Ferries to Limhamn (Sweden)

History

The Dragør pilots were the first in the country to receive royal permission to discharge this service. During the 19th c. the Dragør shipping fleet enjoyed a heyday, plying not only between Copenhagen and the Danish provinces, but also between other harbours along the Baltic coasts and even to English ports. With the advent of steamships at the end of the last century the fleet's routes became restricted again to Danish waters.

Many of the houses in Dragør are protected as monuments. The oldest fisherman's house dates from 1682. It is situated by the harbour (Havnepladsen) and has an exhibition showing the historical development of seafaring in that area (open: May to Sept.: Tues.–Fri. 2–5pm, Sat., Sun. noon–6pm).

Dragør Museet

Mølsteds Museum in the Bledersstræde (no. 1) contains paintings and drawings of Dragør from the period 1862–1930 (open: May to Sept.: Sat., Sun. 2–5pm).

Mølsteds Museet

In the south of the island lies Store Magleby, once known as the "Dutchmen's Town". The first inhabitants of the island, who were Dutch, settled here in the early 16th c. during the reign of Christian II. They drained the land and brought it into cultivation. The Amager Museum, which occupies an old half-timbered farmhouse dating from the 18th c. (Hovedgaden 12), houses a collection of material illustrating the peasant tradition of the Dutch immigrants (open: May–Sept.: Tue.–Sun. noon–4pm; Oct.–Apr.: Wed., Sun. noon–4pm).

Store Magleby, Amagermuseet

★ Amagertorv (Amager Market; pedestrian zone)

H7

The Amagertorv, which runs between Hyskenstræde and Østergade and today forms part of the Strøget pedestrian zone, has been an important junction since the Middle Ages, linking the settlement at Gammeltorv with the market at Nikolaj Plads (see entry). Its name Amagertorv (Amager Market) is mentioned for the first time in 1472. In the 16th and 17th c. the street was from time to time the scene of chivalrous tournaments, even though the day-to-day occupants would have been the farmers and smallholders of Amager. As a result of the trading law enacted in 1684, all foodstuffs and flowers produced on the island of Amager (see entry) had to be sold at this market. In the adjoining buildings several merchant's shops were quickly established and at the corner of Østergade from 1656 the gentry used to drop into the fashionable inn known as "Store Lækkerbidsken" ("Large Titbits").

Location
Between Hyskenstræde and Østergade

Buses
8, 28, 29, 41

The "Stork" Fountain on the Amagertorv

After Copenhagen's second Great Fire of 1795, when the Højbro Plads (see entry) was laid just to the south, a crossing was built linking it to Amagertorv. The sales stands disappeared after 1868 when the market was resited at Christianshavn (see entry).

Storkespring-vandet

After the square lost its role as a market-place, the city's messengers and errand boys used to gather at the water pump at Amagertorv. The old pump was replaced in 1894 by the Storkespringvandet (stork fountain), which even today is one of the most popular meeting places of the young people of Copenhagen. It is flanked by the busy cafés named the "Europa" and the "Norden".

★Royal Copenhagen

The red-brick building (no. 6), which was built in 1616 in the Dutch Renaissance style for the city councillor, later mayor, Mathias Hansen, has rich sandstone decorations. Today it houses exhibitions of goods produced by Royal Copenhagen (royal porcelain manufacturers), the Holmegaard glass works and the porcelain manufacturers Bing & Grøndahl (see Facts and Figures, Danish Design). On Fri. and Sat. visitors can watch porcelain being hand-painted.

★Georg Jensen

In the house next door (no. 4) there are salesrooms and the museum belonging to the firm of silversmiths Georg Jensen (open: Mon.–Thur. 10am–6pm, Fri. 10am–7pm, Sat. 10am–5pm). Silversmiths can be seen at work every Fri. and Sat.

The beautiful patrician house no. 9 was built between 1789 and 1800 for the cloth merchant J. A. Bechmann. Its façade was remodelled between 1830 and 1870. Anyone interested in smoking utensils and old pipes should pay a visit to the Pipe Museum founded in 1864 by W. Ø. Larsen (open: Mon.–Thur. 10am–6pm, Fri. 10am–7pm, Sat. 10am–2pm), which includes hand-carved meerschaum pipes, ornate tobacco tins and clay and water pipes among its treasures. Opposite, in Ole Larsen's tobacco shop, the enthusiast can choose his favourite mixture from among the many fragrant "Selected Blends" of the court purveyors of tobacco.

★W. Ø. Larsens Pipe Museum

In the building next door (no. 10) the visitor will find in Illums Bolighus Danish furniture of all kinds (see Facts and Figures, Danish Design).

★Illums Bolighus

A good example of the historicist trend of the 19th c. is "Ole Haslund's House" (no. 14), which was completed in 1867. Typical of this period are the pillars crowned by busts of men, which serve as window-jambs.

Ole Haslund's House

★★Amalienborg Slot (Amalienborg Palace)

J6

The Rococo palace of Amalienborg, which since 1794 has been the royal residence, was built between 1749 and 1760 for King Frederik V by the famous Danish court and city architect Niels Eigtved (1701–54). Two of the palace's four wings (not open to the public) are occupied by the royal family, whose presence there is marked by the raising of the Dannebrog flag, whilst the other two are used for state and official functions and as museums.

Location
Amaliengade/
Amalienborg
Slotsplads

Buses
1, 6, 9, 10

With the aid of exhibits from the private apartments, the museum in Christian VIII's palace provides information about the royal family from Christian IX to Christian X (1863–1947). It is open Jan.–Apr.: Tue.–Sun. 11am–4pm, May–mid-Oct.: daily 11am–4pm, mid-Oct.–mid-Dec.: Tue.–Sun. 11am–4pm. Eigtved was the most celebrated architect of his time, who, besides building Amalienborg Palace and the surrounding district, was also responsible for the Prince's Palace (today the Nationalmuseet, see entry) and the Marble Bridge (see entry) on the south side of

Amalienborg
Museum

Den lille Havfrue

© Baedeker

Marmorkirken

Fredericiagade
Amaliegade
Frederiksgade
Frederiksgade
Amaliegade
Toldbodgade
Oslokaj

Nyhavn

Amalienborg
Royal Palace since 1794

1 Levetzau Palace
   (Christian VIII, Christian X)

2 Brockdorff Palace
   (Frederik VIII, Frederik IX)

3 Moltke Palace
   (Christian VII)

4 Schack Palace (originally
   Løvenskjold Palace)
   (Frederik VI, Christian IX,
   Margrethe II)

5 Equestrian statue of King
   Frederik V (1771)

Christiansborg Palace (see entry) and thereby created an area of the city which was in a unified Rococo style. Possibly this vision of the city's architecture originated with King Frederik V, who donated land to the rich noble families of Brockdorff, Levetzau, Løvenskjold and Moltke and offered them 40 years of tax exemption to enable them to carry through their building plans. Linked to these gifts was his condition that the four mansions to be built in the middle of the new district of Frederiksstad must be based on plans by Eigtved.

Just a few decades later the palaces were taken into royal ownership after the destruction of Christiansborg Palace in the fire of 1794. In the same year the colonnade designed by C. F. Harsdorff was erected – a wooden construction with Ionic columns which established a link across the Amaliengade between the two palaces.

Statue of Frederik V on horseback

Dominating the centre of Amalienborg Palace is the 12m/39ft statue of Frederik V on horseback (J. F. Saly, 1711), a present from the East India Company in acknowledgement of the Danish crown's support for their colonial conquests.

★★Changing of the guard

The soldiers on guard at Amalienborg Palace, who stand in front of their guard-huts in their bearskin helmets and blue, white and red uniforms, are one of Copenhagen's most photogenic attractions. Every day, when Queen Margarethe II is in residence in Copenhagen, the changing of the guard takes place punctually at noon with music and standards. If the Queen Mother Ingrid is alone at Amalienborg, the changing of the guard takes place with music but no standards. The new soldiers march from their barracks in Kongens Have (see Rosenborg Palace) just before 11.30am. The route they take leads along the Gothersgade as far as Norrevoldgade, then on down the Frederiksborgade, the Købmagergade (see entry) and the Østergade, then over the Kongens Nytorv (see entry) and on along the Bredgade and Frederiksgade to the palace.

Changing of the Guard outside Amalienborg Palace

The modern Arken Museum in Ishøj – built in the shape of the stern of a huge ship

★Arken – Museum of Modern Art

The Arken scandal was in fact a huge hoax which had all Denmark laughing: Anna Carstberg, the museum's founding director, was attributed with all kinds of unfortunate make-believe qualities and even sacked – a wrong decision on the part of local politicians which proved very costly. However, in spite of all its financial problems which the new director Christian Gether now has to solve, the Museum of Modern Art, which opened in 1995, proved to be one of the successes of the Copenhagen Year of Culture.

The design for this eccentric concrete "sculpture" among the dunes of Ishøj was the work of the architectural student Søren Robert Lund and is an stunning concept based on an interchange of narrowness and width. Whitewashed walls and three sloping roofs point to the sky like the stern of a giant prefuturistic ship, a striking collage of concrete and steel against a backcloth of dunes and the sea.

From the 150m/490ft long main nave in the form of a bow and arrow the visitor enters separate display areas and well-lit outer enclosures, spacious halls and galleries housing tranquil designs. The twin-pronged ground plan of the "Arch" provides some 4000sq.m/43,000sq.ft of exhibition space for contemporary, mainly Danish art. The museum will, however, offer more than just pictures and sculptures; it also contains a large concert hall, theatre and ballet workshops and has its own chamber orchestra and a professionally equipped cinema.

Location
Skowej 100
Ishøj

Bus
S-bane to Ishøj,
then bus 128

Opening times
Tue.–Sun
10am–5pm
Wed. to 10pm

Arkitekturcentret Gammel Dok

See Christianshavn

★Assistens Kirkegård (Cemetery)   F6

Location
Kapelvej 2
Buses
5, 16, 7E

Copenhagen's largest and probably most interesting cemetery was laid out by royal command in 1757 following the plague epidemic of 1711. It was initially a makeshift additional cemetery, as its name indicates (Assistens Kirkegård = relief churchyard). The original brick wall with its niches, which surrounds part of the cemetery, was built by Philip de Lange, but the site was subsequently enlarged on a number of occasions. Today the Assistens Kirkegård serves at the same time as a park where people are always to be found on the grass between the graves, relaxing with a picnic or just enjoying the sun.

The cemetery and park are open from sunrise to sunset.

Graves

Tombstone of Søren Kirkegaard

Many famous people are laid to rest in the cemetery; there is a board at the Nørrebrogade entrance listing their names and where they are buried.

Amongst the most famous graves is that of the poet and fairy-storyteller, Hans Christian Andersen (see Famous People), which is to be found in Section P of the cemetery. In Section B the philosopher Søren Kierkegaard (see Famous People) is buried, while in Section D there is the mausoleum of Peter von Scholten, Governor General of the former West Indian islands of St Croix, St John and St Thomas, who in 1848 on his own initiative abolished slavery on the islands following an uprising among the slaves there. Near the entrance can also be found the grave of the Danish workers' poet, Martin Andersen Nexø (see Famous People). Also worthy of special mention are the graves of the physicist and Nobel prizewinner Niels Bohr (see Famous People) and the Danish writer Poul Martin Møller (1794–1838), whose posthumous masterpiece "En dansk students eventyr" (1843), was the first fantasy novel to be written in Denmark.

★Axeltorv (Axel Market; pedestrian zone)   G7

Location
Between
Hammerichsgade
and
Vesterbrogade

S-bane
Vesterport

The Axeltorv, newly designed by Mogens Breyen at the end of the 1980s, and boasting a number of statues by Mogens Møller, is an example of the latest city architecture in Copenhagen. The sky is reflected in the water of the large granite pool above a Venetian mosaic symbolising the sun. The nine sculptures close by are abstract interpretations of the planets of the solar system. At the end of the square the eye is caught by the colourful complex of the great Palad cinema-temple (no. 9; see Practical Information, Cinemas).

The new Scala shopping and entertainment centre (no. 2), alongside a row of shops and boutiques, also houses cinemas, discothèques and a fitness centre, as well as cafés and restaurants, where visitors can take a break while shopping.

Scala

★Bakken (Amusement park)

Founded in 1583, the Dyrehavsbakken, called Bakken for short, is the oldest amusement park in the world. It lies on the edge of the Dyrehaven (see entry) in Klampenborg Park and stretches as far as the Øresund. At the end of the 16th c. visitors used to spend time at the nearby spring "Kirsten Piils Kilde", in order to find a cure for their ills. They were followed by traders and travelling entertainers who set up their stands here and on the adjoining hill; from 1746 this became a permanent fixture.

The Bakken is the popular answer to the Tivoli (see entry), with over 120 amusement rides and stalls as well as restaurants. These include the Kasperl Theatre and the Pierrot, merry-go-rounds and a giant roller-coaster, shooting-ranges, tombolas, music-halls, bars and restaurants with dancing. In the high season a children's day is held every Wednesday, when all the amusements are available at half price (open: Apr.–Aug.: daily 2pm–midnight).

Location
Dyrehavsbakken

S-bane
Klampenborg, then on foot (10mins) or by carriage

Buses
160, 178, 188

Blixen Museet

See Karen Blixen Museet

Bakken amusement park

Bolten's

See Kongens Nytorv

★Botanisk Have (Botanical Garden)   H6

Location
Gothersgade 128

S-bane
Nørreport

Buses
5, 7, 14, 16, 24, 40, 43, 84, 384

Opening times
Oct.–Mar.
8.30am–4pm;
Apr.–Sept.
8.30am–6pm

The Botanical Garden between Sølvgade and Gothersgade was laid out between 1871 and 1874 according to plans by the landscape gardener H. A. Flindt. The lake was originally part of the city's defensive moat.

As well as the greenhouses with their tropical and subtropical plants (open: daily 10am–3pm), the palm house (open: daily 10am–3pm) and the cactus house (open: Sat., Sun. 1–3pm) are well worth seeing. The recently restored hothouses, made of glass, cast-iron and wood, which were probably designed by J. C. Jacobsen and Tyge Rothe, have as their model, among others, the palm house at Kew Gardens in London, designed by the English landscape gardener Joseph Paxton.

In one part of the garden it is possible to admire all the wild plants of Denmark in artificially created habitats of marsh, heath and dune. In addition there is an Alpine garden with mountain plants from all over the world.

Burmeister and Wain Museet

See Christianshavn, B & W Museet

The City Museum, a gouache by I. M. Wagner (1807)

Københavns Bymuseum & Søren Kierkegaard Samlingen   G7
(City Museum)

The city museum, which is being re-arranged, offers an overall view of the history of Copenhagen. Since 1956 it has been housed in the building of the Royal Copenhagen Shooting Society (built in 1787). From 1901, when it was opened, until that date it was located in the City Hall. The first four rooms cover 800 years of history, from medieval

Location
Vesterbrogade 59

Buses
6, 16, 28, 41

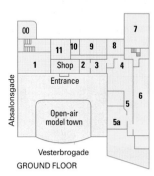

GROUND FLOOR

City Museum

Københavns Bymuseum und Søren Kierkegaard Samlingen

Opening Times
Oct. 1st–Apr. 30 Tue.–Sun. 1–4pm
May 1st–Sept. 30 Tue.–Sun. 10am–4pm

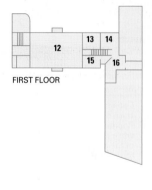

FIRST FLOOR

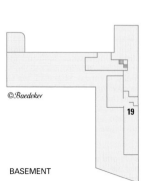

BASEMENT

ATTIC STOREY

1 Royal chamber in 19th c. style
2–5 From Høje Taastrup 1995 to Sømmel Strand 1167; from modern city to small medieval port
5a Pictorama (film and slide show)
6 Episcopal seat and royal residence: from 11th c. trading post to 17th c. Renaissance town under Christian IV
7 Garden room with paintings, silver, 18th c. porcelain and earthenware
8–11 Absolutist rulers: Copenhagen's flowering 1660–1840; Søren Kierkegaard collection (opening 1998)

12 Banquet hall with portrait of Hans Hansens by Frederick VI (1818)
13–16 Middle-class Copenhagen (1840–1908); Liberal constitution and marked industrial advances
17–18 Democratic Copenhagen (1908–2000) Development of democratic-parliamentary monarchy: Copenhagen today and tomorrow
19 Copenhagen underground: Canal system, archaeological finds and a murky capital with prostitution and crime

51

In the Bymuseum the history of Copenhagen is available to all

Copenhagen to the city as it is today. Room 5 portrays the Renaissance town of the 17th c. during the reign of Christian IV (see Famous People). Rooms 8–9 are devoted to the absolutist rulers between 1660 and 1840, while rooms 10–13 cover building changes, industrialisation and the rise of the middle-classes in the 19th c. Finally, in rooms 14 and 15, the visitor will find extensive material on the development of Copenhagen in the 20th c. and the very latest changes in the townscape. The basement portrays the capital of Denmark "underground", from the canal system and archaeological finds to its darker side such as crime and prostitution. The banquet hall and garden room give an idea of how the upper classes used to live.

Søren Kierkegaard Samlingen

A special exhibition is devoted to the life and works of the philosopher Søren Kierkegaard (see Famous People). On display are some pieces of furniture and personal mementoes, including a portrait of his parents and a picture of his friend, Regine Olsen.

Museum street

In 1980 the neighbouring Absalonsgade was successfully opened as a museum street, fitted out with signs, water hydrants, street lamps, letter-boxes, telephone booths and cobble-stones dating from 1850 to 1940.

City model

In front of the museum in the summer months visitors can admire a model of Copenhagen in Reformation times.

★Børsen (Old Stock Exchange)   H7

Location
Børsgade

On the palace island of Slotsholmen opposite Christiansborg Palace (see entry) lies the old Stock Exchange. It is one of the most beautiful buildings in Copenhagen and one of its most characteristic.

This long low Renaissance structure was built for King Christian IV

The Former Exchange, one of the symbols of the city

(see Famous People) between 1619 and 1640 by the Dutch brothers Lorenz and Hans Steenwinckel the Younger. At the wish of the king the Exchange was given decorative gables which face at right angles on to the canal, and the roof was crowned with a 54m/177ft high tower. Its spire, completed in 1625, consists of four stylised intertwined dragon's tails, which were based on a design by the firework-maker Ludvig Heidritter. The copper roof with its patina of green is the building's other characteristic feature.

Buses
1, 2, 5, 6, 8, 9, 10, 28, 29, 31, 37, 43

Originally there was a trading hall on the ground floor, while the upper storey – approached by a ramp on the west side and a staircase on the east – was reserved for businesses and shops. Two statues by J. C. Petzhold, "Mercury" and "Neptune", commissioned by the merchant A. Bjørn, were added to the ramp during restoration work in 1745 by the court architect Nicolai Eigtved.

In the middle of the 19th c. the Exchange was taken over by the union of wholesale merchants, who had to undertake to preserve the architectural style of the building and not to alter anything without the consent of the state.

Today the exchange shops are no longer here but have been displaced to Fonnesbech House on Nikolaj Plads (no. 8; see entry). The old exchange building now belongs to and is the seat of the Chamber of Commerce of Copenhagen. As a general rule the building is not open to the public.

The mosaic work in the entrance hall on the ground floor illustrates the historical development of the Exchange. The great exchange room is spacious with pillars, wooden panelling, gilded leather-clad walls and an elaborate coffered ceiling. At the end of the room stands the bronze figure of Christian IV, the work of the sculptor Bertel Thorvaldsen (see Famous People).

Caritas Springvandet (Caritas Fountain)

Location
Gammeltorv

Bus
5

Erected in 1608 on the Gammeltorv and subsequently restored several times, the Caritas Fountain must be considered one of the most beautiful works of art of the Renaissance period. The group of figures round the copper bowl of the fountain, a pregnant woman with two children, symbolise brotherly love (Caritas = charity). At her feet are sprawled three dolphins with gargoyles.

★Carlsberg Brewery   E/F8

Location
Ny Carlsbergvey
140

Buses
6, 18

Conducted tours
Mon.–Fri.
11am, 2pm

The Carlsberg Brewery, one of the largest in the world, is also rich in tradition. Visitors to Copenhagen are not only offered a conducted tour of the brewery, but are also allowed to sample the beer. The Carlsberg Museum, which was founded in 1882 is located at Valby Langgade 1 (open: Mon.–Fri. 10am–3pm).

A Toast to the Arts

From the four stone elephants guarding the brewery entrance, the decorated "elephant gate", the Carlsberg dynasty's feeling for fine things can be appreciated. For a long time the brewery has supported from its profits Danish cultural life, putting on its lorries the motto "Skål for Kunsten" (a toast to the arts). The founder of the brewery, J. C. Jacobsen, had already established a foundation for research in 1876, the aims of which also included the maintenance of the National Historical Museum in Frederiksborg Slot. His son Carl shared his interest in the arts and among other things authorised the building of the spire of the Nikolaj Church and the campanile of the Jesus church. In addition he extended the scope of the foundation and set up the Ny Carlsberg Glyptotek with its unique collection of classical and modern art. Today the Ny Carlsberg Foundation also contributes to the upkeep of Kronborg Slot and the Louisiana Arts Museum. The latest financial investment is the new wing of Ny Carlsberg Glytotek opened in 1996 to house a collection of French Art.

In November 1847 J. C. Jacobsen (1811–87) produced the first Bavarian beer to be brewed in Denmark in his newly-built brewery in Valby, outside the walls of Copenhagen. The brewery was named Carlsberg by him after his son Carl, who studied brewing both in Denmark and abroad and, by extending the production capacity of the brewery in 1871, started the first Ny-Carlsberg Brewery, although he was to open his own brewery with the same name ten years later. For economic reasons the two factories were amalgamated in 1906. Because of increasing international competition Carlsberg finally merged with the Tuborg Brewery (see entry) in 1970, which resulted in the "De forenede Bryggerier A/S", now Carlsberg A/S. The various types of beer produced (see Practical Information, Food and Drink, Beer) are today exported to more than 130 countries.

The production plant of the first brewery, the "Gamle Carlsberg", was restored in 1982 and today can be visited by arrangement.

Four large granite Indian elephants guard the entrance to the Carlsberg Brewery ▶

The brewery also financed the new wing of the Ny Carlsberg Glyptotek (see entry) which was opened in 1996.

Christiania   J7

Location
Christianshavn district

Bus
8

In 1996 Christiania celebrated its "silver wedding" with the state of Denmark – something that even those who founded the "Free State" in 1971 could never have foreseen. The "free state" of Christiania, which was legalised in 1991, lies on the island of Amager (see entry) and belongs to the district of Christianshavn (see entry). As it was originally intended to offer protection to the royal fleet from Christianshavn, military installations were initially built on the site. In 1971 the garrison and barrack area, which amounted to 34ha/840 acres, was cleared in order to make way for dwellings and parkland. Instead of this the area was occupied by drop-outs, hippies and seekers of an alternative life-style. On November 13th 1971 they founded an independent community, the "Free State of Christiania", which was declared illegal. All attempts by the Danish authorities to get rid of them failed. In the end the place was recognised as a "social experiment", although it continued to attract controversy. Massive external pressures led to the drop-out society being legalised on its twentieth anniversary. In 1991 representatives of the grass-roots democratic full assembly of Christiania signed a long-debated agreement, in which for the first time the inhabitants of the free state undertook to meet the costs of rent and other additional services and to maintain around 150 buildings deemed worthy of preservation as well as the extensive green areas. In return the inhabitants were guaranteed usufruct by the Copenhagen authorities.

Critics still regard Christiania as a trouble-spot and a "hotbed of crime" (in the words of the Danish Justice Minister), partly because of the high poverty levels in the free state (over 50% of the adults live on social security, almost 20% are drawing a pension early or are in receipt of other benefits) and also because of the pervasive consumption of drugs such as hashish and marijuana. Supporters, however, see in the drop-outs' republic an unprecedented attempt to move towards a new type of society and point to the positive successes: since 1979, through the voluntarily set up "Junk Blockade", the consumption of hard drugs virtually no longer exists; in order to safeguard the environment, compost production, sorting of rubbish and recycling have all been introduced to car-free Christiania as part of an alternative energy strategy, and experiments have been made with solar and wind energy. In addition there is a communal child-minding service provided in the nursery and youth-club, which, together with other social services, has been financed by takings in the bars and restaurants.

★★Christiansborg Slot (Christiansborg Palace)   H7

Location
Christiansborg Slotplads

Buses
1, 2, 5, 6, 8, 9, 10, 28, 29, 31, 37, 41, 43

Christiansborg Palace, situated on the island of Slotsholmen, has been the seat of the Danish parliament since 1918 (Folketing; see Facts and Figures, Danish Parliament). In addition the Foreign Ministry and the High Court of Justice are housed here. The royal audience rooms are also located in the castle and, like the parliament itself, can only be visited on a conducted tour.

When leaving Slotsholmen Island in the direction of the Nationalmuseet (see entry) the visitor crosses the Frederiksholms Canal by the Marble Bridge (see entry) designed by Nicolai Eigtved.

Opening times
old castle ruins

Oct.–Apr.: Tue., Thur., Sat., Sun. 9.30am–3.30pm;
May–Sept.: daily 9.30am–3.30pm.

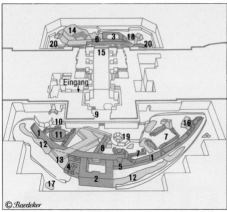

Christiansborg

1167	Bishop Absalon of Roskilde begins the construction of a fortified castle
1368–9	Destruction of castle, followed by rebuilding and extension
Beginning of 15th c.	Castle taken over by Danish crown
1552–6	Building of King's Wing
1733–45	Rebuilding in Baroque style: Christiansborg 1
1794	Destruction by fire
1803	Rebuilding begins: Christiansborg 2
1884	Destruction by fire
1907–19	Rebuilding: Christiansborg 3

© Baedeker

Excavations

Bishop's castle (12th–14th c.)

1 Outer wall
2 West tower
3 East tower (?)
4 Privy Chamber
5 Drain from courtyard
6 House wall (ruined)
7 Small buildings
8 Two-roomed house
9 Wooden well
10 Limestone well
11 Oven

Medieval castle (14th–18th c.)

12 Outer wall
13 South gable of Knights' Hall wing
14 Foundations of Blue Tower
15 Foundation of King's Wing
16 Foundations of church wing
17 Remains of 16th c. foundations
18 Base of chimney
19 Well
20 Water supply pipe of first castle

Danish Parliament (Folketing): June–Sept.: Mon.–Fri., Sun. on the hour 10am–4pm; Oct.–May: Sun. on the hour 10am–4pm

Royal reception rooms (Conducted tours in English): Oct.–Apr.: Tues., Thur. and Sun. 11am, 3pm; May, Sept. daily 11am, 3pm. June–Aug.: daily 11am, 1pm, 3pm.

Conducted tours through parliament and the palace

History

The palace dominates the square where in the spring of 1167 Bishop Absalon (see Famous People) began the building of a fortress and founded Copenhagen. The fortifications were destroyed in 1259 by the Wends and in 1368–69 by the Lübeckers, only to be later extensively rebuilt. When the present palace was built, these ruins were left uncovered and have for some years now have been open to visitors.

The late medieval castle, which under Eric of Pomerania passed to the crown, was altered and extended several times during the 15th, 16th and 17th c. Thus the Knights' Hall was extended on the occasion of the marriage of Christoph III of Bavaria to Queen Dorothea of Brandenburg in 1445, and then in the middle of the 16th c., on the site of the dried-up moat, Christian III added a wing for the king and his bodyguards, which was to contain the second largest room in the whole castle.

The old castle buildings no longer proved adequate for the demands of Baroque grandeur in the 18th c.: after Frederik IV had as late as 1720 ordered all the wings of the castle to be brought to the same height by having additional storeys superimposed, Christian IV (see Famous People) in April 1733 laid the inaugural stone in the building of a magnificent three-storey palace. In November 1740 the royal family moved in, although it was not possible to complete the magnificent Knights'

Christiansborg Palace: the seat of the Danish parliament since 1918

Hall until 1766. The entire kings's apartments were decorated through-out with French mirror glass and the other 348 rooms received the most elaborate fittings. For the Knights' Hall Nicolai Abilgaard contributed 22 paintings on the subject of the history of the Danish monarchy. The palace had four wings and was in the Viennese Baroque style. It was still unfinished when it burnt down in 1794. Only the buildings belonging to the riding arena survived.

In the early years of the 19th c. the second, more austerely conceived, version of the palace was built under Frederik VI to designs by the neo-classical master C. F. Hansen, with its Knights' Hall decorated by Corinthian columns and an ornate coffered ceiling. In 1849 the new parliament moved into the building, which was seldom used as a royal residence. This building also fell victim to a fire in October 1884. Those parts that remain include the palace church, built by C. F. Hansen and consecrated in 1846, the dome of which was embellished with figures of angels and statues of apostles by Bertel Thorvaldsen (see Famous People).

The design for the "third", Christianborg Palace, built between 1907 and 1928, was the work of Thorvald Jørgensen. He had the difficult task of incorporating the remaining parts of the old building into a new set-ting, something in which he was only partially successful. The great four-winged palace is distinguished today by its 90m/295ft high tower and the façade, imposingly clad in Bornholm granite and stone, which was provided by the Danish municipalities. The throne room and the 40m/131ft long Knights' Hall are especially worth visiting.

Statue of Frederik VII on horseback

On the square in front of the palace can be seen a statue of Frederik VII on horseback, which was created by one of Thorvaldsen's pupils, H. V.

Bissen and was erected to commemorate the passing of the first Basic Law in 1849.

In the lobby of the Folketing it is worth noticing the shrine in which the charter of the constitution is kept. From one of the central boxes in the Folketing Hall the visitor has a good view of the chamber, the dimensions of which correspond to those of the "mother of parliaments", the British House of Commons. In contrast, however, to the latter, where the members sit on benches along the length of the room, the Danish representatives are grouped in a horse-shoe shape around the central table and the seat of the parliamentary chairman, and whereas the British lower house does not have enough seats for its 650 members, the 179 representatives of the Folketing each have their own allotted seat with a desk. Following the pattern of the National Assembly which met during the French Revolution, the right-wingers are placed on the right of the chairman and the left-wingers on the left. Even though new parties and internal party regroupings have brought about changes in the seating plan, it is still the case that – looking from the chairman's position – the Conservative People's Party sits to the right of the Venstre liberal party, which in turn sits to the right of the liberal left Venstre Radical Party, itself positioned to the right of the Social Democrats. Only the Socialist People's Party sits somewhat illogically between the Liberal Left and the Social Democrats, whilst the smaller parties are usually relegated to the rear seats.

The seating of representatives is also determined by length of parliamentary service, with party leaders and political spokesmen sitting in the first row. The government is to the left of the parliamentary chair-

Folketing

59

man. The front row is reserved for the Prime Minister, Foreign Minister, Finance and Justice Ministers, with the other ministers behind, their seating order being decided by length of service.

The triple podium (to the left of the speaker's desk) was carved by Anny Berntsen-Bure, daughter of the then Prime Minister Klaus Berntsen, out of a thousand-year-old trunk of oak which had served as the central structure of a mill on the island of Møn. A tapestry by Berit Hjeholt, which bears the title "Like a fleet yearning to set sail", hangs over the podium.

Kongelige Stalde og Kareter, Teatermuseet

An archway leads from the Folketingsgården to the equestrian arena and the Royal Stables (see Practical Information, Museums). Old carriages, harness and livery dating from 1778 onwards can be seen (open: Oct.–Apr.: Sat., Sun., 2–4pm, May–Sept. Fri.–Sun. 2–4pm).

★Teatermuseet

In 1766 N. H. Jardin fitted out the Royal Court Theatre above the riding-stables. It was here that Count von Struensee (see Famous People), powerful minister and lover of Queen Caroline Mathilde, was arrested on Jan. 17th 1772. Shortly afterwards he paid for his liaison with the queen with his life.

In 1842 Jørgen Hansen Koch modernised the theatre, the auditorium of which had remained unaltered until that date. The Theatrical Museum was opened in 1922 and portrays the history of both the Danish and the international theatre from the time of Ludvig Holbergby (see Famous People) until the present day by means of photographs, old prints and colourful costumes (open: Wed. 2–4pm, Sat., Sun. noon–4pm).

★Christianshavn (City district)   H–K6/7

Location
Amager Island

Buses
2, 8, 9, 31, 37

The district of Copenhagen known as Christianshavn is situated opposite Slotsholmen, on the island of Amager (see entry). King Christian IV (see Famous People), who reigned from 1588 to 1648, ordered the building of a new town here which initially did not form part of Copenhagen at all. With its parallel streets lying at right angles to its central canal, it calls to mind Amsterdam. On the side facing away from the sea the town is enclosed by thick walls.

Christianshavn is a tourist attraction in itself. It is reached by the Langebro and Knippelsbro bridges. With the building of this "city in miniature", which took place from 1618 onwards following the Dutch model of streets and canals laid at right angles to one another, King Christian IV gave to the city of Copenhagen its own personal stamp. Up until 1674 Christianshavn remained independent, but then for financial reasons it had to accept annexation to Copenhagen. That there are a striking number of old houses still preserved here is due to the fact that Christianshavn was to a large extent spared the terrible fires that Copenhagen suffered. Up to now it has been possible – despite the unavoidable renovation measures of the last few decades – to preserve in its essentials the historic fabric of buildings such as the many patrician houses and lovingly fashioned courtyards in the Strandgade, where the Danish sailor Peder Tordenskjold (1691–1720) and the educationalist and founder of adult education centres, Nicolai Frederik Severin Grundtvig (see Famous People) were born, the buildings along the Christianshavn Canal, which is included in harbour and canal boat tours, the half-timbered buildings in the Amagergade, the old ramparts, the Vor Frelser Kirke (Church of the Redeemer; see entry) and the Rococo style Christians Kirke (see entry).

Anyone coming over the Knippelsbro Bridge to Christianshavn will see first of all the unattractive building of the Foreign Ministry on the left and a bank complex on the right which was formerly the administrative offices of the shipyard Burmeister & Wain. A few minutes further on, the

Christianshavn Canal

Gammel Dok architectural centre

Christianshavn Torv (market) in the centre of the town is reached, from where a tour on foot can be made of the surrounding streets.

B & W Museet
(Burmeister &
Wain Museum)

In an old warehouse on the Strandgade (no. 4) Copenhagen's largest company, the shipyard Burmeister & Wain, has set up a museum in which models of ships and diesel engines are displayed (open: Mon.–Fri. and first Sun. in the month 10am–1pm).

The Burmeister & Wain shipyards are situated further north on Refshaleøen.

Arkitekturcentret
Gammel Dok

The former storage house no. 27 in the Strandgade is now the home of the Gammel Dok Architecture Centre. Architectural and design exhibitions are regularly held (open: Tues., Thur.–Sun. 10am–5pm, Wed. 10am–8pm). From the windows of the café in the cultural centre the visitor can watch the ships going past in the Inderhavnen.

Christians Kirke

See entry

Orlogsmuseet
Royal Naval
Museum

Visitors who are interested in historic model ships, nautical instruments or naval uniforms (17th c. to the present-day), underwater archaeology or maritime art should pay a visit to the Royal Naval Museum (Orlogsmuseet, Over gaden Oven Vandet 58; open Tues.–Sun. noon–4pm).

Vor Frelser Kirke

See entry

Christiania

See entry

Christians Kirke (Church)   I7

Location
Strandgade

Buses
2, 8, 9, 31, 37

On the west side of the Christianshavn Canal in Christianshavn stands the Christianskirke. This Rococo church, built by Nikolai Eigtved between 1755 and 1759, was the place of worship of the German Lutheran community until 1886. With the approval of King Frederik V the building costs were financed by a lottery, which earned the church the nickname of the "lottery church". Officially the church was initially known as Frederiks Tyske Kirke (Frederick's German Church), whilst it acquired its present-day name in 1901. Its tower, crowned by a sphere with a flag, dates from 1769; the stonework on the tower was the work of C. F. Stanley. Of interest inside the church are the three-storey gallery, the font made of Norwegian marble, a baptism bowl with a German inscription dating from 1759, as well as the crypt with its 48 burial chapels, which were erected in the 18th and 19th c. (open: Mar.–Oct.: 8am–6pm; Nov.–Feb.: 8am–5pm).

Cirkusbygningen (Circus buildings)   G7

Location
Jernbanegade 8

S-bane
Vesterport

The first cylinder-shaped circus and varieties building was built by the architect H. V. Brinkopff in 1885 and opened in April 1886. One of the earliest attractions was the "Black Opera" of the 1890s, a musical show which relied solely on coloured performers. In 1914 the circus arena fell victim to a fire, with only the stone circular wall remaining intact. The rebuilding of the circus was entrusted to the firm of Christiani & Nielsen under the direction of the architect Holger Jacobsen, while the frieze on the exterior wall, showing various scenes of classical horse-races, was the work of U. A. F. Hammeleff. The Schumann Circus then moved into the building for a number of years, until it was taken over by the permanent Benneweis Circus, a family concern founded in 1887. Today the circus building is used for concerts and stage shows. Tickets can be obtained at the box office which is open between noon and 5pm (Tel. 33 15 01 11).

Crown Prince Ferderik (1787) ...   *... and an Indian miniature drawing (16th c.)*

★C. L. Davids Samling (Museum of art)   H6

The former private art collection of C. L. David is housed in an old patrician house built in 1807 by J. H. Rawert. Both the works of art and the building, rather plain in appearance from the outside, were bequeathed to the Danish state in 1945 by the lawyer C. L. David.

The museum has on show outstanding examples of Islamic art from Persia and the surrounding countries dating from the 8th to the 16th c. (brocades, carpets, glassware, ceramics, manuscripts, miniatures and silver tableware). The collection also includes pieces of English furniture, a French Rococo sopraporte by François Boucher, furniture from the workshop of David Roentgen, paintings, in particular Danish painters of the 19th c., Danish silver from 17th and 18th c., and a collection of porcelain from the early period of Royal Danish factory (see Facts and Figures, Danish Design).

Location
Kronprinsesse-
gade 30

Buses
7, 10, 43

Opening times
Tues.–Sun. 1–4pm

Dragor

See Amager

Dukketeatermuseet, Priors Papirteater (Puppet Theatre Museum)   H6

The Dukketeatermuseet, which is situated in a pedestrian zone on the Købmagergade (see entry) near the Rundetårn (see entry), shows the art of puppet theatre from various periods and countries. Companies from Denmark, Germany, England and France cover a diverse repertoire, ranging from fairy tales to Shakespeare. Both large and small-scale

Location
Købmagergade 52

S-bane
Nørreport

Buses
5, 7, 14, 16, 24,
43, 84

puppet theatres can also be bought here – there is no obligation to buy, although the temptation to do so can be considerable (open: May–Mar.: Mon., Wed.–Fri. 12.30–5pm).

★Dyrehaven (Deer park)

Location
Klampenborg
(10km/6miles to
the north of the
city centre)

S-bane
Klampenborg

Opening times
All day

Dyrehaven Nature Park, which adjoins the highly popular amusement park of Bakken (see entry), is where herds of several hundred deer and sika live in a wooded area of about 10sq.km/4sq.miles (hunting rights exclusively belong to the Queen).

The "Hermitage", a Rococo hunting lodge displaying rich ornamental and sculptured decoration, was built by Laurids de Thura for King Christian V in 1734–36. It is only roused from its "Sleeping Beauty" slumber by the presence of the Queen.

At the S-bane station at Klampenborg a horse-drawn carriage can be hired in order to cross the park – just as the Danish kings used to.

Theodor Fontane, the German writer and theatre critic, describes this enchanted castle in the middle of the game park in his novel of 1891, "Unwiederbringlich" ("Gone for ever"):

"The path which they had to take lay along the edge of the park near the village, for the most part under tall-trunked plane trees, whose dangling branches covered in yellow foliage obscured their view with the result that it was only on emerging from this avenue of trees that they became aware of the "Hermitage" standing in the middle of its bright woodland glade ... Holk and the woman ... came to an involuntary halt and stared, almost in consternation, at the castle, towering in the distance in the clear autumnal sky, enveloped in the spell cast by its very seclusion. No smoke was rising and only the sun lay over the wide flat expanse of thick, lush grass, whilst up in the steely blue sky hundreds of sea-gulls hovered, and, in a long column, flew over from the sound in the direction of their long-favoured destination which lay further inland, Fura Water ... Already, in the background, the whole wide silvan canvas was coming alive, and likewise, just as hitherto only isolated herds had darted out from those spots nearest to them, now from the furthermost depths of the woodland emerged hundreds of deer, which, not wishing to fail to appear on the parade ground directly in front of them, started up a lively trot, at first in a wild and almost crazed confusion, until, on drawing nearer, they all formed orderly groups and in sections now filed past the Hermitage."

★Exsperimentarium (Museum)   H3

Location
Hellerup,
Tuborg Havnevej 7

Bus
6

In 1991 the Danish Science Centre Exsperimentarium was opened in the old bottling hall of the Tuborg Brewery (see entry). The building was renovated at a cost of 125 million krone and in its workshops and experiment rooms the new museum offers research opportunities in natural sciences and new technologies. In about 300 experiments – ranging across such topics as magnetism, aerodynamics, polarised light and gyroscopics, sources of energy, anatomy, astronomy and environmental influences – the visitor is enabled in an easily understandable way to draw nearer to the processes and laws of science and technology. The experimentarium is seen as a point of contact between the general public and organisations concerned with trade, industry and research, which, by means of lectures and presentations of new discoveries, are constantly bringing up to date and enlarging the scientific information available within the museum (open: Mon., Wed.–Fri. 9am–5pm; Tue. 9am–9pm; Sat., Sun. 11am–5pm.)

Scientific experimental rooms in the Exsperimentarium

Fiskerkone

See Gammel Strand

Folketing

See Christiansborg Slot

★★Fredensborg Slot (Fredensberg Palace)

This spring and autumn residence of the royal family, situated on the Esrumsø, was built between 1719 and 1722 by J. C. Krieger in the Italian Baroque style. King Frederik IV gave the palace the name "Fredensborg" in memory of the peace which ended the 2nd Nordic War (1700–20). The present appearance of the palace with its classical façade goes back to the architect Caspar Frederik Harsdorff.

If the Queen is present a changing of the guard takes place every day at noon. The palace can only be visited during the month of July (daily 1–5pm).

In the palace park stretching north-westwards to Lake Esrum, Frederik IV had 69 statues of artisans, farmers and fishermen ("Nordmandsdalen") erected. These are perfectly preserved even today. With its avenues and statues, the palace park, which is open all the year round, is considered one of the most beautiful parks in Denmark.

Location
40km/25 miles
north of
Copenhagen

Railway station
Fredensborg

Buses
336, 384

★Frederiksberg Have (Park) E7

Location
Roskildevej/Pile
Allé/Allégade,
Frederiksborg

Buses
18, 28, 41

Opening times
All day

Close to the Zoologisk Have (Zoo) lies Frederiksberg Palace in the middle of a picturesque park criss-crossed by canals. In former times members of the court used to arrange boating parties here; today Frederiksberg Have is a popular destination for weekend outings with the people of Copenhagen. Inside the park, the crowning attraction of which is an avenue of linden trees 270 years old, there is a succession of bars and cafés where visitors can also consume food they have brought with them.

One of the peculiarities of Copenhagen is that, although it is not far from the city centre, Frederiksberg is an independent municipality with its own council. This affluent suburb of Copenhagen has its own coat of arms and its citizens pay fewer taxes than the people of Copenhagen itself.

Frederiksborg Slot

Frederiksberg Palace dates from 1732–38 during the reign of King Christian VI, although a start had already been made on the building of a summer residence back in 1699. Laurids de Thurah built the symmetrically conceived palace on Valby Hill (today Frederiksberg Hill) in the baroque style of an Italian mansion. The rooms contain massive baroque paintings by the Danes, Coffre and Krock, encircled with stucco decorations by Italian masters such as Carbonetti, Quadri and Rigas, as well as tapestries and wall hangings. In 1770 the palace was renovated and some of the rooms redesigned, the Knights' Hall acquiring the appearance that it still has to this day with wall decorations coming from Hersdorff. Since 1869 the palace has been the home of the military academy, founded in 1713 by Frederik IV (the Hærens Officersskole). Only the palace chapel in the east wing, now restored with all its original features, is open to the public.

Frederiksberg Palace

The palace garden was originally laid out in 1711 by Hans Henrik Bruhn. Its design was geometric, following French models, with a large number of fountains, statues and exotic plants. Between 1789 and 1800 it was completely relandscaped by Peter Petersen. He inclined to the English tradition and created a romantically scenic park with tiny islands and meandering rivulets. He left intact the two main avenues lined with linden trees, but replaced the others with small groups of trees. A tour by rowing-boat is recommended: these are provided by Flemming Svendsen – the only person to have royal permission to do so.

Frederiksberg
Have

★★Frederiksborg Slot (Frederiksberg Palace; National Historical Museum)

Since 1884 the National Historical Museum has been housed in the most beautiful Renaissance palace in Denmark, situated on three islands in the middle of the tiny Frederiksborg Lake. The palace was built for King Christian IV (see Famous People) between 1602 and 1620 by the Fleming Hans van Steenwinkel the Elder and his son Hans van Steenwinkel the Younger. It was erected on the site of an older castle belonging to Frederik II and after a fire in 1859 was restored in the old style.

Until Fredensborg Palace was built, the palace at Frederiksborg provided the Danish monarchs with a fitting venue for their coronation ceremonies. All the absolute monarchs during the period 1671 to 1840 initiated their reign here in the palace church. Moreover the Order of the Elephant was newly established in Frederiksborg Palace, the Dannebrog Order introduced in 1671 and in 1693 the palace church was promoted to the role of chapel of the Order of Knights, a role which it still has to

Location
Hillerød (35km/
22 miles north
of Copenhagen)

S-bane
Hillerød;
then bus 701, 703

Opening times
Apr., Oct.:
daily 10am–4pm
May–Sept.:
daily 10am–5pm
Nov.–Mar.:
daily 11am–3pm

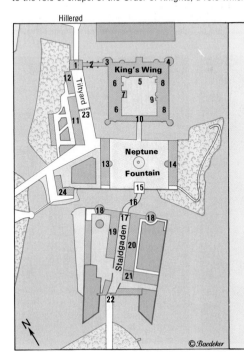

Hillerød

Frederiksborg Castle

1 Audience Chamber
2 Long Corridor
3 Mint Tower
4 Jägerberg Tower
5 Grand Gallery
6 Church Wing
7 Church tower
8 Princesses' Wing
9 Kitchen Fountain
10 Terrace Building
11 Store-rooms
12 Tea rooms
13 Castellan's Lodging
14 Chancery Building
15 Gatehouse
16 S bridge
17 Christian VI's Gateway
18 Frederik II's Round Towers
19 King's Stables
20 Hussar Stables
21 Herluf Trolle's Tower
22 Town Gate
23 Tiltyard Gate
24 Restaurant

King's Wing

Tiltyard

Neptune
Fountain

Staldgaden

© Baedeker

Frederiksborg Slot

this day. After the Second Nordic War it was at Frederiksborg that the peace treaty between Denmark and Sweden was signed in 1720, ending centuries of enmity between the two countries.

In the 1720s J. C. Krieger began the task of laying a garden to the north of the palace. In 1737–40 the living quarters were modernised. With the completion of Fredensborg Palace, Frederiksborg began to take on the air of a museum in the latter part of the 18th c. and the 19th c. The Knights' Chamber was turned into an art gallery and in 1812 Frederik VI set up a portrait collection. Frederik VII made the palace a royal residence once more and, after a fire in December 1859, had it extensively restored under the direction of Ferdinand Meldahl. After his death the state had no more use for the palace and on April 5th 1878, at the instigation of the brewer J. C. Jakobsen (see Carlsberg Brewery), it was officially designated by the king as a museum of Danish history. By 1884 the Knights' Chamber, king's wing and prince's wing and the church had been restored, and in 1907 the audience room was made part of the museum, while Christian IX and Frederik VIII used the palace rooms on isolated occasions for receptions. The size of the collection of valuable furniture and historically important objets d'art can be ascribed to the fact that at that time there was no other museum for arts and crafts in Denmark and therefore everything of any worth was brought here. Even the existing portrait collection of Frederik VI was incorporated into the museum and added to.

Palace grounds

In its architectural style the whole palace complex shows itself heavily influenced by the Dutch Renaissance. From the southernmost island a continuation of the Staldgaden is linked by an S-shaped bridge to the outermost palace courtyard. This is reached through a massive gate-tower which was built by Hans van Steenwinkel the Younger between 1618 and 1623.

Frederiksberg Palace: a magnificent bed

Portraits from the time of Frederick VI

Between the chancellery and the lord of the castle's house there has stood since 1888 in the forecourt of the second island a copy of a Neptune fountain made by Adrian de Vries in 1623, which was taken to Sweden in 1658; the original bronze figures were stolen by the Swedes during the siege of Copenhagen in 1660 and today are to be found in the grounds of Drøttningholm Castle outside Stockholm.

On the third island the actual castle is reached. The oldest part is the king's wing at the north end; of later date is the church wing on the west side as well as the church tower and the princess's wing on the east side. The middle island is connected by a low terraced building. As a link between the mint tower and the audience house the Long Passage, built in grey brick, was added in 1613.

Main building

The palace church, which survived the fire of 1859 unscathed, is located in the west wing. The nave, with its Gothic stellar vaults, is supported by golden sandstone buttresses. Marble marquetry, alabaster figures, inlay work in ebony and other rare woods complete the grand design. The altar and pulpit, also of ebony, are decorated with silver reliefs depicting biblical scenes by the Hamburg artist Jakob Mores. The silver font was made in 1920, based on a drawing by Mores dating from the 16th c. At the end of the church the shields of the Order of the Elephant can be seen – among them the shield of the atomic physicist Niels Bohr (see Famous People), at the sides hang the shields of the Knights of the Grand Cross of the Dannebrog Order.

★★Palace church

The organ, one of the most valuable in Europe, was made in 1617 by the Brunswick organ builder Esaias Compenius. It was dismantled in 1693 and left until 1868, but is now played again, and is even used for concerts (every Thursday 1.30–2pm). Its thousand pipes and its sound, still as splendid as ever, have made it famous all over the world.

The Riddersalen (Knights' Hall), is a 50m/160ft long room situated over the palace church which was rebuilt after the fire of 1859. In the time of Christian IV it was aptly named the "Ballroom". The king ordered it to be decorated with magnificent ornaments and silver figures and there are marvellous wood carvings on the ceiling. Originally there were also a series of wall tapestries depicting the coronation in 1596, woven by Karel von Mander in Delft: these unfortunately were destroyed in the 1859 fire. The wooden ceiling has been faithfully restored to the original and shows a water mill, nautical instuments, a printing works, a clock-maker's, a foundry for cans and mugs and finally the royal coat of arms with the motto "Regna firmat pietas" ("Fear of God strengthens the earthly realms"). The walls are covered with Gobelin tapestries depicting scenes from the Kalmar War and the coronation procession of 1596. The fireplace is made of black Belgian marble and dates from 1880, while the patterns on the marble floor have also been reconstructed according to the originals. The great chandeliers were designed around 1900 by the architect Carl Brummer. In addition there are portraits of Christian IX and his ruling descendants.

★Knights' Hall

The ceiling painting in the Angels' Hall (no. 37) is a small-scale version of a ceiling in the Doge's Palace in Venice. Its carvings, which are by Franz Schwartz and date from 1883, depict Frederik III surrounded by the four estates of the kingdom and by "War" and "Peace". The great wall painting of 1879–83 deals with the Swedish War and the introduction of absolutism.

Other rooms

The furniture in Room 42 provides a highly impressive example of the grandiose displays of splendour which were seen as befitting an absolute monarch. The focal point is a large ebony-carved four-poster bed which was made for the wedding of Count Danneskiold-Samsøe to Christine Catharine von Holstein in 1724 in Paris. The walls are covered with luxurious Gobelin tapestries, while in the two wardrobes on the

Frederiksberg Palace: the Knights' Hall

narrow side of the room there is a collection of silver on display dating from around 1700.

The beginning of the 19th c. was a period when Danish literature, art and science flourished. Pictures of important figures from this time, when Frederik VI was on the throne, are to be seen in Room 55, among them the sculptor Bertel Thorvaldsen (see Famous People), the poet Adam Oehlenschläger (whose own memorial room is no. 60), the physicist H. C. Ørsted, the discoverer of electromagnetism, and the adult educationalist Nicolai Frederik Severin Grundtvig (see Famous People); the pictures of the royal couple were painted by W. Eckersberg in 1825 and 1826. Of especial interest is also the painting of the inauguration session of the constituent royal assembly on October 23rd 1848, which takes up a whole wall in Room 61. At this assembly the king relinquished absolute power. Opposite hang portraits of Danish politicians. The neighbouring room no. 62 is devoted to three men who were to have a profound influence on Danish religious life during the 19th c.: Mynster, Søren Kierkegaard (see Famous People) and Nicolai Frederik Severin Grundtvig (see Famous People).

Frederikskirken

See Marmorkirken

Frihedsmuseet (Museet for Danmarks Frihedskamp 1940 bis 1945; Museum for Denmark's Freedom Struggle 1940 to 1945)   J6

Location
Churchillparken

The Museum for Denmark's Freedom Struggle from 1940 to 1945 is situated on the esplanade in the Churchillparken. An early exhibition,

"Denmark at War", which was held on July 21st 1945 at the Copenhagen masonic lodge, was later taken to Sweden, London and Moscow. To finance the building of the museum a nationwide lottery was held, the proceeds of which came to over 500,000 kroner, with the result that in October 1957 the museum could be inaugurated. The architect Hans Hansen was responsible for the design of the building.

The museum today has a series of outlying branches both in Denmark and further afield. Thus there are permanent exhibitions in such places as the Frøslev camp (Sønderjyllan), from where many Danes were sent to concentration camps, in the Polish concentration camp of Auschwitz and in the concentration camp at Sachsenhausen near Berlin.

S-bane
Østerport

Buses
1, 6, 9

May 1st–Sept. 15th: Tues.–Sat. 10am–4pm, Sun. 10am–5pm; Sept. 16th–Apr. 30th: Tues.–Sat. 11am–3pm, Sun. 11am–4pm.

Opening times

The Museum of Freedom documents the period of the German occupation and Danish resistance between 1940 and 1945 by means of a comprehensive collection of historic photographs, pictures, newspaper articles, letters, weapons and other mementoes. Re-opened in 1995, the exhibition covers the following subjects:

Germany's attack on neutral Denmark and its occupation by the German army in April 1940; passive resistance by the Danish population; the internment of Communists 1941; the Danes serving with the Allies; organisation of the resistance movement; blackouts and the printing of illegal papers; illegal arms and sabotage; everyday life during the war; Dr. Werner Best; the German Eastern Front; German soldiers in Denmark; secret agents; August 29th 1943 (Germany's attack on Denmark's armed forces, followed by the resignation of the Danish government; prisons and prison camps in Denmark; persecution of the Jews in Denmark; organisations in Sweden; German concentration camps; arrest of Danish policemen; Nazi organisations in Denmark; Allied landings in Normandy on June 6th 1944; strike of the Danish population on July 5th 1944; winter 1944/45; Freedom Council and Danish council in London; attacks on Gestapo headquarters; news service; illegal underground work; the "white buses"; the liberation of Denmark in May 1945; the fallen.

Exhibition

Lassen Memorial

In front of the museum there is a memorial to Major Anders Lassen who died in 1945.

Memorial to
A. Lassen

★★Frilandsmuseet (Open air museum)

The Frilandsmuseet (open air museum), which is affiliated to the Nationalmuseet (see entry) (Danish National Museum), is situated 8km/5 miles north of Copenhagen in Lyngby. It covers an area of 35ha/86 acres which the visitor can walk round on foot by means of a circular path 3km/2 miles long. The rural buildings, which date from the 17th to the 19th century, are grouped together according to their geographical origin. In order to get a picture of the various types of houses it is a good idea to visit at least one example of each group. For a walk round the

Location
Lyngby,
Kongevejen 100

S-bane
Sorgenfri

Bus 184

71

A thatched farm-worker's house

Tower windmill of the Dutch type

An old loom (Fünen)

Frilandsmuseet

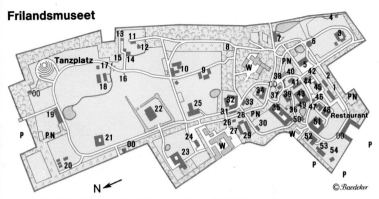

P – Parking, PN – Picnic areas, W – Workshops and stores, OO – Toilets

1 Fisherman's house, Agger, N Jutland

2 Seaman's house, Fanø

3 Farmhouse (early 19th c.), Øster Larsker, Bornholm

4 Watermill, Pedersker, Bornholm

5 Peasant house (end of 16th c.), Ostenfeld, S Schleswig (Germany)

6 Tower windmill, erected on its present site in 1832, in use until 1906

7 Watermill (before 1800), Ellested, Funen (Fyn)

8 Boundary stone (1734), Løve, Central Jutland

9 Farmhouse (c. 1850), Karup Heath, Central Jutland

10 Farmhouse (from 1736). Læsø, Kattegat

11 Peasant house (1866), Múla, Bordoy, Faroes

12 Store hut, Viderejde, Vidoy, Faroes

13 Watermill for domestic use, Sandur, Sandoy, Faroes

14 Buckwheat drying kiln, Múla, Bordoy, Faroes

15 Stone used in weight-lifting contests, Múla, Bordoy, Faroes

16 Milestone (2nd half of 17th c.), Holstebro district, W Jutland

17 Quarry (2nd half of 18th c.), Smedevad, near Holstebro, W Jutland

18 Farmhouse (from 1770), Vemb, W Jutland

19 Barn (originally c. 1600) from a farm at Fjellerup/Djursland, E Jutland

20 Fishermen's houses, Nymindegab, W Jutland

21 Farmhouse (1803), Lønnestak, W Jutland

22 Peasant house (1653), Eiderstedt, SW Schleswig (Germany)

23 Farmhouse (originally 17th c.), Sønder Sejerslev, N Schleswig

24 Pillow-lace-making school (19th c.), Nørre Sejerslev, N Schleswig

25 Crofter's house (18th c.), Rømø

26 Fuel shed, Sode, NE Schleswig

27 Barn (17th c.), Øsby, NE Schleswig

28 Barn (1605), Grønninghoved, NE Schleswig

29 Peasant house (1766), Barsø, NE Schleswig

30 Cottage from Dyndred (2nd half of 18th c.), Alsen, N Schleswig

31 Peasant house with shoemaker's workshop, Ødis Bramdrup, near Kolding, E Jutland

32 Farmhouse (18th c.), True, E Jutland

33 Potter's workshop (1844), Sorring, E Jutland

34 Farmhouse (originally 2nd half of 17th c.), Halland (Sweden)

35 Double farm (18th c.), Göinge, Skåne (Sweden)

36 Bath House, Småland (Sweden)

37 Two-storey storehouse, SE Småland (Sweden)

38 Small watermill, W Småland (Sweden)

39 Smallholder's steading (18th c.), Dörröd. Skåne (Sweden)

40 Weaver's house, Tystrup, Zealand

41 Houses of country craftsmen (17th–19th c.), Kalvehave, Zealand

42 Farm worker's house, Englerup, Zealand

43 Farmhouse (before 1800), Pebringe, Zealand

44 Almshouse (1710), Greve, Zealand

45 Boundary stone (1757), Virum, Zealand

46 Fire station (c. 1850), Kirke Såby, Zealand

47 Small farm (19th c.), Årup, Funen (Fyn)

48 Wooden shoe maker's house (19th c.), Kirke-Søby, Fünen

49 Village green with place of assembly

50 Village smithy (c. 1845), Ørbæk, Funen (Fyn)

51 Farmhouse (1747), Lundager, Funen (Fyn)

52 Small farmhouse, Dannemare, Lolland

53 Small farmhouse (before 1800), Tågense, Lolland

54 Post-mill (c. 1662), Karlstrup, Zealand (no access)

whole museum site and a short visit to four buildings an hour should be allowed, whereas a visit to nine or ten houses can take just under two hours. Information about guided tours can be obtained at the entrance. In the summer there are also frequent folk music performances. Tours round the park by horse-drawn carriage begin at the 1832 windmill tower (no. 6). Because of the fire risk smoking is strictly prohibited anywhere on the site.

The aim of the Open Air Museum is to document traditional living and working conditions in rural Denmark and its exhibits comprise old farmhouses, cottages, sailor's houses, mills, forges, etc., which have been brought together from their original locations throughout the regions of Denmark and the former Danish provinces in Southern Sweden and Southern Schleswig. The interiors of the buildings have been fitted out with the appropriate old furniture, utensils and working tools. In the parkland surrounding the houses indigenous wild plants can be found, while the gardens of the houses boast traditional types of flowers, colourful vegetable patches and old fruit trees. The range and number of buildings is continually being increased.

Gammel Bryghus (Old Brewery)   H7

The Old Brewery Building (or Royal Brewhouse), which is distinguished by its prominent tiled roof, is among those buildings which were erected under King Christian IV (see Famous People).

The brewery, built between 1616 and 1618 on the south-western fortified wall with three gables and a tiled roof, had to be rebuilt twice, following fires in 1632 and 1767. Today it constitutes one of the oldest industrial concerns in Denmark, although the building was used from the 19th c. as a military depot.

Location
Christians Brygge

Buses
1, 2, 5, 6, 8, 9, 10, 31, 37, 43

Gammel Strand (Old Beach)   H7

Situated opposite Slotsholmen (the palace island), and separated by the canal, is Gammel Strand, where long rows of fishwives once offered for sale fresh fish and other marine produce from Tårbæk and Skovshoved. – At the beginning of the middle ages the coastline still ran along the present-day Løngangsstræde, Magstræde, Snaregade and Fortunstræde. It is assumed that this was where the fishing boats unloaded their catches; in 1337 the area was for the first time mentioned as being "propre mare" (near the sea). From the 15th c. the references varied between "ved Stran-den" (on the beach) and "Strandgade" (beach road), while the name "Gammel Strand" was only used for the first time in 1716.

A reminder of the fish market which up until a few years ago

Location
To the west of Højbro Plads

Buses
1, 2, 6, 8, 10, 28, 29, 41

Boat trips start from Gammel Strand

◄ *Frilandsmuseet: Village forge mid 19th century (Fünen)*

Opening times
Mar. 22nd–Sept. 30th:
Tue.–Sun.
10am–5pm
Oct. 1st–Oct. 19th:
Tue.–Sun.
10am–4pm

was still active is provided by the fishwife's memorial, the stone "Fiskerkone", which was erected in 1940. Its special feature is the fisherman's basket tied to the fishwife's back, in which the women used to carry their husband's catch to the town.

Today boats going on the harbour tour or the canal trip to "Den lille Havfrue" (little mermaid) leave from Gammel Strand. Opposite the mooring place is one of the city's best fish restaurants, Krogs Fiskerestaurant.

★Gefion Springvandet (Gefion Fountain)   J6

Location
Churchillparken

The Gefion Fountain, built in 1909 by the sculptor Anders Bundgaard for the Carlsberg foundation (see Carlsberg Brewery) in what is today the Churchillparken, is one of the most impressive fountains in Copenhagen. Its powerful jets of water can be seen in action from April 15th to October 31st.

S-bane
Østerport

Buses
1, 6, 9

It owes its conception to the Old Norse saga, the "Ynglingesaga der Heimskringla". According to this, the goddess Gefion, who had been ordered by Odin to obtain land, was promised by King Gylfe of Sweden as much land as she could plough up in one night. The goddess thereupon betook herself to Jotunheim where she bore a giant four sons, whom she turned into bulls. With these she ploughed up an area the size of Zealand. The ploughed land was lifted up out of Sweden and set down in the Baltic (the "hole" left behind is the Vänern Lake): this was how Zealand was formed.

Glyptotheque

See Ny Carlsberg Glyptotek

The Gefion Fountain

Grundtvig Church

★Grundtvigs Kirke (Church) E4

This church is named in honour of Bishop Nicolai Frederik Severin Grundtvig (see Famous People), the father of the adult education movement, which was the first to be established in Europe.

   This modern church was built between 1921 and 1940 on the Bispebjerg, in brick, in an unusual style reminiscent of an organ. Its proportions are massive: inside length 76m/249ft, inside width 35m/115ft, inside height 22m/72ft, exterior height 30m/98ft. Its nave can accommodate 1800 people. 6,000,000 bricks, all yellow, a typical Danish building material, were used for the construction of the church, which employed the six best masons in Denmark for 19 years. The architect was P. V. Jensen-Klint, whose son Kaare completed the building after his father's death. The great Marcus organ is used for concerts throughout the year.

Location
På Bjerget,
district of
Bispebjerg

Buses
10, 16, 19, 43

May–Sept.: Mon.–Sat. 9am–4.45pm, Sun. noon–4pm; Oct.–Apr.: Mon.–Sat. 9am–4pm, Sun. noon–1pm.

Opening times

★Den lille Havfrue (The little mermaid) J5

On the promenade at Langelinie sits Copenhagen's best-known attraction – the Little Mermaid.

Location
Langelinie

1, 6, 9, June 15th–Sept 1st: special buses from the Rådhuspladsen (city hall)

Buses

Østerport.

S-bane

77

A Fairytale in Bronze and Stone:
Den Lille Havfrue

Sitting on a stone by the harbourside at Langelinie, the delicate figure of the Little Mermaid, undoubtedly the most photographed symbol of Copenhagen, looks out over the Øresund. Perhaps some who see it are transported back to the fairy-tale days of their own childhood when they listened raptly to the tale of the youngest and most beautiful daughter of the sea-king who sacrificed herself in vain for the earthly prince with whom she had fallen in love. This subtly effective sculpture of

the Little Mermaid was erected in 1913, based on the character of the fairy-tale of the same name, written in 1837 by Hans Christian Andersen.

The immediate inspiration for the statue was the première in 1909 of the ballet about the little water-nymph with the fish's tail, who once upon a time came up out of the depths of the sea because she loved a prince and who, as Andersen portrayed in his story, had to forsake the world of humans once more because the prince did not return her love. During the performance in the Royal Theatre the art-loving brewery proprietor Carl Jakobsen had the idea of presenting Copenhagen with a statue of the legendary creature. The model was to have been the prima ballerina Ellen Price, who had danced the fairy-tale heroine. As she was predictably little inclined to pose nude as a model for the sculptor Edward Eriksen, he based only the face of the bronze sculpture on that of Ellen Price and for the body used that of his beautiful wife. His patron Jakobsen wanted the mermaid to be given a fish's tail, but Eriksen had read Andersen's story very thoroughly and knew that the little sea nymph had given the old sea witch her golden hair and her sweet voice in order to gain two legs like a human. As a compromise Eriksen designed a veil-like tail within which two legs were easily recognisable.

On the promenade at Langelinie the Little Mermaid keeps watch for her Prince

After an American newspaper had published a photograph of it the statue of the Little Mermaid, which until then had not attracted much interest, rapidly became the city's most popular tourist attraction and a part of contemporary folk-lore.

★Helligåndskirken (Church of the Holy Spirit) H7

The oldest church in Copenhagen dates back as a monastery church to the year 1400 when a basilica with three naves was built here in brick. After it was partially destroyed by a fire in 1728 it was rebuilt in 1880 in the New Renaissance style.

The sandstone entrance portal, originally intended for the Old Stock Exchange building (see Børse), dates back to 1620. The altar, donated in 1732 by Christian VI, was the work of Didrik Gercken, the sculptures are by Just Wiedewelt, the altarpiece depicting the ascension of Christ by Hendrick Krock. On the north side of the church is the burial chapel of a Danish minister of state, which was erected in 1670.

In the tiny churchyard there is a memorial honouring the Danish victims of Nazi concentration camps. Behind the church stands the House of the Holy Ghost, dating from about 1300, and part of the monastery of the Holy Ghost.

Location
Amagertorv

Buses
28, 29, 41

Opening times
daily 11am–4pm

★Hirschsprungske Samling (Hirschsprung art collection) H6

The Hirschsprung art collection, which was assembled in the 1940s, comprises 600 paintings, 200 sculptures and well over 1000 watercolours and drawings from the period 1800 to 1910. It brings together the works of many Danish artists of this period and is also highly informative in the way it mirrors the Danish way of life at this time. Among the main representatives of this period are C. W. Eckersberg and his pupils C. Kobke, P. C. Skovgaard and Constantin Hansen as well as the Skagen painters P. S. Kroyer and Anna and Michael Ancher, who represent the "modern breakthrough" which came about 1880. There is also work on display by Vilhelm Hammershøj, Ejnar Nielsen and L. A. Ring.

The collection goes back to a foundation by Heinrich Hirschsprung, a famous Copenhagen cigarette manufacturer, who in 1902 left his works of art to the Danish state. A picture of Hirschsprung, together with his wife Pauline, their daughter and four sons, hangs in the second room. It was painted by P. S. Krøyer, who enjoyed Hirschsprung's patronage.

The building in which the collection is housed was completed in 1911 and has a main façade which juts forward like the front of an ancient temple. Its triangular gable is decorated by a relief which was created by the artist Kai Nielsen.

Location
Stockholmsgade 20

Buses
10, 14, 24, 40, 43, 84

Opening times
Thur.–Mon. 11am–4pm
Wed. 11am–9pm

★Holmens Kirke (Church) H7

The Holmenskirke was built in 1619 by the canal of the same name under King Christian IV (see Famous People) by converting an anchor smithy which had been set up by Christian II. In the middle of the 17th c. Leonhard Blasius added the transepts to the Renaissance building. The splendid main portal on the east side (the "King's Portal", 17th c.) came originally from the cathedral in Roskilde (see entry).

The king had the church built specially for sailors, but today it is also used by the royal family. In 1967 Queen Margrethe II and Prince Henrik were married here. The long chapel added in 1705–08 is dedicated to Denmark's sea heroes and contains two models of ships hanging from the ceiling. Of especial artistic value is also the superb brass screen in the interior of the church, with its 38 balusters, which separates the choir from the nave, as well as the brilliantly carved altar and the oak pulpit extending right up to the roof – the largest in Copenhagen.

Both of these were completed in the second half of the 17th c. by Abel Schrøder the Younger.

Location
Holmens Kanal

Buses
1, 2, 6, 8, 9, 10, 31, 37, 43

Opening times
May 15th–Sept.15th:
Mon.–Fri. 9am–2pm, Sat. 9am–noon; Sept. 16th–May14th: Mon.–Sat. 9am–noon

Holmens Kirke

★Højbro Plads (High Bridge Square) H7

Location
by Gammel
Strand

Buses
1, 2, 6, 8, 10, 28,
29, 41

The spaciously laid out Højbro Plads, situated at the end of the Amagertorv, is one of the most frequented squares in Copenhagen.

In the centre stands a monument erected in 1901 for Bishop Absalon (see Famous People), which represents the founder of the city as a powerfully armed knight. This statue on horseback was the work of Ch. G. Vilhelm Bissen, while the plinth is by Martin Nyrop and bears the inscription "He was courageous, wise and far-sighted – a friend of scholarship – in the intensity of his striving a true son of Denmark".

The Højbro Plads looks out on to the island of Slotsholmen and Christiansborg Slot (see entry), the Børsen and Thorvaldsens Museum (see entries), while there are also views of Holmens Kirke and Gammel Strand (see entries).

Statue of Absalon

House nameplates

Before 1771, when house numbers were introduced in Copenhagen – following the French model – by the Count of Struensee (see Famous

House nameplate

People), citizens and visitors had to find their way around by means of nameplates which made some reference to the profession of the owner, or to plants, animals or celestial bodies, etc. in pictorial form and were fixed to the outside of the houses. While simple signs were used in the Middle Ages, the wrought-iron ones of the 17th and 18th c, displayed elaborate shapes and embellishments – for example, the richly decorated house sign of the hatmaker, N. Jørgensen, in Vandkusten, made in 1723, with a golden hat symbolising the business that was pursued there. Under Christian II inns had already had to make the nature of their trade explicit by means of a sign displaying the name of the hostelry or tavern. In the 18th c., especially after the appalling fire of 1728, there was a trend towards stone signs, bearing the emblem of the building and placed over the entrance portal or door.

Karen Blixen Museet (Museum)

In May 1991 a museum dedicated to Karen Blixen (see Famous People) was opened in the manor house on her parents' estate. The Danish writer was born here and also lived here after her return from Africa until her death in 1962.

Karen Blixen wrote her first stories here at Rungstedlund, before she went out to East Africa with her husband, the Swedish Baron Bror von Blixen-Finecke, to manage a coffee plantation there for 17 years. Even during this period the authoress returned to Denmark on numerous occasions. In 1958 she presented the estate to the Rungstedlund foundation, which in 1991 set up the museum.

Location
Rungstedlund
Rungstedstrandvej
111

Opening times
May 1st–Sept. 30th:
daily 10am–5pm;
Oct. 1st–Apr. 30th
Wed.–Fri. 1–4pm
Sat., Sun.
11am–4pm

Karen Blixen: portraits of a man and woman of the Kikuyu tribe

In the rooms of the house furniture and mementoes from Kenya are to be seen, such as the gramophone mentioned in her book "Out of Africa", a present from her friend Denys Finch Hatton.

Of particular interest are her portraits of members of the Kikuyu tribe. The picture "The History of the Kingdom of Denmark", in which the work of the same name by the Danish dramatist Ludvig Holberg (see Famous People) is depicted with a decoratively placed toucan bird, was painted by her in Africa and given by her there to Denys Finch Hatton. After his death in 1931 Karen Blixen received the painting back.

★Kastellet (Castle; Citadellet Frederikshavn)   H5/6

Location
Langelinie

S-bane
Østerport

Buses
1, 6, 9

The castle on the Langelinie, which today houses the Livjäger Museum and the Royal Garrison Library, was built under Frederik III by the Dutchman Henrik Ruse in 1662–63, in the place where under Christian IV (see Famous People) in 1629 the St Annæ entrenchment had been established. The five-cornered fortress was erected with a double moat and was given the name of Citadellet Frederikshavn after its founder. Between 1662 and 1725 the fortification was considerably enlarged by Frederik's successors.

The buildings comprise the main police station, the prison of 1725, in which, among others, Johann Friedrich Count of Struensee (see Famous People) was held prisoner before his execution; the two-storey commandant's house, also built in 1725 to plans by E. D. Häusser; old storehouses as well as two fine fortress portals: the Zealand Gate at the south end of the castle, built in 1663 (the Sjællandsporten), which is adorned by a bust of King Frederik III by the sculptor fr. Dieussart, and the Norway Gate (Norgesporten), completed in the same year, which was blown up by the Germans in 1940, but later rebuilt. The church, consecrated in 1704, was conceived in such a way that the prisoners were able

Kastellet: the Commandant's House

to follow the service without entering the church. The park and lawns around the castle are open daily from 6am until dusk.

Kierkegaard Samlingen

See Københavns Bymuseum & Søren Kierkegaard Samlingen

Kongelige Teater

See Kongens Nytorv

Kongens Have

See Rosenborg Slot

★Kongens Nytorv (New Royal Market)   H/J6

Kongens Nytorv, which is reached from the Rådhuspladsen (City Hall Square) at the end of the Strøget (see entry) pedestrian zone, is Copenhagen's largest square. A dozen or so streets lead off it.

Location
on the Strøget

This important traffic junction was laid out in 1680 by King Christian V. From here it is only a very short walk to the museum ships at Nyhavn (see entry).

Buses
1, 4H, 6, 7, 9, 10
10H, 28, 29, 31, 41

In the direction of the New Port stands the palace of Charlottenborg (Kongens Nytorv 1). It was built between 1672 and 1683 for the half-brother of Christian V and governor of Norway, Ulf Frederik Gyldenløve in the Baroque Dutch Palladian style. Today it is the home of the Academy of Arts and is used for exhibitions.

Charlottenborg
Slot

The Ravhuset (Kongens Nytorv 1) houses an interesting Amber Museum and a shop selling pieces of the "Gold of the Baltic".

Ravhuset
Amber Museum

This building, Kongens Nytorv no. 3, was designed by the architect Caspar Harsdorff in 1777 in the classical style. It has been made a listed building for preservation purposes and today houses the school of architects.

Harsdorffs House

On the north-east side of Kongens Nytorv is situated Thotts Palais (no. 4), which was built in 1685–86 in the Dutch Palladian style for Admiral Niels Juel and which since 1930 has housed the French Embassy. After Count Otto Thott acquired the building in 1760, the wall pillars of the main façade were given Corinthian capitals and the balustrade, crowned with figures and a cartouche with a coat of arms, was added.

Thotts Palais

The south-east side of the square is dominated by the Theatre Royal, founded in 1748, in which plays, operas and ballets are presented (see Practical Information, Music). The present-day building was erected in 1872–74 to designs by Vilhelm Dahlerup and Ove Petersen in the New Renaissance style. The inscription on the main façade "Ei blot til lyst" ("Not just for pleasure") goes back to the original building erected in 1748 by Nicolai Eigtved, while the decorations in the auditorium (1500 seats) are the work of the painter C. Hansen. In 1931 the theatre had an additional auditorium created, the "New Scene" (1050 seats), designed by the architect H. Jacobsen.

★Kongelige
Teater (Theatre
Royal)

In Ravhuset lovers of amber can buy pieces of the "Baltic gold"

Corinthian capitals adorn Thotts Palais – today the home of the French embassy

Early booking of tickets – especially for the ballet – is recommended. (See Practical Information, Advance Booking Offices)

The two statues on either side of the main entrance are of the poets Ludvig Hohlberg (see Famous People) and Adam Oehlenschläger (1779–1850). Oehlenschläger is considered to be Denmark's national poet, having written the Danish National Anthem as well as many plays.

Memorials to L. Hohlberg and A. Oehlenschläger

The main building belonging to the department store Magasin du Nord is also situated on Kongens Nytorv. It was built in 1893–94 in the French "chateau" style by A. Ch. Jensen and H. Glæsel on the site of the elegant "Hotel du grand Nord" which had been opened in 1796.

Magasin du Nord

See Practical Information, Hotels

★Hotel d'Angleterre

In the middle of the square is the statue of Christian V on horseback (1687), the work of the French sculptor Abraham-César Lamoureux, which is almost concealed by a garden which was laid out in 1855–56. It depicts the king in the robes of a Roman emperor. At his feet are Minerva symbolising wisdom, Alexander the Great symbolising courage, Hercules symbolising strength and Artemis symbolising honour.

Statue of Christian V on horseback

Musical events and temporary exhibitions are also offered on Kongens Nytorv by the new Copenhagen Cultural Centre Bolten's, where there are also several cafés and restaurants (open: 10am–5am).

Cultural Centre Bolten's

★★Kronborg Slot (Kronborg Castle)

Within Kronborg Castle there are today 27 rooms devoted to a trade and seafaring museum (Handels- og Søfartsmuseet), which documents the history of Danish seafaring, as well as displaying exhibits from earlier Danish settlements in Greenland and the West Indies.

As early as 1420 Erich the Pomeranian had established a castle called the "Krogen" ("hook") here at the narrowest point in the Øresund, where a sandy tongue of land protrudes close to the coast of Schonen in Sweden, with the express purpose of demanding a toll on ships passing through the sound – a substantial source of revenue for the king.

In 1558–59 Christian II had the wall encircling the castle strengthened with corner bastions under the direction of the Saxon fortress builder Hans von Dieskow. In 1574–85 under Frederik II the site was converted into a magnificent four-winged Renaissance castle under the Dutchmen Hans van Paeschen and Antonius van Opbergen and was given the name "Kronborg". After a fire in September 1629, in which only the church was left unscathed, Christian IV (see Famous People) had the castle rebuilt by Hans van Steenwinckel the Younger in 1635–40 without any alterations. When the Swedes took the castle in 1659 they carried off many treasures, among them the famous "table canopy" of Frederik II, woven from gold and silver thread by Hans Knieper, which is today to be found in the National Museum in Stockholm. Under succeeding kings the castle received further extensions and alterations and between 1785 and 1922 it was used as a barracks.

Between 1924 and 1935 the castle was completely restored by J. Magdahl-Nielsen and refurbished in the style of Frederik II and Christian IV.

The upkeep of the palace has been subsidised for many years by the Ny-Carlsberg Foundation (see Carlsberg Brewery), while the collection of paintings from the 16th and 17th c. is continually supplemented by loans from the Copenhagen Statens Museum (see entry) and the

Location
Helsingør

Railway station
Helsingør

Opening times
May–Sept.:
daily
10.30am–5pm;
Nov.–Mar.:
Tues.–Sun.
11am–3pm;
Apr. and Oct.
11am–4pm

Kronborg Castle

National Historical Museum at Frederiksborg Palace (see entry) in Hillerød.

"Hamlet's Castle"

Shakespeare's play "Hamlet" is set in Helsingør (Elsinore) and thus Kronborg has become "Hamlet's Castle". Even if this is not really historically correct, the castle courtyard makes an outstanding backdrop for the occasional festival performance of the play. Famous actors who have performed here include Sir Laurence Olivier, Sir Michael Redgrave and Kenneth Branagh.

Tour of the castle

Over the main entrance portal there is an inscription confirming that Frederik II had the castle built in 1577 and named it "Kronborg". Above can be seen the oriel belonging to the royal apartment.

The former royal apartments with superb ceiling paintings dating from the middle of the 17th c. are situated in the north wing. Of the original fittings and furnishings scarcely anything remains, the greater part of the furniture on display there having been made in the 17th c.

The Knights' Hall or ballroom with its 62×11m/203×36ft proportions is the largest and also one of the most beautiful Renaissance rooms in the whole of Northern Europe. Its enormous paintings were originally intended by Christian IV for Rosenborg Palace (see entry), as were the pictures in the queen's gallery. The theme running through the pictures is that of the power of the planets over the course of the lives of mortals.

In the west wing the Small Hall, besides its Renaissance furniture, still boasts seven of the original fourteen magnificent Gobelin tapestries dating from 1582 which used to decorate the ballroom. The other seven wall hangings are now to be found in the Nationalmuseet (see entry).

The south wing contains the castle chapel, consecrated in 1582, which by virtue of its stone vaulting was able to withstand the fire of 1629. Its sumptuous Renaissance interior fittings dating from the 16th c., with elaborate wood carvings by German masters, are well worth seeing. The golden alabaster relief of the "Crucifixion" over the altar was completed in 1587, while the valance covering the lower part of the altar was provided by the clothmakers Kirsten and John Becker in 1982.

Finally the visitor also has access to the castle casemates with their gloomy dungeons. From the south-west "trumpeters' tower" (approached by a spiral staircase with 145 steps) a wonderful view across the Øresund can be enjoyed. A walk along the western bastions is equally rewarding for the wealth of views which it affords.

★Kunstindustrimuseet (Museum of Decorative and Applied Art)   J6

The Museum of Decorative and Applied Art encompasses European arts and crafts from the Middle Ages up to the present time, as well as material from China and Japan. Its collections are housed in nearly 60 rooms, three of them, with the Rococo and silver collection, on the first floor. The main emphasis of the exhibits is on living room furniture and fittings. Thus there are carpets, 18th c. crockery from the royal porcelain manufacturers, faience, Danish silver, chinoiserie, Art nouveau work, glass, textiles, furniture, jewellery and scientific instruments. Modern Danish design is also represented. The museum is housed in the Rococo building of the former Frederik Hospital which was built in 1757 by Niels Eigtved and Laurids de Thura. The museum was set up in 1890 by the Ny-Carlsberg Foundation (see Carlsberg Brewery) and has been located here since 1926. The house has a garden which is open to visitors. A series of sculptures are to be found there, including "The Sea Horse" (1916) by Niels Skovgaard and a "Figure of a Woman" and a "Vase" (about 1750) by J. C. Petzold.
Garden

Location
Bredgade 68

S-bane
Østerport

Buses
1, 6, 9

Opening times
Middle
Ages–1900:
Tue.–Sat. 1–4pm;
1900 to today:
Tue.–Sat.
10am–4pm
Sun. 1–4pm

Articles of modern furniture in the Kunstindustrimuseet

Museum of Arts and Crafts: "Seahorse" ...   ... and Delft tiles (c. 1729)

Købmagergade (Pedestrian zone) H6/7

Location
Between Kultorvet
and Højbro Plads

The Købmagergade pedestrianised zone which runs between Kultorvet and Højbro Plads (see entry) was very likely from the 13th c. onwards part of the main thoroughfare between Roskilde (see entry) and the "Købmændenes Havn" (merchant port). In the 15th c. the butchers (kød-mangere) of Copenhagen settled here and gave the street its name "Købmagergade". In the middle of the 16th c. the butchers moved to the Skindergade, but the street retained the original name, albeit in its present slightly altered form. Today the Købmagergade is a lively pedestrian area with many shops, fashion boutiques such as Red/Green, Carli Gry and Lene Sand, restaurants, bars and cafés.

Royal Porcelain Factory

The Royal Porcelain Factory had its first premises between 1775 and 1882 at Købmagergade no. 5. Within only a few years of its opening it had become internationally renowned for its dinner and tea services, vases and porcelain busts and figures.

Statue of Mercury

From the roof of the red-brick house at no. 42 (1896) the visitor is greeted by a statue of Mercury, the Old Roman god of trade and crafts who was based on the Greek god Hermes.

Erotica Museum

At Købmagergade 24 stands the world's oldest museum of erotica. Decoration, sculptures and wall-reliefs, explicit photographs and monitors portray the history of erotica from ancient times until the present day (open: Oct.–Apr.; daily 11am–8pm, May–Sept.: daily 10am–11pm).

Danish designer clothes and erotic art – both can be found in Købmagergade

Legetøjsmuseet (Toy Museum)   G8

The little toy museum on the Valkendorfsgade was set up on the initiative of Fritz Hartz, who assembled the first exhibits from antique markets in London.

This lovingly-assembled private collection in Sommerstedgade was formed on the initiative of Olgas Lyst in 1997. Some 400 dolls and 50 dolls' houses are exhibited in a display area of 150sq.m/1600sq.ft; included are several British and Danish dolls' houses dated ca. 1800 as well as old toys which were made in Danish prisons at the turn of the century (open: Sat. 1–5pm; also guided tours on request, tel. 31 23 85 58).

Location
Sommerstedgade 11

S-bane
Dybbel

Buses
10, 16

★Lejre Forsøgscenter (Lejre historical and archaeological research centre: "Prehistoric dwelling places")

At the Lejre historical and archaeological research centre the aim is to bring the past back to life. The "social and material culture of prehistoric times" is represented here with the main attraction a reconstructed "iron-age village" set in attractive scenery, the tour of which is just under 3km/2 miles long.

Historically authentic prehistoric workplaces have been set up: a forge, pottery, brickworks and weaving, as well as stalls for domestic animals – especially popular with children. At the "valley of fire" the visitor has the opportunity to bring meat or bread and roast it over prehistoric hearths.

Beyond the grounds of the museum, the estate of Ravnshøjgård was

Location
Slangeallé 2, Lejre (38km/24 miles south-west of Roskilde)

Railway station
Lejre; then bus 233

89

Opening times
May–mid-Oct.
Tue.–Sun.
10am–5pm
(daily mid-June to
mid-Aug.)

also acquired by the research centre. On this old farm the type of agriculture practised before the Second World War has been revived.

Nearby there are stone settings in the form of ships: according to Viking belief, when a person died he went to the Kingdom of the Dead in one of these vessels.

Little Mermaid

See Den lille Havfrue

Louisiana (Art museum and cultural centre)

Location
Humlebǽk,
Gl. Strandvej 13
(35km/22 miles
north of
Copenhagen

Railway station
Humlebǽk,
then bus 388

Opening times
daily 10am–5pm,
Wed. 10am–10pm

Information
Tel. 49 19 07 91

The Louisiana Museum of Art and Cultural Centre lies in a beautiful park high above the Øresund, with a view of the Swedish coast. Here art, architecture and landscape blend in a uniquely harmonious way. The range of contemporary art on display in these relaxed surroundings seems almost inexhaustible. Whitewashed exhibition pavilions nestle among old trees and bushes, together with hidden walks and illuminated winter-gardens. The museum was founded in 1954 by the industrialist Knud Jensen, who initially intended it merely to be a home for Scandinavian art. Thanks to generous endowments, especially on the part of the Ny Carlsberg Foundation (see Carlsberg Brewery), however, the museum soon developed one of the best collections of modern art in the world. The entrance to the Louisiana is marked by an old ivy-coated summer villa. Its previous owner, who built the house and laid out the park in 1955, was married in turn to three women called Louise, hence the name of the collection "Louisiana". The new buildings which merge so well with their surroundings were designed between 1958 and 1991 by the architects Jørgen Bo and Vilhelm Wohlert, aided later by Claus Wohlert. More recently, in 1990–91, a basement graphics wing was opened, turning what had until then been a semi-circular set of buildings into a closed complex. The gardens are the work of Vibeke Holscher, Lea Nørgaard and Ole and Edith Nørgaard.

**Permanent
collection**

The permanent collection was started after the Second World War, when Danish artists such as Robert Jacobsen and Richard Mortensen went to Paris where they met a number of gifted sculptors and painters, includ-

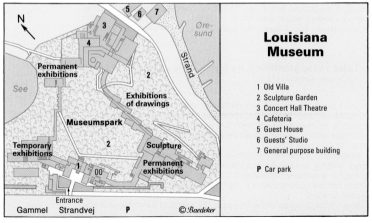

Louisiana Museum

1 Old Villa
2 Sculpture Garden
3 Concert Hall Theatre
4 Cafeteria
5 Guest House
6 Guests' Studio
7 General purpose building

P Car park

© Baedeker

An elegant group sculpture by Henry Moore in the Louisiana Museum of Art

Louisiana: monochrome colour plates by Yves Klein

ing Vasarély, Herbin, Dewasne, Albers, Gabo, Rickey and Calder, whose work can be now be seen in Louisiana. The avant-garde Cobra group is represented with paintings by Appel, Alechinsky, Lucebert etc. Other art movements of the 1950s include sculptures by Giacometti and Richter as well as paintings by Dubuffet, Bacon, Matta, Saura and Sam Francis, Mark Rothko and Reinhardt. Jean Tinguely's spectacular open-air sculpture "Sketch of the End of the World" is a mement of the wild sixties, while examples of the pop-art of that period are works by Roy Lichtenstein, Robert Rauschenberg, Andy Warhol, Dine and Oldenburg. Sculptures of great presence by Morris Louis, Noland and Frank Stella are also worthy of particular note. The 1970s and 1980s are represented by Josef Beuys, Ryman and Richter as well as Per Kirkeby and Richard Serra and German artists such as A. R. Penck, Georg Baselitz and Anselm Kiefer. Special attention should also be paid to the graphic collection in the new wing. Highlights of the sculpture collection are without doubt the well-lit Giacometti Room and the outstanding bronze sculptures by Henry Moore, Max Ernst and Alexander Calder in the extensive parkland. In addition, the Louisiana organises six to eight special exhibitions each year.

Visitors are welcome to relax on the grass or enjoy a view of the sea from the cafeteria.

Marble Bridge (New Bridge, Main Bridge, Palace Bridge)　　　H7

Location
Frederiksholms Kanal

Buses
1, 2, 5, 6, 10

The marble bridge which spans the Frederikskanal between the island of Slotsholmen and the National Museum (see entry) is considered one of the masterpieces of Nicolai Eigtved. King Christian VI had issued instructions for the building of the bridge in 1739 but it was not possible to finish the sculpture work until 1745. From a technical point of view the bridge's special advantage lay in the flat construction of its arches which

The Marble Bridge over the Frederikskanal – a masterpiece by Nicolai Egtved

meant that the road over the bridge could be almost completely horizontal.

The central pillars bear elegant classical portrait medallions with Rococo decorations, while the central arch is adorned with a head of Medusa. The French sculptor Louis-Augustin le Clerc, also hard at work at Christiansborg Palace (see entry), was given the task of carrying out all this decorative work on the bridge.

In his workshop he created out of Saxon sandstone the heavily symbolic portraits which, framed by reeds, rocaille and two foam-belching sea monsters, offer homage to the sea. Whether they actually represent the ancient gods Poseidon, Amphitrite, Oceanos and Tethys is debatable.

Officially the bridge is actually called the New Bridge, Main Bridge or Palace Bridge, although the name it is unofficially known by is the "Marble Bridge" on account of its marble-surfaced pavements. At the beginning of the 1970s a comprehensive restoration of the bridge was initiated under the direction of Erik Erlandsen and this continued until 1993.

★Marmorkirken (Marble Church; Frederikskirken)   J6

Officially called the "Frederikskirken", the place of worship which has always been known by the people of Copenhagen as just the "Marble Church" was designed in 1740 as the central church for the new city district of Frederiksstad by the famous court architect Nicolai Eigtved, who died in 1754 during the course of its construction.

King Frederik V laid the foundation stone in October 1749, but work on the building was brought to a halt in 1770 by Count von Struensee (see Famous People) on account of the high costs. Its eventual completion, using Danish limestone instead of the expensive Norwegian marble, did

Location
Frederiksgade 4

Buses
1, 6, 9

Opening times
Mon.–Sat.
11am–2pm;
Sun. 10.30am

Grundtvig monument ...

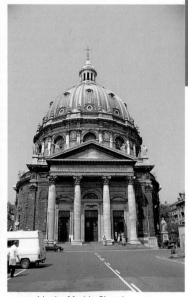

... outside the Marble Church

The Marble Church: interior of the Rotunda

not come about until 1894, after the great industrialist C. F. Tietgen had bought the ruin with the proviso that thechurch should be finished.

Eigtved's original building plan was now altered by the architect Ferdinand Meldahl, who added a 46m/151ft high cupola in the Roman baroque style. The cupola has a diameter of 33m/108ft and is one of the largest in Europe. Inside the rotunda are 12 towering marble pillars and coloured frescos in blue, gold and green. Particularly worth noticing are an ivory crucifix in the choir, a German oak relief of the Descent from the Cross in the front chapel, a marble font by Joakom Skovgård, Grundtvig's seven-armed gold chandelier and a relief by Niels Skovgård which commemorates C. F. Tietgen and his wife. The church is lined with statues of famous Danes from church life, including Søren Kierkegaard (see Famous People), St Ansgar, Denmark's patron saint, the reformer Martin Luther and the priest Nicolai Frederik Severin Grundtvig (see Famous People). The figures are by, among others, H. V. Bissen, J. F. Willumsen and K. Nellemose. On the roof projection there can also be seen enthroned 12 sculptures of famous representatives of religious and ecclesiastical history.

Mindelunden (Memorial to Danish resistance fighters)   G3

Location
Tuborgvej, Ryparken

S-bane
Hellerup

Buses
21, 23

The Mindelunden memorial is dedicated to all Danes who were killed in the struggle for their country's freedom during the German occupation from 1940 to 1945. On the Mindelunden site the corpses of 199 executed resistance fighters were found after the Second World War.

A commemorative wall designed by Axel Poulsen bears their names together with a poem by the Dane, Kaj Munk, who himself became a victim of fascism. In the small wood behind the memorial there are 31 graves which bear witness to those who were killed in German concentration camps. In the pergola which lies to the east, 141 memorial tablets have been erected to victims of the Nazi tyranny who disappeared without trace.

On August 20th 1945, after the German withdrawal, the first interments took place and the official opening of Mindelunden followed on May 5th 1950. The subsequent artistic design of the remembrance groves was carried out by Kaj Gottlob, while the landscaping of the park was entrusted to Axel Andersen from Gentofte.

Dec., Jan.: 10am–4pm; Nov., Feb.: 10am–5pm; Mar., Oct.: 10am–6pm; Apr., Sept.: 10am–7pm; May, Aug.: 10am–8pm; June, July: 10am–9pm.

Opening times

★Musikhistorisk Museum og Carl Claudius' Samling   H6
(Museum of Musical History)

The Museum of Musical History, which was originally attached to the Museum of Industrial Art (see Kunstindustrimuseet), was founded in 1898. Since 1966 it has been located in its present home, a two-storey building restored between 1963 and 1966 by Jørgen Bo and Vilhelm Wohlert. The comprehensive collection comprises some 2000 historical instruments of various types, including a harmonium belonging to King Christian VII, a violin belonging to Niels W. Gades and a piano from the collection of Carl Nielsens. In 1941 the museum received an extensive addition of instuments bequeathed by the Consul General, Carl August Claudius. There is a library joined to the museum with a wide-ranging collection of musical literature.

On certain Saturdays and Tuesdays (see announcements) the museum arranges concerts on historical instuments.

Location
Åbenrå 30

S-bane
Nørreport

Buses
5, 7, 14, 16, 43, 73E, 184

Opening times
May–Sept.,
Fri.–Wed. 1–4pm;
Oct.–Apr. Mon.,
Wed., Sat., Sun.
1pm–4pm

Nationalhistoriske Museum

See Frederiksborg Slot

★★Nationalmuseet (National Museum)   H7

The Danish National Museum is situated on the Frederiksholms Kanal opposite the island of Slotsholmen and Christiansborg Slot (see entry), which can be reached from here by crossing the Marble Bridge (see entry).

The museum, which is devoted to Danish cultural history from prehistoric to more recent times, comprises the Prince's Palace, which was built by Nicolai Eigtved in 1743–44 and wings of the palace added on at a later date which are on the Stormgade, the Ny Vestergade and the Vester Voldgade, as well as several departments located outside the main site.

Between 1989 and 1992 the National Museum was completely modernised and refurbished and considerably enlarged (details printed in Danish and English).

Location
Frederiksholms
Kanal 12;
Entrance: Ny
Vestergade 10

Buses
1, 2, 5, 6, 10

Prehistoric period, Middle Ages until 1660, Modern Age from 1660, classical antiquities, coin and medal collection, ethnographic collection with exhibitions of non-European cultures, and a children's museum: Tues.–Sun. 10am–5pm.

Opening times

The cultural history collection is divided into three areas. The early and pre-history department contains exhibits from the Stone, Bronze and Iron Ages and from the Viking era. Especially interesting are the sun cart

Collections

95

A typical 17th century middle-class bedroom

Secrets of the past: Viking rune inscriptions

from Trundholm (c. 1200 B.C.), the reproduction of a cult vehicle with a gold sun-screen, and the famous Bronze Age helmets with horns.

In the Middle Ages section there are gold altars on show, including the gold altar of Lisbjerg, Romanesque and Gothic church fittings, tools and furniture, as well as seven Gobelin tapestries, which were designed in 1582 for the decoration of the Knights' Hall at Kronborg Slot. The period after 1660 is represented by a series of living rooms belonging to the upper middle classes, for example a room in Ålborg dating from the middle of the 17th c., Rococo rooms and rooms directly planned for the Prince's Palace.

The collection of antiques has exhibits on display covering the classical eras of Greece and Italy, while the coin and medal collection concentrates above all on work from Denmark and the other Scandinavian countries.

In the ethnographic collection, the oldest in the world, the most striking section is the one dealing with the way of life of the Eskimos in Greenland, Canada and Alaska. There are also sections on Asia, Africa, Oceania and the culture of the Indians.

The children's museum is aimed especially at children between the ages of 6 and 12. It provides information about school life about 1900, 1950 and 1990, as well as of the nomadic life led by the Tuarags in the Sahara. Youngsters can also learn about a medieval castle and a Viking ship.

Children's Museum

Finally a visit should be made to the Victorian House, built in 1851–52, in which can be seen the contents of an upper-class household of 1890 belonging to the Danish businessman Rudolph Christensen (Conducted tours: June 16th–Sept. 15th: Thur.–Sun. noon–3pm on the hour; Sept. 16th–June 15th: Sat., Sun. noon–3pm on the hour).

Victorian House

Nikolaj Plads (Nicholas Square)   H7

Nikolaj Plads takes its name from the massive Nicholas Church (Nikolaj Kirke), built in the 13th c., which was completely burnt down in the great conflagration of 1795, except for the tower. Subsequently the butchers of Højbro Plads set up their stalls or "Maven" (stomachs) in the abandoned churchyard. The use of the area as a market did not come to an end until 1917 when the rebuilt Nicholas Church which we know today was opened. The spire of the new church, which was completed in 1910, was financed by a donation from the brewery owner Carl Jacobsen (see Carlsberg Brewery).

Location
East of Højbro Plads

Buses
1, 2, 6, 8, 10, 28, 29, 41

Today the Nicholas Church is no longer used for religious services, but instead is a venue for concerts and art exhibitions. The building also has a small restaurant.

In the summer months Nikolaj Plads is the setting for theatrical and musical events, in particular the Copenhagen Jazz Festival: one of its most famous venues is the bar, "De tre Musketérer" ("Three Musketeers"), at no. 25 in the square.

Nicolaj Kirke

Ny Carlsberg Glyptotek (Glyptotheque)   H7

The famous Ny Carlsberg Glyptotek boasts one of the largest and most important collections of ancient sculptures north of the Alps as well as one of the finest collections of 19th c. French art from David to Paul Gauguin. It was founded by the brewer Carl Jacobsen and his wife Ottilia (see Carlsberg Brewery), who decided in 1888 to donate to the nation their extensive collection of sculptures embracing ancient finds and works by members of the Thorvaldsen school as well as by con-

Location
Dantes Plads 7

S-bane
Main railway station

Ny Carlsberg Glyptotek

Buses
1, 2, 5, 10, 14, 16, 28, 29, 30, 32, 33, 34, 41

Opening times
Tue.–Sun.
10am–4pm

temporary artists. The Ny Carlsberg Foundation has continued to develop and add to the collection by gifts of antique pieces as well as 19th and 20th c. works, and also financed the latest extension to house the collection of French paintings. The oldest section of the museum was built in 1897 to designs by Vilhelm Dahlerup, and Hack Kampmann drew up the plans for an extension in 1906. The glass wing which was opened in 1996 and contains French Impressionist paintings was the work of the top Danish architect Henning Larsen.

Winter Garden

The central point of the museum is a wonderful winter garden with a Mediterranean climate, where the visitor can relax and enjoy the atmosphere similar to that in which a substantial part of the works on display were created. In the centre of the room can be seen a fountain-group by the Dane Kai Nielsen entitled "Water Mother with Children".

Egypt

Rooms 1–4
The Egyptian Collection, with exhibits dating from 3000 B.C. to A.D. 100, deals mainly with funerary art. Especially worthy of mention is the beautifully wrought head of an Egyptian princess (ca. 1360 B.C. and the "Horse of the Nile" (ca. 3000 B.C.) in Room 3.

Near East

Room 5
Room 5 is devoted to antique art of the Near East from the 3rd to the 1st c. B.C. The oldest piece on display is the seated figure of a Sumerian which can be dated to about 2500 B.C.; in addition the visitor will find Assyrian, Persian, Phoenician and Cyprian art.

Greece

Rooms 6–10
The collection of Greek art from the Archaic, Classical and Hellenic periods (7th–1st c. B.C.), which to a large degree was assembled with the help of the German archaeologists W. Helbig and P. Arndt, can claim to be one of the finest north of the Alps. Outstanding are the "Rayet Head" (6th c. B.C.) in Room 6 and the Roman copies of Greek portraits from the Hellenic era in Room 10.

Roman Empire

Rooms 11–18
The Roman portraits, including busts of Pompey, Augustus, Caligula and Livia (Room 12), date from the Late Republic to the decline of the Empire (1st c. B.C. to 5th c. A.D.). Idealised heads, portraits of divine rulers or almost unmercifully realistic likenesses – almost all were produced by Greek sculptors in leading Roman workshops. In the Festival hall (Room 18), which is used for concerts and lectures, can be seen numerous portrait statues and sarcophagi from the period of the Roman Empire.

Etruria

Rooms 19–21
The major part of the Etruscan collection was already in the glyptotheque at the time of Carl Jacobsen. The crematory urns, vases, stone and terracotta figures from the 8th–2nd c. B.C. reflect Greek influences. Particularly noteworthy is a gravestone (cippus) from Chiusi with elaborate relief decorations depicting a burial ritual (6th c. B.C.).

Southern Italy, Sicily

Rooms 22, 23
The finds displayed here reveal that the Greek colonies in Southern Italy and Sicily played an important intermediary role in exports of art to Etruria.

Palmyra

Rooms 24, 25
The grave portraits from the heyday of the oasis town of Palmyra (1st–3rd c. A.D. form the most extensive collection outside Syria.

Cyprus

Room 25a
The vases, stone and clay figures from Cyprus date mainly from between the 7th and 4th c. B.C.

Roman figures from the time of the Late Republic to the Empire

Egyptian grave drawings (c. 480 B.C.)   *Paul Gaugin: "Girl from Tahiti" (1891)*

Ny Carlsberg Glyptotek

Danish Painting

Rooms 26–28
Denmark's "Golden Age" between 1800 and 1850 is marked by paintings by C. W. Eckersberg ("Double portrait of Preben Bille-Brahe and Johanne Caroline Wilhemine f. Falbe", 1817), Jens Juel ("Mother and Son", 1800), Købke, Constantin Hansen, Lundbye and Skovgaard, together with some sculptures by H. W. Bissen, a pupil of Thorvaldsen.

Danish Sculpture

Rooms 29, 30, 48, 49, 52 and 53
The glyptotheque is the main museum of Danish sculpture after Bertel Thorvaldsen (see Famous People), whose classic lines were copied by his pupils H. W. Bissen and J. A. Jerichau (Rooms 28, 29, 43–45, 48). A more strongly naturalistic style was adopted by the next generation of sculptors (Såbye, Stein and V. Bissen), while Kai Nielsen (Room 30) and Gerhard Henning (Rooms 47, 47A) mark the breakthrough into the 20th c.

French Sculpture

Rooms 33–38, 43, 44
Some of the French sculptures, such as the Degas bronzes, are exhibited in the New Building (see below). The remainder are in the Dahlerup Building; they form a collection so complete that its equal can be found only in France itself, with works by Auguste Rodin (Rooms 33, 34) and a first-class collection of the "salon" sculptures, represented by Carpeaux, Dubois and Barrias.

Icons

Room 38A
A collection of 17th–19th c. Greek and Russian icons can be seen in Room 38A.

Open Magazine

Room 54
In the "Open Magazine" can be found 19th and 20th c. paintings and sculptures by both Danish and foreign masters.

New Building French Painting

Rooms 56–66
A well-lit glass arcade leads from the Winter Garden to the New Building for French 19th c. paintings. The ground floor (Rooms 56–60) is devoted to the forerunners of the Impressionists such as Géricault and Delacroix, and the "Barbizon painters" Camille Corot ("View of the Grand Trianon", 1866), Gustave Courbet ("Three English Maidens", 1865) and Edouard Manet ("The Execution of Emperor Maximilian I of Mexico", 1867), who had detached themselves from the French Classical movement. On the first floor (Rooms 61, 62) are works by all the leading Impressionists: Monet, Sisley, Pissarro, Renoir and Degas. Thanks to a generous gift from the founder's son Helge Jacobsen in 1927 the museum owns a first-class collection of works by Paul Gauguin which can be seen on the upper floor (Rooms 63–66). Among his 35 exhibits are the painting "Girl from Tahiti" (1891) and twelve ceramics, the latter being a gift from the Ny Carlsberg Foundation to mark the opening of the building in 1996. The post-Impressionists on display include Van Gogh ("Countryside near St Rémy, 1889), Cézanne, Toulouse-Lautrec, Signac, Bonnard, Vuillard and Maillol. All the Degas bronzes are also exhibited here, including the enchanting figure of the little ballerina in genuine tulle costume.

Bronze figure of a ballerina by Degas

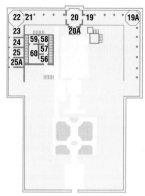

©Baedeker

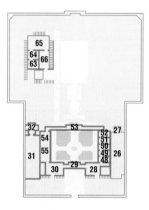

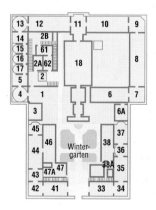

Ny Carlsberg Glyptothek

The major features of the museum are sculptures from the past 3500 years and 19th c. and contemporary French painting

Rooms 19–21: Etruscan Collection
Most of the items are associated with burials, including crematory urns, sacrophagi, vases and bronzes.

Rooms 22 and 23: Southern Italy, Sicily

Rooms 24 and 25: Art from Palmyra (Syria)

Room 25A: Cypriot Collection

Rooms 56–60: French Painting
Forerunners of Impressionism, including Courbet, Corot and Manet.

Rooms 26–28: Danish Painting
Especially works from the 19th c., the "Golden Age" (1800–1850): Eckersberg, Lundbye, Købka, etc.)

Rooms 29 and 30, 48 and 49, 52 and 53: Danish Sculpture
The glypotheque is the major museum of post-Thorvaldson sculpture: works include those by Såbya, Stein, V. Bissen, Kai Nielsen and Gerhard Henning.

Room 54: "The Open Magazine"
Paintings and sculptures by Danish and foreign artists of the 19th and 20th c.

Rooms 63–66: French Painting
The Post-Impressionists:
35 works by Paul Gauguin, as well as some by Van Gogh, Toulouse-Lautrec, Signac and Bonnard.

Rooms 1–4: Egyptian Art
Burial art: gods, animals, people.

Room 5: Ancient Oriental Art
Assyrian, Persian, etc., sculpture.

Rooms 6–10: Greek Art
Vases, bronzes, sculptures.

Rooms 11–18: Portraits
Greco-Roman portrait art.

Rooms 33–38, 43–45 and 47: French and Danish Sculpture
Some of the French sculptures are exhibited in the old building, including the Rodin Collection.

Room 38A: Icons

Rooms 61 and 62: French Painting
Impressionists; Monet, Degas and others.

★Nyhavn (New harbour) J6

Location
Kongens Nytorv

Buses
1, 6, 7, 9, 10, 28, 29, 31, 41

The Nyhavn is the name of a canal which was dug between 1671 and 1673 in order to connect the port of Copenhagen with the Kongens Nytorv (see entry). The harbour promenade of the same name runs along it and on the north side it is today a pedestrian zone and one of the most popular places in the whole city. In summer the Nytorv is especially "hyggelig", as the Danes say, which means more or less "very friendly" but furthermore conveys the charming atmosphere of this colourful harbourside street.

Nyhavn, where the writer Hans Christian Andersen (see Baedeker Special "A Fairytale in Bronze and Stone") once lived (in nos. 18, 20 and 67), used to be considered a kind of counterpart to the Hamburg Reeperbahn. On what was formerly the "seedy" side, in the now extensively restored brightly painted old gabled houses on the quayside, a large number of restaurants have been set up. They offer the visitor not only the traditional Danish "Kolde Bord" but also superb fish dishes and foreign specialities. On summer evenings the people of Copenhagen like to meet on the Nyhavn "just for a glass of beer", with which they can relax on the quayside and enjoy the romantic view of the old sailing ships mirrored in the water.

The oldest building on the Nyhavn is house no. 9. It dates from the year 1681 and provides an example of the type of buildings which existed prior to the devastating fire of 1728. One of the curiosities to be found among the small shops which have grown up here is the studio belonging to Ole, the "King of Tattooists", which is in the cellar of no. 17.

An anchor was placed at the end of the Nyhavn as a memorial to Danish sailors who lost their lives during the Second World War.

Old threemasters and lightships on Nyhavn make a picturesque scene

Nyhavn is a "museum harbour" for the picturesque museum ships of the National Museum (see entry) and other lovingly restored ships. There is also a lightship at anchor here dating from 1885 (Fyrskib XVII) which once did service as the "Gedser Riff" lightship.

Museum harbour

From Nyhavn the visitor can take harbour and canal trips to the Little Mermaid (see Den lille Havfrue) and Christianshavn (see entry).
See also Practical Information, Boat trips.

Harbour and canal trips

Orlogsmuseet

See Christianshavn

Peblinge Sø

See Sankt Jørgens Sø • Peblinge Sø • Sortedams Sø

Reformert Kirke (Reformed Church)   H6

After the German, French and Dutch Calvinists were given the right to freedom of religious worship in 1685, building of the Dutch–French Reformed Church was begun in 1688 and was completed just a year later. The stonemason Henrik Brockham was the architect of the rectangular Baroque building made with red Dutch bricks. The church suffered severe damage in the fires of 1728 and 1731 but was afterward completely restored.

Location
Gothersgade 111

Buses
7, 17, 43

Inside the church, special attention should be given to the wonderful carved pulpit by Friedrich Ehbisch, the galleries and the monarch's throne. The placing of the altar and the pulpit on the same side and the lack of any figurative decorations are characteristic of buildings of the Reformed Church.

Regensen (Collegium Regium; students' college)   H6

In 1569, in order to help students with inadequate means, Frederik II founded a society offering 100 free scholarship places. The Regensen students' college was built between 1623 and 1628 in red brick under Christian IV (see Famous People). The royal benefactor is remembered by a plaque on the Købmagergade (see entry). The hostel, which was able to accommodate just under 100 students in 48 rooms, was officially called Collegium Regium in 1628 but within a year the name Regensen came into use.

Location
Store Kannike-stræde 2

The only part of the building to survive the great fire of 1728 was the wing on the Store Kannikestræde, the rest being rebuilt in 1731. Further additions and alterations to the building followed at the end of the 18th c. and the beginning of the 20th c.

In the courtyard of the Collegium, which is still used today as a students' hostel, there is a linden tree, which was planted in the 1950s. It replaced the famous linden tree which was planted by the Regensen provost A. C. Hviid on May 12th 1785, the anniversary of which is celebrated every year.

Buses
5, 7, 14, 16, 17, 24, 43, 84

★★Rosenborg Slot (Rosenborg Palace)   H6

Since 1833 the collections of the Danish kings have been on display to the public in Rosenborg Palace, which was built at the same time as Frederiksborg Palace (see entry). The palace dates back to the reign of

Rosenborg Slot

Location
Øster Voldgade
4A
S-bane
Nørreport

Buses
5, 7, 10, 14, 16, 17,
24, 43, 84

Christian IV (see Famous People), who initially had the south part built in 1606–07 and then in 1613–17 had it considerably extended by the addition of the square west tower designed by Bertel Lange. Between 1633 and 1634 the eight-sided staircase tower was added on the front of the east façade, most likely by Hans van Steenwinckel the Younger. The palace was built in the Dutch Renaissance style as a spring and autumn residence of the Danish kings and was used as such until the middle of the 18th c.

Opening times

May 1st–May 31st, Sept. 1st–Oct. 21st: daily 11am–3pm; June 1st–Aug. 31st: daily 10am–4pm; Oct. 22nd–Dec. 14th, Jan. 1st–Apr. 30th: Tues., Fri. and Sun. 11am–2pm.

Visit

Rosenborg Slot today contains, in the 24 rooms on show, a wealth of objets d'art associated with the Danish royal house, as well as the unusually charming original furniture, which contributes to the palace's immense appeal.

The following are especially worth seeing: Christian IV's study, decorated with elaborate panels and ceiling paintings, where the king carried out his extensive correspondence sitting at a gold-painted writing cabinet made in 1580 in Augsburg; the Winter Room of Christian IV, in the panelling of which Dutch paintings from Antwerp have been inset; Frederik III's Marble Room, originally the bedchamber of Christian IV's

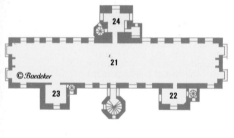

Rosenborg Slot

SECOND FLOOR

21 Long Room
22 Glass Chamber
23 Porcelain Chamber
24 Regalia Room
(at present closed)

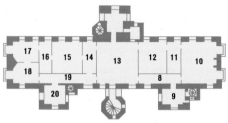

FIRST FLOOR

8 Frederick IV Corridor
9 Lacquer Cabinet of Princess Sophie Hedwig
10 Frederick IV's Apartment
11 Frederick IV's Study
12 Christian VI's Apartment
13 "The Rose" Anteroom Mirror Cabinet
14 Frederick VI's Study
15 Christian VII's Chamber
16 Frederick IV's Chamber
17 Christian VIII's Chamber
18 Frederick VII's Chamber
19 Corridor of Christian VII and Frederick VI
20 Bronze Room

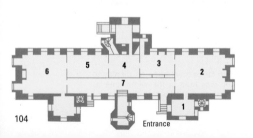

GROUND FLOOR

1 Christian IV's writing cabinet
2 Christian IV's Winter Room
3 Christian IV's Bedroom
4 Dark Room
5 Frederick III's Marble Room
6 Royal Chamber of Christian V
7 Stone Passage

Entrance

Rosenborg Slot: a picture-book castle in magnificent parkland

A royal apartment in Rosenborg Slot

consort, decked out in a very formal baroque style; the King's Chamber, with Dutch Gobelin tapestries by M. Wauters and formal portraits of King Christian V and Queen Charlotte Amalie (both paintings by J. D'Agar); the painted chamber, decorated in 1663–65 for Sophie Amalie, the wife of Frederik III, with sumptious chinoiserie, turquoise and mother-of-pearl; the hall of Frederik IV, adorned with gobelins from Audenarde of (c. 1700); the "Rose" ante-chamber, with paintings and furniture from the time of Frederik V; the mirror chamber, fitted out in 1700 for Frederik IV following the model of Versailles; a 24-arm amber chandelier made in 1743–56 by L. Spengler; the Flora Danica dinner service for 100 people, produced in 1803 by the Royal Porcelain Factory, the floral decoration of which is from a design by G. C. Oeders; the Glass Chamber, fitted out with Venetian glass in 1714 by Frederik IV after his tour of Europe; and the Long Banqueting or Knights' Hall. It was the last room to be completed in 1624. Only two fireplaces remain from the original fittings. The stucco ceiling, installed at the beginning of the 18th c. by Frederik IV, shows the royal coat of arms, flanked by the Order of the Elephant and the Dannenborg Order.

★★Treasure Chamber

Opening times
Jan.–Apr.,
Oct. 22nd–Dec.
14th
Tue.–Sun.
11am–3pm
May, Sept.–Oct.
21st.:
daily 11am–3pm;
June–Aug,:
daily 10am–4pm

Occupying three well-secured rooms in the vaults is the Treasure Chamber, opened in 1975 and now on show to the public. Here are to be found the imperial regalia, which have been held in Rosenborg Palace for safe keeping since the end of the 17th c., as well as other royal treasures, including the golden crown of the absolute monarchy, made in 1670 by Poul Kurtz in Copenhagen with diamonds, sapphires and rubies, which was worn by the kings of Denmark for 170 years and which even today is placed on the sarcophagus of a monarch lying in state. In addition the crown of Christian IV, made in 1595–96 by the goldsmith Dirk Fyring in Odense, can be seen, as well as various crown jewels, an enamelled silver drinking horn of 1465 and the symbol of the Order of the Garter, founded in 1348 by Edward III, with its famous motto "Honi soit qui mal y pense". There is also the saddle of Christian IV, embroidered with gold, jewels and pearls, and finally the imperial regalia, made in 1648 for the coronation of Frederik III. The sceptre symbolises authority and power, while the orb with its cross symbolises the earthly ball, with God's anointed ruler at the head of its church.

★Kongens Have

Forming part of the palace is the Kongens Have (also called Rosenborg Have), which was laid out in 1606 under Christian IV and is the oldest park in Copenhagen. It contains many statues, including one of Hans Christian Andersen (see Famous People) surrounded by eagerly listening children. The barracks of the Royal Guards are also situated here and the new guard leaves here shortly before 11.30am for the changing of the guard at Amalienborg Palace (see entry).

Livgårdens
historiske
Samling

In the 200 year-old barracks (Gothersgade 100) uniforms, weapons and paintings document the history of the Life Guards from 1658 to the present day (open: May–Sept.: Tue., Sun. 11am–3pm, Oct.–Apr.: Sun. 11am–3pm).

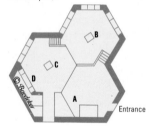

Treasury
Rosenborg Slot

A Christian IV's Collection

B Christian IV's Royal Crown

C Royal Crown from Christian V to Christian VII

D Crown Jewels and Regalia

Roskilde

The town of Roskilde lies on the fjord of the same name, which cuts deep into the island of Sjælland (Zealand). Founded according to legend by King Ro, but in point of fact by the Vikings in 980, the town became the seat of the Zealand bishops in about 1020 and rapidly developed into a centre of royal power. It was also from time to time used as the town of residence of the royal family. Today Roskilde is the largest provincial town in Zealand and is the seat of a university. The celebrated Roskilde rock-festival is held here every summer.

Location
30km/19 miles west of Copenhagen

Railway station
Roskilde

★★Roskilde Domkirke (Cathedral)

The Cathedral of St Luke at Roskilde is one of Denmark's national monuments. The imposing building of red brick faces across the fjord from its slight elevation. Its main features date from the time of Bishop Absalon (see Famous People). Building of the cathedral was begun in 1170 in the Romanesque style at the place where earlier around 1020 under Harold Bluetooth a wooden church had stood. In 1170 the church was extended in the Northern French Gothic style while in the chapels and entrance halls which were added later, various other directions of Danish architecture can be observed. The two west towers were added in the 14th c., their slim, copper-covered helm roofs dating from 1635–36. The basilica is 85m/280ft long, with three naves, and inside has a height of 24m/79ft. The royal door between the two west towers is only opened for royal funerals, so visitors enter through the side-door on the south side.

Location
Town centre

Opening times
Apr., Sept. Mon.–Fri. 9am–4.45pm;
Sat. 11.30–4.45pm;
Sun. 12.30–3.45pm;
May–Aug. Mon.–Fri. 9am–4.45pm
Sat. 9am–noon
Sun. 12.30–3.45pm
Oct.–Mar. Mon.–Fri. 10am–2.45pm
Sat. 11.30am–2.45pm
Sun. 12.20–3.45pm

Roskilde Cathedral

Visit   The cathedral is the final place of rest for the Danish monarchs since the early 15th c. The alabaster and marble gravestones of 38 Danish queens and kings buried here – from Margarete I (d. 1412) to Frederik IX (d. 1972) – are one of the main attractions of the church. Frederik IX's sarcophagus, which also originally stood in one of the chapels, was given its own resting-place – an octagonal edifice of hand-painted tiles – outside the cathedral in 1985. Inside the church the superb 15th c. carved choir stalls are especially worth seeing.

Above the choir stalls there are wooden reliefs with pictures from the Old Testament (south side) and the New Testament (north side) with a noteworthy depiction of the Ascension, showing Christ's footprints left behind in the ground, while his feet can be seen at the top of the picture.

The great golden winged altar (16th c.) comes from Antwerp and was originally intended for the church of Frederiksborg Palace (see entry). The altar was faultlessly restored after a fire in 1968, and the side-panels depict Christ's life and Passion.

On the north wall can be seen the "Throne of Christian IV", dating from the Renaissance, with its richly decorated canopy; opposite it stands the organ which was restored in 1988–91. Organists of international renown give concerts every Thur. at 8pm during the summer months. A figure of St John from the early 16th c. (in the middle one of the three chapels in the north transept), the pulpit (1609) made of sand-

Roskilde Cathedral

© Baedeker

A   Entrance
B   Christian I's Chapel
    (chapel of the three kings)
C   Frederik V's Chapel
D   Chapterhouse
E   Oluf Mortensen's Porch
F   Christian IV's Chapel
G   St Andrew's Chapel
H   St Birgitte's Chapel
J   N Tower Chapel
K   S Tower Chapel
L   Absalon's Arch

1   Main entrance
2   Royal Column
3   Monument of Christian III and Queen Dorothea
4   Tomb of Christian I and Queen Dorothea
5   Monument of Frederik II and Queen Sophie
6   Tomb of Caroline Amalie
7   Tomb of Sophie Magdalene
8   Tomb of Christian VIII
9   Tomb of Marie Sophie Frederike
10 Tomb of Queen Louise
11 Tomb of Frederik V
12 Tomb of Juliane Marie
13 Tomb of Christian VII
14 Tomb of Frederik VI
15 Tomb of Louise Charlotte

16 Tomb of Christian VI
17 Tomb of Frederik VII
18 Helhestens Sten
19 Gravestone of Bishop Peder Jensen Lodehal
20 Monument of Duke Christopher
21 Tomb of Frederik IV
22 Pillar with remains of Svend Estridsen
23 Tomb of Christian V
24 Tomb of Charlotte Amalie
25 Pillar with remains of Estrid, Knud the Great's sister
26 Tomb of Queen Louise
27 Tomb of Queen Margaret
28 High altar
29 Choir-stalls (1420)
30 Font

31 Tomb of Frederik III
32 Tomb of Sophie Amalie
33 Tomb of Anne Catherine
34 Tomb of Christian IV
35 Tomb of Prince Christian
36 Tomb of Queen Alexandrine
37 Tomb of Christian X
38 Double tomb of Christian IX and Queen Louise
39 Double tomb of Frederik VIII and Queen Louise
40 Tomb of Anne Sophie Reventlow
41 Kirsten Kimer, Per Døver and St Jørgen
42 Vincentz Hahn's armour
43 Royal Gallery
44 Organ
45 Pulpit (17th c.)
46 Tomb of Federik IX

stone, alabaster, marble and black limestone, and the bronze font of 1602 are also well worth seeing.

The royal tombs in the burial chapel offer a unique basis for comparing the various fashions in monumental art from the early 15th c. to the present century. The most valuable piece is the supine statue of Queen Margarethe I, behind the high altar, a Gothic piece in alabaster made in 1414 by the Lübeck artist, Johannes Junge. The burial chapel of Christian IV (on the north side), with its massive ogival vaulting, displays wall paintings by Wilhelm Marstrand and a bronze statue of the king (by Bertel Thorvaldsen). Also situated on the north side are the chapels of Christian IX, St Bridget and St Andrew. On the south side is the completely classical chapel built for Frederik V, with a dome and high windows which allow plenty of light into the building. On this side there is also the Chapel of the Three Kings, the granite pillar of which supports ribbed vaulting. The heights of various kings are marked on this pillar – Christian I claimed to be the tallest and he marked his height as 2.1m/6ft 10½in. but in fact his skeleton measures just under 1.9m/6ft 3 in.

Royal tombs

★★Vikingeskibshallen (Hall of Viking ships)

After the Viking ship museum in Oslo, the hall of ships at Roskilde offers the best coverage of the shipbuilding history of the Vikings.

The museum has been under construction since 1969. In 1991 the permanent exhibition of ships of the Viking age was completed. In the middle of 1997 a new museum harbour and an island were added. While the harbour was being deepened workmen stumbled across the wreck of a medieval vehicle which is to be carefully examined and preserved in the coming years.

In the hall there are five Viking ships dating from the period 1000–50, which were recovered from the sea in 1962 and subsequently restored. They had been weighed down with stones so that they sank into the Roskildefjord to mark the limit of a navigation channel and to protect Roskilde from attacks from the sea. The ships on display are of various sizes and types and their state of preservation is not uniform. They comprise an ocean-going ship (length 16.5m/54ft), a longship (28m/92ft) which was salvaged in two parts, a trading ship (13.3m/44ft), a warship (18m/59ft) and a ferry (12m/39ft).

The exhibition also covers the historic development of Viking times; a film provides information about the salvaging and conservation of the ships and the building of the replica ship the "Roar Ege" and the sailing expeditions made in her. Copies of Viking jewellery can be purchased in the museum shop.

At present, using Viking tools and methods, a replica of the little ship called the "Skuldelev" is being constructed. In the workshops opposite visitors can try their hand at rope and sail-making or taste the dried fish from the barrel in which they were stored and then slake their thirsts. In the archaeological section visitors can watch the wreck which was raised in 1997 being examined for traces of pitch and paint and see these described and dated.

In the new harbour old Nordic ships lie at anchor, including a smart four-sail boat.

In the summer months educational and tourist trips are organised (for information tel. 46 30 02 00, fax 46 32 21 15).

Location
Strandengen

Railway station
Roskilde

Buses
in Roskilde no. 123

Opening times
Apr.–Oct.:
daily 9am–5pm;
Nov.–Mar.:
daily 10am–4pm

★**Rundetårn** (Round Tower)　　　　　　　　　　　　H6

The Round Tower, which can be reached from the Nørreport S-bane station by crossing the Købmagergade (see entry), is another of the

Location
Købmagergade

Rundetårn

buildings associated with King Christian IV (See Famous People). It was erected by him as an observatory in 1642. At 35m/115ft the tower is one of the most striking buildings in the city (open: June–Aug.: Mon.–Sat. 10am–8pm, Sun. noon–8pm; rest of the year Mon.–Sat. 10am–5pm, Sun. 10am–4pm, Oct.–Mar. also on Tue., Wed. 7–10pm).

Visit

The ascent of the tower is not made by a staircase, but instead by a winding 209m/686ft long passage, up which the heavy equipment, which can now be seen in an astronomical collection, could more easily be transported. The story is told that Tsar Peter the Great rode up it in 1716, accompanied by his wife in a six-in-hand coach, which, given the measurements, seems difficult to imagine. In 1902 the first car drove up and today unicycle races take place in the tower every year.

On arriving at the top the visitor will notice a "planet machine", set up in 1928, which shows, with the northern starry sky as a background, the sun and six planets circling round it. From the very top platform, which in 1643 was provided with an elegant iron railing by the master smith Caspar Fincke, there is a superb panoramic view over the old city of Copenhagen.

Trinitatis Kirke

The tower is part of the Trinitatis Kirke (Trinity Church), begun in 1637 to designs by Hans von Steenwinckel the Younger, which was consecrated on June 1st 1656 by the Bishop of Zealand in the presence of Frederik III. The sacred building was intended to serve both as a church, as a university library (in the roof) and with the Round Tower as an observatory. The precious collection of manuscripts in the library fell victim to the fire of 1728, whilst in 1862 the observatory was transferred to the Østervold and the library to the Fiolstræde. Of special interest inside the Trinitatis Kirke is the altar, made by Friedrich Ehbisch in 1731 in the Baroque style and the beautiful wooden pulpit, also by Friedrich Ehbisch. Opposite the pulpit there is a splendid golden Rococo clock dating from 1757 which

The Round Tower: from the top is a panoramic view of the city

Bronze Age musicians: the lure blowers

has three faces. On the north wall of the choir can be seen a marble epi-
taph dating from 1689 commemorating the Danish field marshal Hans
Schack (d. 1676), framed by his battle equipment.

★★Rådhus and Rådhuspladsen (City Hall and City Hall Square)   G/H7

Copenhagen City Hall, seat of the city's administration, is easily reached
from the Vesterport and main railway station S-bane stations. It is the
fifth in the city's history. It took 13 years to build and was opened in 1905.
The architect was Professor Martin Nyrop (1849–1921), himself a
member of the city administration.

    The city hall covers an area of 7000 sq.m/75,350 sq.ft. Within its rec-
tangular plan are located a covered central hall and also an open courtyard planted with flowers. The administrative offices are to be found in
three wings of the building (open: Mon.–Fri. 10am–3pm; conducted
tours: Mon.–Fri. 3pm, Sat. 10am).

    Flanked by six stone guards the Danish flag today flutters on the
ridged roof of the front part of the building. Above a small balcony on
the façade is the golden statue of the founder of the city, Bishop Absalon
(see Famous People), by C. G. V. Bissen.

    Conducted tours of the city hall start in the central hall, which has an
area of 44×24m/144×79ft and a height of 9m/30ft and has a glazed roof
as well as balconies and galleries on the upper floors. The hall serves as
a polling station for elections to the City Council Assembly and for the
Folketing, but it is also used as a concert and exhibition hall. It contains
busts of four famous Danes and freemen of the city: the first shows the
architect of the building, the others the sculptor Bertel Thorvaldsen, the
physicist Niels Bohr and the writer Hans Christian Andersen (see notes
on all three under Famous People). The oak banisters of the staircase
boast 17 balusters which, according to an old Danish children's rhyme,
represent the architect and the craftsmen entering the city hall. The mag-
istrate's session room, a large banqueting hall with the coats of arms of
Danish cities, the city council chamber and a library complete the city's
"seat of government".

Location
in the south-west
of the city centre

Buses
1, 2, 6, 8, 14, 16,
19, 28, 29, 30, 32,
33, 34, 35, 41, 63,
64, 68

From the entrance hall there is access to the room housing Jens Olsens'
famous world clock (restored in 1997), which he worked at for 27 years
and which was set going in 1955. It is a miracle of astronomy, showing
times throughout the world, the paths of the stars (in particular, the
planets) and the dates of the Gregorian and Julian calendars (open:
Mon.–Fri. 10am–4pm, Sat. 10am–1pm; conducted tours: Mon.–Fri. 1pm,
3pm, Sat. 10am).

Jens Olsens
Verdensur

The city hall tower, at 106m/346ft Denmark's highest tower, offers the
most panoramic view of Copenhagen. The visitor must first climb nearly
300 steps to reach the balcony and then proceed along narrow passage-
ways to the foot of the spire. The peal of bells in the tower is used as a
time signal by the Danish radio service. (Conducted tours: Oct.–May:
Mon.–Sat. noon; June–Sept.: Mon.–Fri. 10am, noon, 2pm, Sat. noon.)

Tower

On the imposing square in front of the city hall stands the Dragon's Leap
Fountain, the statue of which depicts a bull fighting with a dragon. The
bronze statue was made by Joachim Skovgaard in 1923.

Dragon's Leap
Fountain

The terminal of the transport services which was erected here in 1995
has met with limited approval. Most people would like to see the black
edifice removed.

Transport
services
terminal

In front of the city hall there also stands a bronze basin made by Martin
Nyrop in 1908 which bears the inscription "A beautiful city, you our

Bronze basin

Seat of the city's administration: Copenhagen City Hall with Denmark's tallest tower

mother, you look tenderly on the sound. Your mouth smiles lovingly on your children, both big and small."

Lure Blowers

Between the city hall and the Palace Hotel can be seen two bronze lure blowers by the sculptor Siegfried Wagner which were erected here in 1914. Their bronze horns, bent into an S shape, are 1.70m/5½ft and 1.80m/6ft long. During the Bronze Age in Northern Europe the lures were sacred musical instruments. More than 30 of such instruments were found in Denmark, 18 of which can now be seen in the National Museum (see entry).

Andersen Monument

On the square in front of the city hall there is also a monument to the writer Hans Christian Andersen (see Baedeker Special).

Saint Alban's Church   J6

Location
Esplanaden

Buses
1, 6, 9

The Anglican Saint Alban's Church is situated between the Frihedsmuseet and Gefion Springvandet (see entries). It was built in 1885–87 in the English Gothic style to a design by the English architect A. W. Blomfield. English language services have been held here right up to the present day.

In the adjacent Churchillparken there is a monument to the British politician Sir Winston Churchill (1874–1965).

Sankt Ansgar Kirke (Church)   J6

Location
Bredgade 64

The Roman Catholic St Ansgar Church was built in 1841–42 in the Neo-Romanesque style next to the Kunstindustrimuseet (see entry). Since

Catholics were not granted permission to ring the bells for mass until the Constitution of 1849, the church originally possessed no tower. The present bell-tower was added in 1943. The church now houses a museum on the history of the Catholic church in Denmark since 1654 (open: Tues.–Sun. noon–4pm).

S-bane
Østerport

Buses
1, 6, 9

Sankt Jørgens Sø · Peblinge Sø · Sortedams Sø (Lakes)

G7–H5

Three lakes (søerne) form a semi-circle round the centre of Copenhagen, the tree-lined streets that pass along their banks being connected by four bridges. In summer it is possible to sail or row on the lakes, in winter skaters are to be seen skimming across the ice. To the west of this girdle of lakes – going from south to north – extend the city districts of Vesterbro, Nørrebro and Østerbro.

Location
North-west of the city centre

The southernmost lake is St Jørgens Sø, on the southern bank of which is situated the Tycho Brahe Planetarium (see entry). In front of the bridge (Gyldenløvesgade), which separates off the neighbouring Peblinge Sø, the towers of the Restaurant Søpravillonen (no. 24) dominate the skyline. By the northernmost lake, the Sørtedams Sø, the visitor can stop at "Den franske Café" for coffee and cakes.

Sankt Nikolaj Kirke

See Nikolaj Plads

Sankt Petri Kirke (Church)

H6

Built in 1450, the Sankt Petri Kirke is the church of the German community, which King Frederik II transferred to the Germans resident in Copenhagen back in 1585. From 1681 to 1683 Hans van Steenwinckel the Younger undertook alterations to the building, in the course of which the choir received a Baroque gable. Most of the fittings in the church fell victim to the great fire of 1728, but in 1730–31 the church was rebuilt by J. C. Krieger. Its 78m/256ft tower topped by a spire was added by Boye Junge in 1757. During the bombardment by the English in 1807 the church suffered severe damage but was subsequently completely rebuilt and in 1997/8 restored.

Location
Nørregade/
St Peders Stræde

Bus
5

Conducted tours
Sun., after the service.

Inside the building there are valuable burial chapels, the contents of which include works by the Neo-classical artist, Johannes Wiedevelt.

Skala

See Axeltorv

Sortedams Sø

See Sankt Jørgens Sø · Peblinge Sø · Sortedams Sø

★★Statens Museum for Kunst (State Art Museum)

H6

The State Art Museum houses works by Danish and European masters from the 13th c. to the present day. Illustrious names from the "Golden Age" such as Eckersberg and Købke can be found here, together with painters of the Skagen (The Skaw) and Funen (Fyn) schools and con-

Location
Sølvgade 48–50

temporary artists including Harald Giersing, Kai Nielsen and Gerhard Henning. Other highlights include Dutch and Flemish paintings of the 15th to 17th c., the Venetian school of the 16th and 17th c. and the notable Matisse Collection. The museum's collection was originally derived from the paintings and sculptures belonging to the Danish kings in Christiansborg Palace (see Christiansborg Slot) which, after the fire of 1894, needed new museum space. The present-day complex was built between 1889 and 1896 by Vilhelm Dahlerup and E. V. Møller in the Italian Renaissance style.

S-bane
Nørreport,
Østerport

Buses
10, 24, 43, 84

The collection of paintings includes works by European masters of the 13th to 18th c. The Italian section contains important pictures by Titian, Tintoretto, Guardi and Tiepolo, together with some by Mantegna, Filipino Lippi, Parmigianino and Barocci. The Dutch collection extends from early Flemish art of the beginning of the 15th c. to the heyday of the Dutch school in the 17th c. Included are works by Rubens, Bruegel the Elder, Hans Memling, Frans Hals, Rembrandt, van de Velde, van Goyen, Ruisdael, Jan Steen, Pieter Lastman and Jacob Jordaens. The German collection is notable for paintings by Lucas Cranach the Elder – the most extensive collection of his pictures outside Germany. The French section includes, most notably, 18th c. works by Poussin, Lorrain and Fragonard.

Old European masters

The outstanding Danish artists of the 18th c. include Nicolai A. Abildgaard and Jens Juel, while the "Golden Age" of the early 19th c. is represented by C. W. Eckersberg and his pupils Christian Købke and Constantin Hansen. Among the landscape painters of the second half of the 19th c. J. T. Lundbye, P. C. Skovgaard and Vilhelm Hammershøi are the most notable. Also represented are the Funen (Fyn) painters Peter Hansen, Frits Syberg and Johannes Larsen, as well as Michael and Anna Ancher and P. S. Krøyer of the Skagen colony.

Old Danish masters

The precursors of modern Danish art include the painters Harald Giersing, Edvard Weie and Karl Isakson. Of the sculptors who worked during the first half of the 20th c., particular mention should be made of Kai Nielsen, Gerhard Henning and Astrid Noack. Egil Jacobsen, Richard Mortensen, Robert Jacobsen and Bjørn Nørgaard are further members of the contemporary stream of artists. Thanks to generous gifts the museum also owns a fine collection of works by 20th c. French painters, including Braque, Rouault and Picasso as well as 25 pictures by Henri Matisse. The nine paintings by Emil Nolde were bequeathed to the museum by the artist himself.

Modern art

The gallery of engravings, which was moved here from the Royal Library in 1835, contains some 300,000 European drawings and examples of graphic art from the middle of the 16th c. to the present day, including etchings and engravings by A. Dürer and works by Piranesi, Degas, Toulouse-Lautrec, Picasso and Giacometti.

Gallery of engravings

Storkespringvandet

See Amagertorv

Storm P.-Museet (Storm P.-Museum)   E7

This museum shows the artistic development of the humorous artist Robert Storm Petersen (1882–1949). The collection gained its name from the signature on his works, which was Storm P. (open: May–Aug.: Tues.–Sun. 10am–4pm; Sept.–Apr.: Wed., Sat., Sun. 10am–4pm).

Location
Frederiksberg
Runddel

◀ *The State Art Museum contains masterpieces of painting from the "Golden Age" to the 20th century*

Strøget

S-bane
Frederiksberg

Buses
18, 27, 28, 41

The first room presents the artist's early creative period, influenced by symbolism and Art Nouveau, while the second room contains works on the theme of "the circus", including the work "Green Clown", dating from 1940. The third room is given over to Storm P.'s modern paintings. The drawings in the fourth room are derived from two series, begun in 1916 and 1922, created for the Copenhagen newspaper "Berlingske Tidende". In the fifth room, the reading room, is housed the library. Stage designs by the artist are also set out here.

★★Strøget (Pedestrian zone) H6/7

Location
in the centre
between Rådhus-
pladsen and
Kongens Nytorv

Buses
Rådhuspladsen:
1, 2, 6, 8, 14, 16,
19, 28, 29, 30, 32,
33, 34, 35, 41, 50,
63, 64, 68, 75E
Kongens Nytorv:
1, 4H, 6, 7, 9, 10,
10H, 28, 29, 31, 41

The name Strøget, which basically means "stripe" or "stroke", is today to be found over the signs of the five streets which form the most famous shopping mile in Denmark and longest pedestrian zone in Europe.

The popular name given to the 1.8km/1 mile long traffic artery linking Rådhuspladsen and Kongens Nytorv (see entries) was not recognised officially until the 1980s.

Strøget is Copenhagen's most popular shopping street, and the one with the widest range of goods (see Practical Information, Shopping). Many restaurants, bierkellers and cafés have also been set up here.

The five streets which make up the Strøget were declared a pedestrian zone in November 1962 in spite of considerable misgivings among the residents. The names of the historic thoroughfares leading from the Rådhuspladsen are: Frederiksberggade, Nygade, Vimmelskaftet, Amagertorv (see entry) and Østergade. The two squares, Gammeltorv and Nytorv, with their green spaces and fountains, of which Gammeltorv with the Caritas Fountain (see entry) has the oldest, add to the appeal of the Strøget. Alongside many elegant shops, fashion boutiques,

Café Europa – the place to rest after a shopping expedition in the Strøget

jewellers, booksellers, attractive souvenir shops, delicatessen and specialist shops there are the large department stores of Illum and Magasin du Nord, as well as salesrooms belonging to the Copenhagen Porcelain Factory, the Holmegaard Glassworks and the silversmiths, Georg Jensens (see Facts and Figures, Danish Design). Strøget is the epitome of Copenhagen, typical not just of the city itself, but also of its total informality.

Søren Kierkegaard Samlingen

See Københavns Bymuseum & Søren Kierkegaard Samlingen

★★Thorvaldsens Museum   H7

This museum, which is devoted to the most famous of Danish sculptors, Bertel Thorvaldsen (see Famous People), was founded by the sculptor himself in 1837. However it could only be opened after his death in September 1848 (memorial slab to Thorvaldsen in the inner courtyard). The plot of land used for the museum was a gift from Frederik VI, while Thorvaldsen donated the extensive collection which was formed from his own works and those he had collected. Gottlieb Bindesboll was chosen as architect for the museum and he designed a building in the historicist style, enhancing it with bright colours both inside and outside.

Location
Porthusgade 2

Buses
1, 2, 6, 8, 10, 28, 29, 41

Opening times
Tues.–Sun.
10am–5pm

His design gave the outer walls a vivid pictorial frieze, which on the side looking on to the canal depicts Thorvaldsen's triumphant return from Rome in 1838, while on the other two walls the unloading of the frigate "Rota" and the transporting of Thorvaldsen's sculptures into the museum are portrayed. The main entrance is dominated by a four-horsed chariot driven by the goddess of victory which was executed by Thorvaldsen's pupil H. V. Bissen to plans by the master. The bronze group was a present from King Christian VIII. The ceiling decorations inside the building, which follow antique models, were entrusted by Bindesboll to several artists, including G. C. Hilker, Christian Købke and Jorgen Sonne; the floors were covered with elaborate mosaics and terrazzo work.

Amor and the three Graces

The museum contains a wide-ranging collection of antique figures, sculptures – partly originals, partly models – and details about Throvaldsen's life, such as a demonstration of the artist's methods of working. Thorvaldsen's own collections of paintings and classical antiquities are also on display.

Collection

Thotts Palais

See Kongens Nytorv

★★Tivoli G/H7

Location
Vesterbrogade 3

S-bane
Main railway
station

Buses
Rådhuspladsen:
1, 2, 6, 8, 14, 16,
19, 28, 29, 30, 32,
33, 34, 35, 41, 50,
63, 64, 68, 75E

Opening times
End Apr.
to mid-Sept.:
Sun.–Thur.
11am–midnight
Fri., Sat.
11am–2am

Without doubt the most famous sight of the Danish capital is Tivoli. The amusement park lies right in the city centre, only a stone's throw from the Rådhuspladsen (see entry) and the main railway station. From the very first season it opened the Tivoli has been both a fairground and a cultural centre. When each year at the end of April after the winter break, it again opens its gates, it is a special day for children of all ages. The roundabout with its animals, the wild swans and the flying suitcase from Andersen's fairytales are all there; the old-time cars go again on their circuits with drivers filled with pride at the wheel. In Tivoli business people meet at midday for a Danish lunch, music lovers and ballet fans enjoy a varied programme in the concert hall or on the open-air stage; on the benches sit "Abonninen", loud Danish encylopeadic "pensioners with reduced-price Tivoli season tickets" and "sunshine sweet-eaters", as the Danes call sunbathers. Tivoli is Denmark, even if few things Danish are to be found in the mixture of styles. The buildings are inspired by the Orient, the pantomime theatre is traditional Italian commedia dell'arte, the massive tulips are from Holland – but out of the wide cultural mix has arisen a very pleasing unity from which a lesson can be learnt. Good taste makes Tivoli what it is. Here there is no plastic, no neon lighting, no canned entertainment. Building materials are wood and stone, the subdued light of lanterns in the trees comes from over 100,000 light bulbs, and the plays and music are live. A first visit should take place at dusk, when the old buildings between the magnificent flower beds and the playing water fountains of the garden are illuminated in a rainbow of colours – then Tivoli is transformed into a dream world. The park owes its name to an Italian town near Rome famous for its fountains.

Pleasure for the People

The founder of Tivoli was Georg Carstensen (1812–1857), a world-wanderer, adventurer and rake with a feeling for beauty. Already as a young man this Algiers-born son of a diplomat had made a small fortune as a newspaper publisher. In order to please his sub-scribers, Carstensen gave a rousing festival in Kongens Have, the king's garden. When this was received with enthusiastic approval, he eventually persuaded King Christian VIII to give permission for a permanent amusement area with the argument "if the people are kept amused, then they do not get involved in politics". Whether this was true or not, Carstensen obtained for an annual rent of 472 thalers the 8ha/20 acre site of the Copenhagen glacis, a grass area sloping down from the fort, with its lakes which are the remains of the moats which once surrounded the old city. Even on its inaugu-ration day in August 1843 Tivoli attracted 16,000 visitors and in a very short time it developed into an amusement park where – something which was quite unusual for that time – all social classes could mix together. Today it is a world attraction which has been visited by over 300 million visitors. Carstensen was, however, an artist not a business man and soon was on bad terms with the Tivoli founders and its board of directors because of his increas-ingly wild plans which were not cheap! Disappointed by their petty-mindedness, Carstensen went to the West Indies and New York. Later he made an unsuccessful attempt to open two pleasure gar-dens named Alhambra. Embittered and bankrupt Carstensen died in Copenhagen in 1857 only 45 years old but Tivoli lives and remains a garden for the people and a magic fairytale of children's dreams to this day.

As well as the main entrance on the Vesterbrogade there are three other entrances, including the one on H. C. Andersens Boulevard. In the entrance building are L. Tussaud's Wax Museum (see entry) and the Tivoli Museum, in which the 150-year history of the park is illustrated in a most amusing way (open: in the Tivoli season daily 10am–10pm: rest of the year Tue.–Sun. 10am–4pm).

L. Tussauds' Wax Museum

Entering through the main entrance on the Vesterbrogade the visitor will notice a few steps ahead on the right-hand side a bronze statue of Georg Carstensen, extending a cordial greeting with his top-hat and stick. Yet, even today, the spirit and inspiration of the Tivoli's founder can still be found in the many perfectly preserved original buildings, whose imaginative architecture reflects the oriental influence of Carstensen's childhood and his passion for the Far East.

Carstensen Memorial

The wide-ranging entertainment available to the visitor comprises 26 different attractions, including roller-coasters, roundabouts, a mountain railway, hall of mirrors, chamber of horrors, ferris wheel, flying carpet, electric, rowing and pedal boats, as well as the Valmuen puppet theatre. At least one new attraction is added each year – 1997 saw the construction of a new playground for the tiny tots and the introduction of the "Friday Rock", with Danish musicians performing on the "Plænen" open-air stage (10pm). Refreshments are provided by 28 restaurants at prices to suit every pocket, with menus ranging from a simple sandwich with beer through traditional home cooking and Chinese delicacies to exclusive haute cuisine.

★★**Attractions**

An afternoon or evening visit is especially delightful when the 100,000 lamps of every colour (neon-lights are not allowed) which light up the old buildings, the wonderful flower arrangements, ornate fountains and the reflections on the surfaces of the lakes combine to make the Tivoli an illuminated dream-world.

Carstensen's pantomime theatre in Tivoli – the home of Harlequin and Columbine

Tivoli Amusement Park

©Baedeker

Amusements

1 Grasshopper	10 Roundabout	18 "Little Flyers"
2 Flying Carpet	11 Comet	19 "Animal roundabout"
3 "Ladybird"	12 Vintage cars	20 Odin expressway
4 Children's giant wheel	13 "Flying suitcase"	21 Roundabout
5 Wild swans	14 Tram, line 8	22 Galleys
6 Viking ship	15 Driving School	23 Tub track
7 Boating pool	16 Dodgems	24 Balloon swing
8 "Mini Go Go"	17 Blue cars	25 Scenic Railway
9 Glass house	00 Toilets	26 "Devil's fire"

★Pantomime theatre

Since political theatre was forbidden in absolutist Denmark, Carstensen allowed pantomime to find its home here. The pantomime theatre, which is protected by a preservation order, is the home every evening to – something unique in the whole world – performances of the traditional Italian commedia dell'arte, with the innocent white-painted clown Pierrot appearing on stage with Columbine and Harlequin. Fifteen different pantomimes are included in the theatre's repertoire.

Concert hall

In the concert hall internationally known artists appear regularly as guests with the Tivoli's symphony orchestra. Wind music, jazz sessions and festival concerts can be heard and performances from visiting ballet companies are also arranged.

Open-air stage

International stars also provide the entertainment on the great open-air stage of the "Plænen" theatre, which has space for 50,000 spectators; performances: 4.30pm (every Sat., end Apr.–mid-July and mid-

Chinese Tower reflected in the Tivoli lake ▶

Aug.–mid-Sept.), 7pm (daily except Fri.), 9.30pm (every Sun., end Apr.–mid-June and mid-Aug.–mid-Sept.), 10pm (every Sat.), 10.30pm (every Mon.–Thur. and Sun., end June–mid-Aug.)

Less well known artists perform on several smaller stages located round the park.

★★Fireworks   Particularly impressive are the firework displays which take place on Wednesdays, Saturdays and public holidays at 11.45pm.

★Tivoli Guards   An important symbol of the Tivoli Gardens are the Tivoli Guards, founded in 1844. They consist of 110 boys aged between 9 and 16 drawn from all social classes. Like the Royal Guards they have their own uniform, music corps, flagbearers, marine artillery and a golden coach, in which a tiny prince sits with his tiny princess. The Tivoli Guards march through the park on Saturdays, Sundays and public holidays at 5.30 and 7.30pm – except between July 7th and 25th, when they are on holiday.

Trinitatis Kirke

See Rundetårn

★Tuborg Brewery   H3

Location
Hellerup,
Strandvejen 50

Bus
1

The internationally renowned Tuborg Brewery (Tuborgs Bryggerier A/S) was founded in 1873.

Tuborg, which has been amalgamated with the Carlsberg Brewery (see entry) since 1970, produces over 17 million litres of beer and exports to over 130 countries.

Unfortunately, conducted tours of the brewery are no longer available. Those who are interested in the 400-year history of hops and malt should plan a visit to the Carlsberg Brewery (see entry) and its adjoining museum.

On the 34ha/84 acre factory site there is a 26m/85ft high beer bottle, which was made for the Nordic industrial exhibition of 1888 at the Tivoli Gardens and which then had a lift operating inside it. Its capacity is the equivalent of 1·5 million bottles of beer!

In the former bottling hall of the brewery the Eksperimentarium (see entry), a museum for natural sciences and new technology, was opened in 1991.

★L. Tussaud's Wax Museum (waxworks)   G7

Location
H. C. Andersen
Boulevard 22

S-bane
Main railway
station

Buses
1, 2, 6, 8, 14, 16,
19, 28, 29, 30, 32,
33, 34, 35, 41, 63,
64, 68

Opening times
May–mid-Sept.
daily 10am–11pm;
mid Sept.–Apr.
daily 10am–6pm

The idea and art of waxworks in the form we know it today came about in the 17th c. and spread from Paris to London and Amsterdam. A greatgrandson of the famous Madame Marie Tussaud, called Louis Joseph Tussaud (1875–1940), who had already set up his own waxworks museums in London and Liverpool, brought the art of wax portraits to Copenhagen. The waxworks building, which was opened in 1894, has been renovated and extended on several occasions, the last time in 1988, when additional galleries were added on to make space for further sections of the museum.

The waxworks museum contains likenesses of over 250 personalities from the worlds of politics, the arts, science, the cinema and other areas of public life. These include the oldest king "Gorm den Gamle", the Viking Knut the Great and his successor Knud the Holy, the English princess Caroline Mathilde, who became famous because of her liaison with the Count of Struensee (see Famous People), many Danish monarchs, including King Christian IV (see Famous People), international

Christian II and Christian IV ...

... and the "heavenly" Greta Garbo

Niels Bohr and Albert Einstein in wax

politicians from more recent history, (including Sir Winston Churchill, Mao Tse-Tung, Emperor Hirohito, Indira Gandhi, former Prime Minister of Britain, Margaret Thatcher, the United States Presidents Reagan, Bush and Clinton), the Danish philisopher Søren Kierkegaard (see Famous People), the artists Pablo Picasso, Vincent van Gogh and Salvador Dalí, the composers Mozart, Beethoven and Edvard Grieg, the writers Ernest Hemingway, Henrik Ibsen and Karen Blixen (see Famous People), the Danish poet Hans Christian Andersen (see Famous People), surrounded by his fairy-tale characters, the physicists Albert Einstein and Niels Bohr (see Famous People), the Wright brothers, famous as pioneer aviators, stars of theatre and screen, such as Laurel and Hardy, Charlie Chaplin, Marilyn Monroe, Jean Harlow, the "Goddess" Greta Garbo, Elizabeth Taylor, Peter Sellers, Liv Ullmann, John Wayne, Ingrid Bergman and Humphrey Bogart in the café in "Casablanca" and great names of the music scene, including Elvis Presley, the Beatles and Charles Aznavour.

Chamber of Horrors

In the basement there is a "Chamber of Horrors", where Madame Tussaud is to be seen at work, making death masks from the heads of guillotine victims during the French Revolution. Also on display here are the "Phantom of the Opera", Alfred Hitchcock's "Psycho" cellar, Frankenstein and Count Dracula, as well as Queen Marie Antoinette on the way to her execution.

★Tycho Brahe Planetarium   G7

Location
Gl. Kongevej 10

Buses
1, 14

Opening times
daily 10.30am–9pm

This planetarium, which was opened at the beginning of November 1989, owes its name to the great Danish astronomer Tycho Brahe (see Famous People). Over 400,000 visitors come every year to what is to date the largest planetarium in Western Europe. Its cylinder-shaped building was built to designs by the Danish architect Knud Munk.

In the planetarium's permanent and temporary exhibitions, which are accompanied by explanations in Danish and English, the visitor has the opportunity to become acquainted with the fascinating variety of the universe. With the help of a computer-assisted Zeiss projector, a night sky with around 9000 planets, galaxies, comets and stars can be projected on to the roof of the planetarium, which functions as a colossal screen. The visitor can sit back in his "flight seat" and gaze at the complete panorama.

Apart from these public presentations, there are also astronomy courses, an information centre and the "Cassopeia" restaurant, situated on the bank of St Jørgens Sø and named after the constellation in the northern sky where in 1572 Tycho Brahe discovered a new star, the Nova Cassopeia.

Hven Island

On the tiny island of Hven, which lies in the Øresund to the north-east of Copenhagen and today belongs to Sweden, archaeologists have uncovered the remains of the observatories of Stjerneborg and Uraniborg, where Tycho Brahe carried out his earliest astronomical researches. The possible restoration of the ruins, which today can be visited, is under discussion. The local museum on Hven provides an interesting overview of the astronomer's life and work. In winter the island can only be reached by ferry from Landskrona in Sweden, but in summer there are daily crossings by hydrofoil from Copenhagen.

Tøjhusmuseet (Arsenal museum)   H7

Location
Tøjhusgade 3

This museum of military history, which was set up in 1928, is housed in the Royal Arsenal, which was built in 1598–1604 following Italian

Uniforms and weapons from five centuries are on display in the Arsenal Museum

models, in particular the arsenal in Venice. Its ground floor consists of a cannon hall, in which aeroplanes can also be seen; its first floor has a hall of weapons and a collection of uniforms. The exhibits are gathered together under the following themes: handguns, armour (including that of Duke Adolf von Gottorf, 1560) and swords from 1400, cannons, flags, coats of arms and uniforms (open: Apr.–mid-Oct. Tue.–Sun. 10am–5pm, mid-Oct.–Mar. Tue.–Sun. 10am–4pm).

Buses
1, 2, 5, 6, 8, 10, 31, 37, 43

The ground floor of the arsenal forms the longest vaulted hall in the whole of Europe: 163m/535ft long, 24m/79ft wide, 27m/89ft high, with the cross vault being supported by 16 central pillars.

Universitet (University)

H6

The old buildings of the university, which was set up in 1479 by Christian I, are situated opposite the Vor Frue Kirke (see entry) in the centre of the old Latin quarter, which with its little alleys full of corners is very reminiscent of the Quartier Latin in Paris. Even today the students of the university continue to put their stamp on the surroundings and ambience of this quarter, although in point of fact most of the university departments have been moved to the island of Amager (see entry).

Location
Frue Plads

Bus
5

The university complex has been destroyed by fire on several occasions during the course of its history. The present main building, in which Peter Malling combined classical architectural trends with Neo-Gothic stylism, dates from 1831–36, as a Latin inscription on the façade proves: "Fredericus sextus instauravit anno MDCCCXXXVI" (opened by Frederik VI in 1836). It was built on the ruins of a medieval bishop's palace. At the instigation of the theologist Matthias Hagen Hohlenberg, an enormous eagle was placed over the main entrance to the university with the inscription: "Coelestem adspicit lucem" ("He saw the heavenly light").

On the neighbouring Frue Plads there is a row of busts commemorating distinguished graduates of the university, including one of the physicist and Nobel prizewinner Niels Bohr (see Famous People). Inside the main building the visitor should make a special note of the old university banqueting hall with its historic paintings, the entrance hall with its painted frescoes and the Gobelin hall with Belgian Gobelin tapestries of the 17th c.

University library Only a short walk away in the Fiolstræde (no. 1) is the university library (open: Mon.–Fri. 9am–6pm, Sat. 9am–4pm), which was moved from its original home in the Trinitatis Kirke (see Rundetårn) in 1862. The red-brick building was erected by J. D. Herholdt between 1857 and 1861. The decorations in the reading room were the work of Georg Hilker.

Bust of Niels Bohr

★Vor Frelser Kirke (Church of the Redeemer)   J7

Location
St Annægade

Situated in the district of Christianshavn (see entry), the Church of the Redeemer was built between 1682 and 1696 out of sandstone and brick

Church of the Redeemer

Church of Our Lady

under the direction of the royal architect, Lambert van Haven. However the upper part of the tower with the external spiral staircase was added later in 1752 by Laurids de Thura, whose inspiration for this addition was the Baroque church of Sant' Ivo alla Sapienza in Rome. The top of the tower is crowned by a globe with a 3m/10ft high golden figure of Christ, which was made by the coppersmith Jacob Høvinghoff. A visit to the tower involves an ascent of more than 400 steps, of which a third are on the outside of the tower and should only really be negotiated in good weather. There is no truth in the story that the builder of the tower plunged to his death because he had designed the spiral incorrectly!

The interior of the church is just as worthy of attention as the ascent of the tower is spectacular. The high altar, designed in the Italian Baroque style by Nicodemus Tessin the Younger, is elaborately decorated with figures and cherubs. Other outstanding features are the choir screen with its carved angels, a baptismal font of white marble and the organ, begun in 1698 by Christian Nerger, with its carved wooden casing. The gallery of the church with its two-storey organ is supported by two magnificent stucco elephants.

Buses
2, 8, 9, 31, 37, 72E, 73E, 79E

Opening times
Mar.–May, Sept., Oct.: Mon.–Sat. 9am–3.30pm, Sun. noon–3.30pm, June–Aug. Mon.–Sat. 9am–4.30pm, Sun. noon–4.30pm

Vor Frue Kirke (Church of Our Lady)   H7

Copenhagen's "cathedral" is the sixth church to have been built on this site. After the fifth church was burnt down during the bombardment of the city in 1807, C. F. Hansen was given the task of rebuilding the church, which he did between 1811 and 1829 in the neo-classical style with a well-defined design. The triangular gable on the temple-like front facing on to the Nørregade is decorated by a group of statues by Thorvaldsen (see Famous People). The interior, spanned by massive whitewashed barrel-vaulting, contains further examples of works by Thorvaldsen (see Thorvaldsens Museum). Especially noteworthy are the figure of Christ behind the altar, twelve apostles on the walls and the font with its kneeling angel. The characteristic square tower is flat-roofed and is topped by a gleaming cross. (Open: June–Sept.: Mon.–Sat. 9am–5pm, Sun. noon–4pm; Oct.–May: Sun. noon–1pm, 3–4pm.)

The square adjoining the university (see Universitet) is often the venue in summertime for open-air dramatic and musical performances.

Location
Nørregade 8

Bus
5

★★Zoologisk Have (Zoo)   E7

Copenhagen's zoo is one of the oldest in Europe and, with over 2500 animals, one of the largest. The zoo was founded in 1859 by the ornithologist Niels Kjærbølling. Most of the present stock of animals were either born in Copenhagen or in other zoos. Their enclosures are laid out in such a way that as far as possible they approximate to their natural environment in the wild. Information signs and boards provide the visitor with details about the origins of the individual species.

The zoo has been extensively modernised during the last few years – the newest acquisition being the large tropical house, at the entrance to which a 44m/144ft outlook tower gives an overall view of the zoo, or during the summer months it is possible to view the complex by taking a ride on a miniature railway.

The zoo consists of the following sections: opposite the entrance lies the gibbon island and the bird lake with storks, pelicans and geese; the lions' enclosure; the parkland with its pink flamingoes; the enclosure for animals from the far north, such as seals, polar bears, musk-oxen and reindeer; pandas, marabous, capybaras from the far east; in the giraffe house a dozen new calves were born during the last ten years; the aviary, where pheasants and scarlet ibiss from South America can be

Location
Roskildevej 32

Buses
28, 39, 41, 175

Opening times
Apr.–May 9am–5pm; June–Aug. 9am–6pm; Sept.–Oct. 9am–5pm; Nov.–Mar. 9am–4pm

Animals

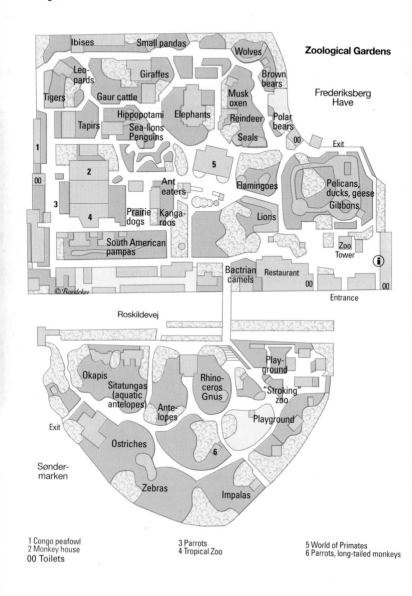

Zoological Gardens

Frederiksberg Have

Ibises
Small pandas
Wolves
Leopards
Giraffes
Brown bears
Tigers
Gaur cattle
Musk oxen
Hippopotami
Elephants
Reindeer
Polar bears
Tapirs
Sea-lions
Penguins
Seals
1
00
2
5
3
Ant eaters
Flamingoes
Pelicans, ducks, geese
Gibbons
4
Prairie dogs
Kanga-roos
Lions
South American pampas
Zoo Tower
ⓘ
Bactrian camels
Restaurant
00
00
© Baedeker
Entrance

Roskildevej

Play-ground
Okapis
Sitatungas (aquatic antelopes)
Rhino-ceros
Gnus
"Stroking" zoo
Ante-lopes
Playground
Exit
Ostriches
6
Sønder-marken
Zebras
Impalas

1 Congo peafowl
2 Monkey house
00 Toilets

3 Parrots
4 Tropical Zoo

5 World of Primates
6 Parrots, long-tailed monkeys

128

The "King of the Jungle" waits quietly for feeding time

The Zoo: polar bears ...

... and pink flamingoes

Zoologisk Museum

admired; the tigers' open enclosure; the cages for the snow-leopards and black panthers; the enclosures for shabrack tapirs, boars, gaurs, antelopes, okapis, zebras, rhinoceroses and hippopotamuses, Nile crocodiles, camels, kangeroos and prairie dogs; the elephant house famous for its success in breeding; the nocturnal zoo with bats, South American armadillos, African galagos; insects and other articulates. The chimpanzees and gorillas live in an ape house which, with its tropical forest vegetation and tropical climate, simulates a jungle atmosphere. In the Søndermark section is a 4500sq.m/5380sq.yd enclosure for African savanna animals, together with a popular children's playground and "stroking zoo" with young fawns and a rabbit colony.

At the same time all kinds of activities have been devised for the occupants of the zoo. Thus the ant-eaters for example can dig down in artificial ant-hills for their favoured syrup-like food, and in the climbing trees and rigging frames of the monkey house there hang wooden blocks, the hollows of which are stuffed with dainties which the monkeys can tease out for themselves.

★★Zoologisk Museum (Zoological Museum)   G5

Location
Universitetsparken
15

Buses
18, 42, 43, 184,
72E, 79E, 173E

Opening times
Tues.–Sun.
11am–5pm

The Zoological Museum is one of the most popular museums in Copenhagen among visitors. The reason for this is the up-to-date and highly impressive representation of animals in their natural environment, which for visitors both young and old is an extremely interesting experience.

An early zoological collection was assembled in Copenhagen over 300 years ago by Ole Worm (1588–1654). This museum was taken over by Frederik III and incorporated in his "Royal Chamber of Arts", which existed for around 200 years and in part is preserved today in the Zoological Museum. Around 1770 the university assembled a zoological collection of its own which was not made accessible to the general public until the first half of the 19th c. when it was amalgamated with the "Royal Natural Science Museum". This museum was closed in 1967 and its stock transferred to the new exhibition building in the university park.

The Zoological Museum is divided into two large parts: "Denmark's Animal Kingdom" begins with the migration of the various animal species into Denmark at the end of the last ice age around 15,000 years ago and covers not only the individual natural Danish habitats with their typical flora and fauna, but also the animal species to be found in the urban areas. The section "From pole to pole" outlines the animal world to be found in the various types of natural landscape across the entire planet. Thus the living conditions of animals is shown not just in the proximity of the North and South poles, but in the endless expanses of the tundra; life is documented in coastal areas, on islands, in the vast forest regions of the northern hemisphere, in mountain areas, deserts, steppelands and tropical rain forests; information is given about the special features of freshwater species as well as about the distinctive forms of life to be found in the ocean (from its uppermost layers to its depths).

The museum is manned by students who can give detailed information and explanations to visitors. In addition a list of the names of Danish animals with translations is available.

The Principal Sights at a Glance

**Practical
Information
from A to Z**

Air Travel

Airport

Copenhagen's airport is at Kastrup on the island of Amager, some 10km/6 miles south-east of the city centre. Its transit and departure concourse features a bright new shopping zone, with duty-free shopping there likely to continue at least until 1999.
Getting to Copenhagen: see entry
Internal flights fly from Copenhagen to Esbjerg, Karup, Skrydstrup, Stauning, Sønderborg, Thisted, and Ålborg and Århus (Tirstrup) in Jutland, Odense (Beldringe) on Funen (Fyn) and Rønne on the island of Bornholm (40–60 minutes). There are air taxis to the islands of Anholt, Læsø and Ærø.

Air Terminal

The journey to the airport from the air terminal at Central Station opposite Tivoli takes about 25 minutes and departs approximately every quarter of an hour between 5.40am and 9.45pm. For more detailed information on bus times: tel. 32 57 17 01.

Flight
information

Flight information from Kastrup:
tel. 32 47 47 47

Airlines

British Airways
Vesterbrogade 2; tel. 33 14 60 00

Scandinavian Airlines System (SAS)
SAS Building, Hammerichsgade 1–5
Flight information: tel. 32 57 17 01
Domestic flight reservations: tel. 70 10 20 00

Antiques

Farvergade,
Kompagnistræde,
Læderstræde

Copenhagen is one of Europe's very best hunting grounds for antiques. These are to be found in a whole range of places, some of them simply junk-shops, others much more upmarket. Fortunately for the antique hunter, however, most of the shops and dealers are concentrated in a few streets, making it easier to shop around and compare prices. This is particularly true of Farvergade, Kompagnistræde, Læderstræde and Hyskenstræde, the streets parallel with the Strøget pedestrian precinct (see A to Z).

Royal
Copenhagen
Antiques,
Rosenthal
Studio

In the elegant fin-de-siècle surroundings of Royal Copenhagen Antiques (Amagertorv 6) the finest Danish silver and antique jewellery by artists such as Georg Jensen and A. Michelsen, together with Holmegaard glass and services of Royal Porcelain can be found. There are also displays of items by Denmark's great silversmith in the nearby Georg Jensen museum. The English Silver House at 4 Pilestræde is worth a visit, as is the work by the Danish artist Bjørn Wiinblads (see Famous People) on show in the Rosenthal Studio at 21 Frederiksberggade.

Nyhavn,
flea markets

Nyhavn (see A to Z). And on Saturdays in the summer months it is also worth hunting for bargains at the flea markets on Gammel Strand and Israels Plads.

Ravnsborggade

Another good place for bargains is the large cluster of antique shops on Ravnsborggade in the Nørrebro district.

Secondhand
books

Studiestræde and Fiolstræde in the University quarter have plenty of second-hand and antiquarian book shops (see Shopping and Souvenirs).

Lovers of antiques should visit the Saturday flea-market on Gammel Strand

Antique dealers from throughout Denmark take part in the big antiques fair in the old Stock Exchange (see A to Z) every September.

Antiques fair

See below

Auction Houses

Auction Houses

Auction houses in Copenhagen include:

Bruun Rasmussen
Bredgade 33; tel. 33 13 69 11

Lauritz Christensen
Søtorvet 1–3; tel. 33 15 55 12

Herholdt Jensen
Rundforbivej 188, Nærum; tel. 45 50 52 88

Kunsthallen
Gothersgade 9; tel. 33 32 52 00

Københavns Auctions
Æbeløgade 4; tel. 39 29 90 00

Sagførernes Auctions
Nørre Farimagsgade 43–47; tel. 33 11 45 30

Babysitting

HH-Babysitting; tel. 38 74 81 51 and 40 32 87 29
6.30am–10pm daily

Studenternes Babysitters, Smållegade 52A; tel./fax 70 20 44 16
Mon.–Thu.6.30–9am and 3–6pm, Fri. 3–6pm

Beaches

Although presumably hardly anyone is likely to go to Copenhagen for a beach holiday swimming can be enjoyed in the Baltic from a number of beaches that are quite close by. These are mainly around Dragør on the island of Amager (see A to Z), in Charlottenlund beach park 6km/3½ miles north of the city centre, and Bellevue beach park 4km/2½ miles further on. There are also half a dozen beaches along Køge Bay to the south-west of the city, with some particularly good ones for swimming in Køge Bugt beach park. The north and west coasts of Zealand have plenty of fine beaches too, including the broad sands at Hornbæk, Dronningmølle and Gilleleje – about 55km/34 miles north of Copenhagen – and Sejrø bay at Holbœk – 60km/37 miles from Copenhagen. Probably the finest sections are in North Zealand at Tisvildeleje and Liseleje, which are some 60km/37 miles from Copenhagen, and near Nykøbing and Rørvig about 100km/62 miles away. Southern Zealand boasts good beaches at Rødvig (75km/47 miles), Fakse Ladeplads and Karrebæksminde (95km/59 miles).

Bicycles

Free cycles!

Copenhagen has a good network of cycle tracks. What is more, anyone without a machine of their own can borrow one of the two thousand or so city cycles free from one of the 150 marked city-centre sites.

They can be taken out of the cycle rack by inserting a 20 kroner piece – as for a shopping trolley – and when the cycle is returned to a slot the money is refunded.

Cycles can be hired from:

Cykelbørs, Central Station (tel. 3314 07 17) and Gothersgade 157 (tel. 33 11 09 09)

Danwheel Rent-a-bike, Colbjørnsensgade 3; tel. 31 21 22 27

Machines can also be rented from the railway stations in Østerborg, Klampenborg, Lyngby, Hillerød and Helsingør.

Bicycle hire

City Safari

Copenhagen youngsters will show visitors both faces of their city – the good and the bad – on a two-hour guided cycle ride.

Information: tel. 31 24 04 07

Guided tours

Bike Denmark

Individual sightseeing tours by cycle lasting between 3 and 9 hours

Information: tel. 33 33 86 13

Boat Trips

Harbour and canal tours lasting 50 minutes and covering the main sights, including the Little Mermaid, operate daily from the beginning of April to mid-October. They depart from Gammel Strand (Højbro Plads) and Nyhavn (Kongens Nytorv) every half hour from 10am. For further information: tel. 33 13 31 05.

You can also take the waterbus and use the day ticket to travel between the various sights.

Harbour and canal tour

The two-masted schooner "Isefjord" is available for hire between May and October for parties of at least 20 people for trips on the Øresund, departing from the quay by the Hotel Admiral, Toldbodgade. For further information and reservations: tel. 33 15 17 29, fax 33 15 78 90.

Sea trips

Ferries to
Sweden

Trips by hydrofoil from Havnegade to Malmö (40 minutes) and Ven Island (45 minutes); information and bookings: tel. 33 12 80 88

From Dragør to Limhamn: about 20 departures a day (55 minutes); information and bookings: tel. 32 53 15 85

Business Hours

See Opening Times

Cafés

A good way to finish off a stroll around the town is a relaxing visit to one of Copenhagen's many cafés to sample their delicious Danish pastries and cakes. Some konditori also serve smørrebrød and very filling sandwiches.

*Café Europa, Amagertorv 1; tel. 33 14 28 89 (top city-centre hotspot since 1989; super sandwiches)
Café Krasnapolsky, Vestergade 10; tel.33 32 88 00 (Danish cool)

Cafés and konditori (a selection)

★Café Norden, Østergade 61; tel. 33 11 77 91 (always packed, overlooking the lively Amagertorv; irresistible pastries)

★Café Victor, Ny Østergade 8; tel. 33 13 36 13 (smart café/restaurant with classically elegant decor)

★La Glace, Skoubogade 3–5 (Copenhagen's oldest konditori with fabulous ice creams and speciality cakes)

★Kransekagehuset, Ny Østergade 9; tel. 33 13 19 02 (very chic, with garden on Pistolstræde; marvellous in-house jams)

Kul Kaféen, Teglgårdsstræde 5; tel. 33 32 17 77 (Fair Trade coffee)

Marstrand Konditori-Café, Købmagergade 15; tel. 33 14 07 91 (founded in 1740, superb apple tartlets)

Reinhard van Hauen, Østergade 22; tel. 33 13 17 03 (traditional pastrycook with luscious Danish pastries)

★Royal Copenhagen, Amagertorv 6 (excellent coffee and cakes elegantly served on classic porcelain)

Sabines Caféteria, Teglgårdsstræde 4; tel. 33 14 09 44 (popular student rendezvous)

Skt. Peder's Bageri, Skt. Pedersstræde 29; tel. 33 11 11 29 (founded 1652, bizarre specialities include Batman biscuits!)

Calendar of Events

See Events

Camping

Campingrådet, the Danish camping board, inspects campsites every year and divides them up into five categories, awarding them between one and five stars. Most Danish camping sites are 3-star, with a good standard of facilities and round-the-clock surveillance. Camping Danmark, the Camping Board's official guide to the country's classified, approved camping sites, is available from Campingrådet (Hesseløgade 16, DK-2100 København Ø; tel. 39 27 88 44). A leaflet listing the main camp sites can also be obtained from tourist information centres (see Information).

Denmark does not allow overnight camping on anywhere that is not an approved camp site, and this applies to camper vans as well as tents and caravans.

Some camp sites in and around Copenhagen

Absalon
Kordalsvej 132, DK-2610 Rødovre
tel. 31 41 06 00, fax 36 41 02 93; 2 stars
Open: all year round; 1000 places

Bellahøj
Hvidkildevej, DK-2400 København NV
tel. 38 10 11 50, fax 38 10 13 32; 2 stars
Open: June–August; 670 places
Buses: 2, 8, 63, 68 from City Hall Square

Nivå
Campingvej 14, 2990 Nivå
tel. 49 14 52 26
Open: April–September
130 places; about 25km/16 miles north of Copenhagen

Nærum
Ravnebakken, 2850 Nærum
tel. 45 80 19 57, fax 42 80 11 78; 2 stars
Open: mid-March–end September
375 places; 15km/9 miles north of city centre on E55/E47

Strandmøllen
Strandmøllevej, 2942 Skodsborg
tel. 45 80 94 45; 2 stars
Open: mid-May–mid-September
120 places; 14km/9 miles from city centre via Strandvejen

Car Rental

See Motoring

Chemists

See Health Care

Children

Copenhagen has so many distractions to offer its young visitors that there is absolutely no excuse for them to complain of being bored. The city centre is relatively small so it is easy to get round it in an hour on foot, or if you want to go sightseeing by bicycle there over 2000 cycles at your disposal free of charge. Most museums and attractions have special rates for families and children, and many of the large and small museums go to great lengths to make their displays especially appealing to children. Lots of restaurants have children's menus – high-chairs are available as a matter of course – and some even provide entertainment during the meal. If you want to cater for the whole family by renting a city-centre appartment bookings can be arranged through Citilet (see Appartments in the entry for Hotels).

Copenhagen with children

Watching the Changing of the Guard in front of the Amalienborg Palace on the stroke of 12 every day is great fun and costs nothing. Tivoli is of course a must, but Bakken Amusement Park and Lyngby's Open Air Folk Museum are firm family favourites as well. Other hits with children include the zoo, and boat trips around the harbour, the castle island and through the old canals of Christianshavn. Childish dreams of yesteryear can be relived in the National Museum's toy house, while the very latest visions of the future can be experienced in the virtual reality of the Experimentarium. Also vying for attention are Tussaud's Waxworks, Ripley's Believe It or Not and the Guinness World of Records. Copenhagen, with Europe's longest car-free shopping precinct, is a great place for shopping for children's clothes and toys, although these can be on the pricey side.

Activities for children

Cinemas

Copenhagen's cinemas screen foreign films in the original language with Danish sub-titles. Many have cheaper admission prices on Monday–Thursday, and some also have matinées at reduced ticket prices.

Dagmar, Jernbanegade 2; tel. 33 14 32 22
Grand, Mikkel Bryggers Gade 8; tel. 33 15 16 11
★Filmhuset, Vognmagergade 10; tel. 33 74 34 04 (a must for movie buffs, showing highlights from film history, Danish cult movies and experimental work by young film-makers; see also Museums, Danske Filmmuseum)

Selection of cinemas

Palads – a luxury cinema in the Axeltorv

★Imperial Bio, Ved Vesterport; tel. 70 13 12 11 (Copenhagen's finest and largest auditorium with unique amounts of legroom)
Palads, Axeltorv 9; tel. 70 13 12 11 (high-scoring multiplex with over 20 screens; snackbar recommended)
Palladium, Vesterbrogade 1; tel. 70 13 12 11
Scala, Axeltorv 2; tel. 33 13 81 00 (a small movie complex standing where Josephine Baker used to tread the boards)

Copenhagen Card

See Public Transport

Currency

Unit of currency

Denmark's unit of currency is the Danish crown (abbreviated to dkr, i.e. Danish krone), consisting of 100 øre. Banknotes are for 50, 100, 200 and 1000 krone and coins for 25 and 50 øre (copper, without a hole), 1, 2 and 5 krone (silver, with a hole) and 10 and 20 krone (brass, without a hole). There is no limit on the amount of foreign or Danish currency that can be imported into Denmark.

Travellers' cheques, credit cards

All banks and most hotels and shops take travellers' cheques and eurocheques, and the same applies to most international credit cards. These are also usually accepted by car hire firms and the larger hotels and restaurants.
Remember to keep a receipt and record of travellers' cheques separately from the cheques themselves so that they can be replaced if necessary. And keep a note of the number to ring to put a stop immediately on any credit cards, cheque cards, etc. that may get lost or stolen.

Copenhagen has plenty of cashpoints that will take credit cards and eurocheque cards – simply look for the logo that applies to the card being used.

Banks are usually open Mon., Tue., Wed., Fri. 9.30am–4pm and Thu. 9.30am–6pm. Money can also be changed outside these hours at bank cashpoints and exchange bureaux.

Customs Regulations

Member States of the European Union (EU), which includes Denmark, the United Kingdom and Ireland, form a common internal market, and there is theoretically no limit to the amount of goods that can be taken from one EU country to another provided they have been purchased tax paid in an EU country, are for personal use and not intended for resale. Customs authorities have, however, issued guidelines as to the maximum amounts considered reasonable for persons over 17 years of age. These are: 1.5 litres of spirits or 20 litres fortified or sparkling wine, 90 litres of table wine (of which not more than 60 litres may be sparkling wine), no limit on beer; 300 cigarettes or 150 cigarillos or 75 cigars or 400g smoking tobacco. There is no limit on perfume or toilet water.
The allowances for goods purchased in duty-free shops – due to be phased out in 1999 – at airports and on aircraft and ferries are the same as for entry from non-EU countries (see below).

For visitors coming from a country outside the EU, or who have arrived from an EU country without having passed through customs control with all their baggage, the allowances for goods obtained anywhere outside the EU for persons over the age of 17 are: 1 litre spirits or 2 litres of fortified wine plus 2 litres table wine; 50g perfume, 250cc toilet water; 200 cigarettes or 100 cigarillos or 50 cigars or 250g smoking tobacco.

For other English-speaking countries the duty-free allowances are as follows: Australia 250 cigarettes or 50 cigars or 250g tobacco, 1 litre spirits or 1 litre wine; Canada 200 cigarettes and 50 cigars and 900g tobacco, 1.1 litres spirits or wine; New Zealand 200 cigarettes or 50 cigars or 250g tobacco, 1 litre spirits and 4.5 litres wine; South Africa 400 cigarettes and 50 cigars and 250g tobacco, 1 litre spirits and 2 litres wine; USA 200 cigarettes and 100 cigars or a reasonable quantity of tobacco, 1 litre spirits or 1 litre wine.

Diplomatic Representation

Embassies

Kristianiagade 21, 2100 Copenhagen Ø; tel. 35 26 22 44

Kr. Bernikowsgade 1, 1175 Copenhagen K; tel. 33 12 22 99

Østbanegade 21, 2100 Copenhagen Ø; tel. 31 42 32 33

Kastelsvej 40, 2100 Copenhagen Ø; tel. 35 44 52 00

Dag Hammarskjølds Allé 24, 2100 Copenhagen Ø; tel. 35 55 31 44

Disabled Access

Danish government policy is to provide equal opportunities for everyone, and that extends to a policy of integration and equality for handicapped citizens and visitors alike. For further information consult the free "Access in Denmark – a Travel Guide for the Disabled" published by the Danish Tourist Board.

Information about disabled access is also available from:

Bolig-, Motor- og Hjælpemiddeludvalget
Landskronagade 66
2100 Copenhagen Ø
tel. 39 18 26 66

Electricity

Current in Denmark is supplied at 220 volts AC, 50 cycles, which means that two-pin Continental-type adaptors will be required.

Emergency Services

Emergency	Dial 112 (free-phone throughout Denmark)
Medical assistance	See Health Care
Breakdown service	See Motoring

Events

Calendars of events

In April and October every year the Danish Tourist Office (see Information) publishes a free booklet of Coming Events in Denmark for the next six months.

Copenhagen annual booklets

Major events in Copenhagen each year are listed in the Copenhagen booklet published annually by Wonderful Copenhagen Convention & Visitors Bureau, and in the Danish Tourist Board's annual booklet on Copenhagen. For monthly listings of sporting and cultural events look in "Copenhagen this week", which also serves as a mini-guide. All these publications are in English and can be obtained free of charge from the Danish Tourist Board (see Information), hotels and the major banks.

Other What's On listings

For listings check out the current music and movie programmes available at arts venues etc. and the What's On columns headed "Forlystelser" on the back pages of the local newspapers.

Events in Copenhagen

January

New Year's Concert

April

Queen's Birthday (April 16th; march-past by the Palace Guard)

April to mid-September

Bakken Amusement Park; special children's party every Wednesday from end of June to beginning of August.
Tivoli Amusement Park; Sun.–Thu. 11am–midnight, Fri., Sat. 11am–2am; Wed., Sat., public holidays, fireworks at 11.45pm; children's party every Tuesday from end of June to beginning of August.

May

Wonderful Copenhagen Marathon (usually last week in May)

Whitsun

Carnival in Copenhagen
Copenhagen's Rio-type Whitsun Carnival, founded by students and community groups in the early Eighties, has samba in a riot of colourful costumes and parade floats, ending up with a kiddies' carnival.

Sophienholm (Lyngby): Children's programme and promenade concert every Sunday	May to end August
June 23rd (Midsummer's Eve): bonfires north of Copenhagen to drive off witches Dancin' City dance festival, Scandinavia's biggest modern dance festival Roskilde Festival: Denmark's biggest rock festival (last weekend in June)	June
Copenhagen Summer International Stage/Theatre Festival with lots of events indoors and outdoors, in parks and pubs, on the streets and in the castle grounds	June/July
Copenhagen Jazz Festival (nearly 500 concerts and jam sessions over nine days in early July out and about in the city streets, squares and pubs and along the canals) International Rowing Regatta Organ concerts in many of the churches	July
Copenhagen Water Festival (10-day city festival on and around the harbour promenades near Amalienborg Palace with exhibitions, opera, ballet and rock concerts) Classical music in the Ny Carlsberg Glyptotek (from mid-August)	August
Copenhagen Film Festival (a week of previews of new autumn films in the original languages with Danish sub-titles) Amager: music festival (church concerts)	September
Antiques Fair in the old Stock Exchange Kulturnatten: "night of culture" with special performances up till midnight in museums, churches, theatres and cinemas, plus open air shows Copenhagen Choir Festival: concerts at the end of October with the best Danish choirs and international competitors	October
Christmas Fair, big Christmas parade and Christmas concerts	November, December

Excursions

Visitors with the time to spare will find quite a few places in the vicinity of Copenhagen that are well worth a visit. They are easy to get to as well, either by public transport or on a sightseeing tour.

Danish State Railways (DSB) offers special excursion-rate tours to Louisiana and round the Øresund (information: tel. 33 14 17 01):
Louisiana Modern Art Museum (see A to Z, Louisiana)
Every half hour by train from Copenhagen (return fare plus museum admission)

DSB special excursions

Øresund Round the Sound tour
By hydrofoil over the Øresund from Copenhagen to Malmo, then by train through the lovely landscape of southern Sweden to Helsingborg and by ferry over the Sund and back by train down the coast to Copenhagen – or alternatively the journey can be made in the opposite direction.

Local operators and the Tourist Information Centre offer a range of themed tours including Afternoon Hamlet Tours, Castle Tours of North Zealand, Vikingland Tours, etc. For further information see Sightseeing or contact the Danish Tourist Board (see Information) or Copenhagen Excursions (tel. 32 54 06 06).

Sightseeing tours

Excursions

Charlottenlund	Ordrupgårdsamlingen: see Museums
Dronningmølle	Rudolf Tegners Museum: see Museums
Dyrehavn	See A to Z
Esrum Sø	Location: 47km/29 miles north of Copenhagen A number of Romanesque buildings remain from this 14th c. Benedictine monastery on the shore of Lake Esrum.
Farum Bastrup national park	Location: 15km/9½ miles north-west of Copenhagen Farum Bastrup national park, between lakes Farum and Bure, is a charming landscape of lakes and wooded hills formed by the retreating glaciers over 10,000 years ago at the end of the last ice age. Nature-lovers can wander here to their heart's content. A good starting point is the little town of Farum, by the lake, from where a lovely trail leads through the woods to Bastrup Sø and the ruins of Bastrup's medieval tower atop a 40m/130ft hill. You can then take the path from here to Lake Bure passing through Krogelund Slov and Ganløse Eged woods.
Fredensborg Slot	See A to Z
Frederiksborg Slot	See A to Z
Frederikssund	Location: 41km/25½ miles north-east of Copenhagen The town of Frederikssund developed during the Middle Ages by the ferry crossing at the narrowest point on Roskilde fjord, and has become famous for its annual Viking Festival of plays. The yellow building at 4

Frederiksberg Palace

Jenriksvej is a museum devoted to Danish artist and sculptor J. F. Willumsen (1863–1948) and houses many of his works (open 10am–4pm daily).

Location: 57km/35 miles north-east of Copenhagen

Frederiksværk, at the northern end of Roskilde fjord, owes its existence to the opening in 1719 of the canal from Arrsø (at 41sq.km/16sq. miles Denmark's largest lake) to Roskilde fjord. The town was actually founded, however, in the mid-18th c. with the opening of a cannon foundry and gunpowder plant, part of which is now a museum. The former foundry (giethuset) was converted into an art centre in the late Eighties. An impressive row of old houses has been preserved by the canal in the town centre.

It is also worth having a look at the GeoArt Museum at 160 Frederiksvej. Opened in 1991, it has an interesting collection of rocks and minerals and also runs courses on stone polishing in July and August (open daily except Mondays 10am–5pm and until 8pm on Thursdays).

See A to Z

Location: 15km/9½ miles north of Copenhagen city centre

The recreation area around Copenhagen includes three lakes – Furesøen, Lyngby Sø and Bagsvœrd Sø – linked by a canal. These lakes, in their woodland setting, are good for swimming, sailing, windsurfing, rowing and fishing, and long walks through the surrounding woods. The Mølleå, the river that feeds into lakes Fure and Lyngby, powered a number of water mills built on its banks in the Middle Ages and was later a power source for processing copper and making paper. Only a couple of the old mills have survived.

Location: 59km/37 miles north of Copenhagen

Gilleleje, with its bustling fishing port, is on the northern tip of Zealand and has a flat sandy beach with good swimming for children. Its main attractions are the Gilleleje Museum at 56 Vesterbrogade with models of local boats (open June–Sep. Tue.–Sun. 2–5pm) and the pleasant surrounding countryside, with a bird sanctuary at Gilbjerg Hoved. Of the two lighthouses to the east of the town the one furthest to the east, built in 1772, was the first of its kind to be fired by coal.

Telefonmuseet: see Museums

Location: 45km/28 miles north of Copenhagen

Helsingør is the site of Hamlet's Elsinore Castle or, to give it its proper title, Kronborg Slot (see A to Z). Other sights worth seeing include the many half-timbered buildings along Stengade (pedestrian precinct), some of them listed and carefully restored typically 18th c. houses. The church of St Olai, begun in 1200 but not completed until 1559, is Denmark's largest rural parish church and has a beautiful reredos, intricate choir-screen and impressive baptistry. The late medieval church of the Virgin Mary, with its fine organ, just 200m/220yds further north on Sct. Annæ Gade, forms the south wing of the Carmelite cloister. Dating from 1430, this is the best preserved complex of its kind in Denmark, and holds the tomb of Dyveke (d. 1517), mistress of King Christian II. Nowadays the cloister houses the town museum (Bymuseum; open daily 12–4pm). Other places worth a visit include Marienlyst Slot, with its art exhibitions (Marienlyst Allé 32; open daily 12–5pm), and Denmark's technology and transport museum (Danmarks Teknisk & Transport Museum). Exhibits include a car from 1886 and a 1906 plane (Nordre Strandvej 23 and Ole Rømers Vej; open Mon.–Fri. 10am–4pm, Sat., Sun. 10am–5pm). Ferries from this ancient trading port run to Helsingborg in Sweden, only 4.5km/2¾ miles away across the Øresund.

Excursions

Hillerød	Location: 35km/22 miles north of Copenhagen Most visitors to Hillerød come to see Fredriksborg Slot (see A to Z). The town also has an attractive pedestrian precinct, however, along Helsingørgade and Slotsgade which is ideal for window-shopping.
Holmegaard glass works	See Museums
Holte	Søllerød Museum (Vedbæk Finds): see Museums
Hornbæk	Location: 50km/31 miles north of Copenhagen Hornbæk is the oldest fishing settlement on the north coast of Zealand. A very picturesque resort, with its red and yellow painted houses, it has a large marina and a broad beach of fine sand. The blue interior of the 1727 village church symbolises the importance of the sea to the good folk of Hornbæk, and this is reinforced by the row of model ships suspended from the ceiling. The reredos is by Danish artist C.W. Eckersberg. Trees planted as windbreaks in the early 19th c. in the nearby Hornbæk Plantage today form a popular wooded park and recreational area.
Hornsherred, Jægerspris, Selsø	Location: 50km/31 miles west of Copenhagen The megalithic tombs on Hornsherred show that this peninsula between Isefjord and Roskilde fjord was inhabited thousands of years ago, and this is where, in 1987, archaeologists found the site of a house – Denmark's oldest to date – that must have stood here from 3000 B.C. In the north of the peninsula it is worth visiting Jægerspris, the royal hunting lodge built in the 16th c. and renovated in the 18th c. The last people to live here were Frederik VII and his third wife, the illegitimate daughter of a serving maid elevated to Countess Danner upon her marriage. When the King died the Countess set up a foundation here for needy and impoverished young women. The 54 columns commemorating illustrious Danish and Norwegian nobility are an interesting feature of the grounds. Selsø Palace, east of Skibby, was built in the 16th c. and revamped in the 18th c. It is noted for its rooms lined with Versailles-type mirrors (1733) and its paintings by H. Krock.
Hundested	Knud Rasmussens Hus: see Museums
Hørsholm	Danish Hunting and Forestry Museum: see Museums
Karen Blixen Museet	See A to Z
Kronborg Slot	See A to Z
Køge	Location: 32km/20 miles south of Copenhagen The little town of Køge is famous for its quaint 16th and 17th c. half-timbered houses. The Køge Museum (Nørregade 4; open daily 10am–5pm) has interesting displays of old furniture and costumes, while the Køge Skitsesamling (Nørregade 29; open Tue.–Sun. 11am–5pm) specialises in 19th c. drawings and engravings. For a breath of fresh air away from the museum setting try a walk along the 7km/5 miles of beach at Køge Bugt beach park.
Lejre Forøgscenter	See A to Z
Louisiana	See A to Z
Lyngby	Sophienholm: see Museums Frilandsmuseet: see A to Z
Nærum	Sommers Veteranbil Museum: see Museums

Food and Drink

Although the cuisine of Copenhagen does not enjoy the reputation of
that of France, it is possible to eat very well in the city. There is the usual
variety of international dishes, but visitors should not miss the chance to
sample Danish specialities.

Breakfast (*morgenmad*) can be obtained in restaurants and hotels until   Mealtimes
about 11am. It usually consists of rolls, cheese, egg, marmalade and a
variety of assorted cold meats. Lunch is taken between noon and 2pm,
and the evening meal usually between 6pm and 9pm.

Typically Danish are the varied cold and slightly warm buffets spread out   Frokost
in restaurants, which make lunch in Denmark such an important meal.
The first course is always fish – usually marinated herring, followed by
smoked or marinated salmon – and then a choice between rissoles, roast
pork, liver paté or brisket of beef, finishing with cheese (*ost*) served with
a topping of rum. Beer and aquavit are usually drunk with the meal.

The Copenhagen Menu

The legendary *smørrebrød* is an open sandwich topped with every con-   Smørrebrød
ceivable variety of tempting delicacy, such as roast beef, salmon, filleted
fish, smoked eel, liver paté or shrimps. Note that white bread is called
franksbrød and brown bread *rugbrød*. Ready-made smørrebrød can be
bought at lunch-time in most of the city's numerous restaurants – for

The "Snaren" in Kompagnistræde – the place to visit for smørrebrød

Smørrebrød, Pølser and Rødgrød med Fløde

Foreign visitors may find the names on Danish menus something of a tongue-twister, but their taste buds will relish the culinary delicacies that Denmark has to offer. Surrounded by sea, the country can, of course, offer endless varieties of fish and shellfish – as a special treat sample the tender, pink shrimps or marinated herring on leavened bread with a beer straight from the barrel and an ice-cold aquavit. Try the fresh or dried cod in mustard sauce, smoked salmon, *graved lachs*, grilled sole or baked plaice at one of the specialist restaurants in the Gammel Strand quarter, or enjoy the gastronomic delights on offer in the gourmet cellars of the "hyggellig" Nyhavn promenade. The justifiably famous *smørrebrød*,

as the substantial Danish open sandwich is called, normally disappears under appetising toppings of fish, meat or vegetables. Another traditional food is the *pølser*, a bright red fried sausage from roadside stalls – worth trying with sweet gherkins, mustard and fried onions. Roast pork chops with crispy crackling or spicy rissoles are other original Danish dishes. Those who like to nibble at light snacks are well catered for in Denmark. The legendary *rødgrød med fløde* (red fruit pudding with cream) is a "must" for dessert; other popular Danish sweets include marzipan cakes such as *københagener*, *wienerbrød* and *kransekage* and, of course, *fløde-is*, cream ices made to a Danish recipe.

Fish delights: Krogs Fish Restaurant on Gammel Strand

example, in the Tivoli at Vester Voldgade 91 or at Gitte Kik in Fortunstraede near Gammel beach – and in some specialist shops, such as Centrum Smørrebrødsanretning, Vesterbrogade 6C (opposite Central Station).

Fish is prepared in many tasty ways in Copenhagen. Many courses include trout, small flat-fish or fried plaice. Delicacies which should not be missed include smoked salmon or *graved lach*, salmon marinated in a mixture of sugar, salt, pepper and dill.

Fish

Also very popular are the tasty bacon and substantial meat dishes, such as roast pork with crispy crackling and red cabbage (*flæskesteg med røkåi*), fried sausage (*pølser*) from roadside stalls, spicy rissoles of pork or beef, pea-soup with sausages and pork (*gule årter*), and roast venison with cranberries (*dyreryg*).

Meat

See entry

Restaurants

Drinks

The national drinks of the Danes are coffee and beer. Wine, mainly imported from Germany, France and Italy, is relatively expensive, although prices have tended to fall in recent years.

A typical Danish *schnaps* (brandy), often drunk following a greasy meal, is *aquavit* (water of life), a brandy with the aroma of caraway seeds and other spices, with an alcohol content of at least 38%. The most popular brands are Rød Aalborg and Jubilæums-Akvavit. Gammel Dansk is recommended for those who like a bitter drink to settle the stomach. Fizzy drinks are known as *vand*, an abbreviation of *sodavand*; examples are *appelsinvand* (fizzy orange) and *cirtronvand* (fizzy lemonade). Mineral water is called *danskvand*. Meals usually end with coffee, which is served in all pubs and bars.

The usual drink is a light lager (*øl*), normally sold in small bottles. There is also a Danish keg beer, not dissimilar to British beer.

Beer

By far the biggest brewery chain in Denmark is United Breweries Carlsberg and Tuborg, which produces over fifteen different brands for domestic consumption. These include various beers such as the light Grøn Tuborg and Hof by Carlsberg, both with 3·7% alcohol content, and the darker Red Tuborg and Gammel Carlsberg. Somewhat stronger are Carlsberg Guld Export (4%) and Guld Tuborg (4·6%). Stronger still, up to 6·2%, are the light-coloured Elefanten Beer, Tuborg F.F., and Tuborg Påskebryg, as well as the amber-coloured Carlsberg 47, known as C47 for short, the number referring to the year 1847, when the Carlsberg brewery was founded. Gammel Porter is a sweet stout similar in appearance to Guinness, with an alcohol content of 6·1%.

A Danish speciality is what is known as *kande*, much favoured by connoisseurs, a mixture of two kinds of beer (a sort of "black and tan"), plus aquavit, Pernod and lemonade.

Opposite Tivoli, in the "A Hereford Beefstouw" restaurant, Denmark's smallest brewery, the Apollo, brews its own keg beer. With the support of the Wiibroe Breweries this little brewery was set up in the middle of the restaurant.

Some Gastronomic Terms

English	Danish
restaurant	restaurant
cafeteria	cafetaria
breakfast	morgenmad

Food and Drink

English	Danish
lunch	middagsmad
evening meal	aftensmad
food	mad
drink	drikke
much, many	meget, mange
a little	lidt
bill	regning
to pay	betale
at once	straks
menu	spisekort
soup	suppe
meat	kød
grilled	stegt på grill
roast	steg
roast mutton	faresteg
veal	kalv
lamb	lam
beef	okse
ham	skinke
pork	svin
roast pork	flæskesteg
sausage	pølse
fish	fisk
fried	stegt
boiled	kogt
fish dumplings	fiskeboller
cod	torsk
trout	ørred
herring	sild
salmon	laks
smoked salmon, lobster	røget laks, hummer
prawns	rejer
crab	krebs
vegetables	grøn(t)sager
cauliflower	blomkål
beans	bønne
peas	ært
cucumber, gherkin	agurk
potatoes	kartoffel
cabbage	kål
green salad	grøn salat
red cabbage	rødkål
spinach	spinat
tomato	tomat
ice cream	is
stewed fruit, etc.	kompot
red fruit pudding	rødgrød
pudding	budding
whipped cream	flødeskum
fruit	frugt
apple	æble
orange	appelsin
pear	pære
strawberry	jordbær
bilberry, blueberry	blåbær
raspberry	hindbær

English	Danish
cherry	kirsebær
plum	blomme
drinks	drik
beer	øl
coffee	kaffe
milk	mælk
mineral	mineralvand
cream	fløde
tea	te
water	vand
wine	vin
white wine	hvidvin
red wine	rødvin
bread	brød
white bread	franksbrød
rolls	rundstykke
cake	kage

Galleries

Copenhagen has innumerable galleries. These stage a whole host of temporary exhibitions ranging from painting, sculpture, prints, lithography, photography, videos and ceramics to glass and textiles. Up-to-date details of current exhibitions can be found in Copenhagen This Week, published by the Tourist Board (see Information).

Bredgade Kunsthandel, Bredgade 67–69 and Esplanaden 14
Dansk Arkitekturcenter, Strandgade 27B
Galerie Asbæk, Ny Adelgade 8–10
Galerie Gerly, Vandkunsten 13
Galleri Vincent, Fredericiagade 30
Gallerihuset, Studiestræde 19
Glasværkstedet, Kronprinsessegade 34B
Munkeruphus, Munkerup Strandvej 78
Nikolaj, Skt. Nikolaj Plads
Overgaden, Overgaden neden Vandet 17
Politikens Galleri, Vestergade 22
Strandstræde Keramik, Lille Strandstræde 14
Video Galleriet Huset, Rådhusstræde 13

Galleries (a selection)

Getting to Copenhagen

The quickest way to get to Copenhagen from the United Kingdom and Ireland is by air, and there are several flights daily from London, Luton, Birmingham, Manchester, Newcastle, Glasgow and Dublin. There are also several daily and weekly connections from Copenhagen to North America, Africa and Australia (see also Air Travel).

By air

Travel to Copenhagen by road and by rail has been speeded up considerably since the ferry trip between Funen and Zealand has been replaced by a tunnel/bridge motorway. This reduces the time taken by the through train to Copenhagen from the Esbjerg ferry terminal to about four hours.

By rail

Car ferries operate from the United Kingdom to Esbjerg in Jutland out of Harwich and Newcastle. In each case the trip takes about 20 hours. The

By road and sea

E20 motorway runs between Esbjerg and Copenhagen, a distance of about 180 miles. Travellers coming from Germany by road can drive up through Schleswig Holstein or get ferries from Puttgarden to Rødbyhavn and take the E45 to Copenhagen, or from Rostock to Gedser and then take the E55.

Health Care

Emergency	Call 112 (freephone)
Medical emergency service (lægevagt)	In an emergency contact the medical emergency service: inside Copenhagen: Mon.–Fri. 9am–4pm; tel. 33 93 63 00 (or 4pm–8am daily and 24 hours at weekends; tel. 32 84 00 41) outside surgery hours: tel. 38 88 60 41 The doctor's fee must be paid in cash (see Health Insurance).
Dental emergency service (tandlægevagt)	Oslo Plads 14 (by Østerport S-train station) tel. 31 38 02 51 Dental treatment must also be paid for in cash (see Health Insurance).
Hospitals, casualty departments (hospitalet)	All foreign visitors who are in Denmark for a limited period are entitled to free medical or hospital treatment if they are taken ill, if a previously diagnosed chronic condition suddenly deteriorates, or if they are in an accident. The following hospitals have casualty departments with emergency rooms in operation round the clock:

Centre: Rigshospitalet, Blegdamsvej 9
South (Amager): Sundby Hospital, Italiensvej 1
West: Frederiksberg Hospital, Nordre Fasanvej 57
North: Bispebjerg Hospital, Bispebjerg Bakke 23
Suburbs: Københavns Amts Sygehus (KAS), Nordre Ringvej, Glostrup; KAS, Niels Kildegårdsvej, Gentofte; Herlev Sygehus, Herlev Ringvej 75

Chemists	Anyone on regular medication would be well advised to take with them enough to last for their stay in Copenhagen. There are plenty of chemist shops which are open Mon.–Fri. 9am–5.30pm and Sat. 9am–1pm.
Chemists open round-the-clock	City centre: Steno-Apotek, Vesterbrogade 6C (opposite Central Station) tel. 33 91 09 60

On Amager:
Sønderbro-Apotek, Amagerbrogade 158 (near airport)
tel. 31 58 01 29

Suburbs: Glostrup-Apotek, Hovedvejen 101 (road to Roskilde)
tel. 43 96 00 20
Kongens Lyngby-Apotek, Lyngby Hovedgade 27; tel. 45 87 00 96

Health insurance	Citizens of EU countries can get treatment and essential medication under the Danish National Health Service provided they have brought form E111 with them. This has to be signed after treatment and when buying medication. Doctors' and dentists' fees must be paid in cash (see above) but some of this can be refunded at the local Danish health service office on production of the bill and form E111 – consult the Danish Tourist Board (see Information) for details. At chemists if you produce form E111 you only need pay the cost of the medication not covered by health insurance.

Hotels

Denmark is in the process of introducing a star classification system for hotels which are members of HORESTA, its Hotel, Restaurant & Tourism Industry Employers' Association. Hitherto it has had no official hotel classification system as such. Price is no guarantee of quality either. Copenhagen has 90 or so hotels and they tend to be quite expensive, although room rates are usually much lower in winter. Generally speaking most of them are in the top of the medium range category and truly grand hotels are few and far between. If you are travelling by car it is essential to find out about parking facilities in advance since very few hotels have a garage, and car parking is short-stay in most of the city. The hotels listed below are divided into four price categories. Category I is luxury hotels (double room from 1600 dkr), category II upper price range (double room from 1000 dkr), category III medium range (double from 800 dkr) and category IV budget hotels; "r" rooms.

Categories

Rooms can be booked directly with the hotel, through a travel agent or the hotel booking section of Copenhagen tourist information centre:

Hotel booking

Hotel Booking
Wonderful Copenhagen Tourist Information
Bernstorffgade 1, DK-1577 Copenhagen K
tel. 33 25 38 44, fax 33 12 40 45
(Jan.–March, Nov., Dec.: Mon.–Fri. 9am–5pm, Sat. 9am–2pm; May: daily 9am–6pm; June: daily 9am–8pm; July–mid-Sep.: daily 9am–midnight; mid–end Sep.: daily 9am–10pm)

Bookings can also be made by EASY BOOK
Århusgade 33–35, DK-2100 Copenhagen; tel. 35 38 00 37
(Mon.–Fri. 9am–6pm, Sat. 9am–2pm)
Many tour operators include Copenhagen in their tours and can offer good value packages for both groups and independent travellers.

Renting an apartment is an option worth trying for longer stays and for families with children. Centrally located apartments can be booked through:

Apartments

Citilet
tel. 33 91 30 77, fax 33 93 93 08

Rent an Apartment
tel. 33 33 08 05, fax 33 32 08 04

A Selection of Copenhagen's Hotels

★Hotel d'Angleterre
Kongens Nytorv 34; tel. 33 12 00 95, fax 33 12 11 18; 130 r
This very grand de luxe establishment is one of Denmark's best-known hotels (see Quotations, Erich Kästner), and its visitors' book is full of famous names ranging from Winston Churchill and Roald Amunden to Michael Jackson. Wiinblads, its gourmet restaurant, is decorated with masterpieces by Rosenthal artist Bjørn Wiinblad (see Famous People). The palace originally built on Kongens Nytorv in 1630 under Christian V was taken over by gastronome Gottfried Rau in 1795 who transformed it into the elegant Hotel d'Angleterre. It was revamped and extended in the late 19th c. and its ornate façade dates from 1903.

Category I
(de luxe)

★The Plaza
Bernstorffsgade 4; tel. 33 14 92 62, fax 33 93 93 62; 93 r

Opened near the central station in 1913 this grand hotel has all the inimitable style of the British Empire, with rooms the very epitome of well-appointed elegance. Even if you can afford nothing else, savour the pleasure of a quiet drink in the panelled Library Bar. The Alexander Nevsky restaurant serves Russian specialities, while Flora Danica is the place for Scandinavian cuisine.

⋆Palace
Rådhuspladsen 57; tel. 33 14 40 50, fax 33 14 52 79; 162 r
The Palace, a listed building with an imposing tower opposite the Town Hall, was commissioned by Anders Jensen in 1910 from top architect Anton Rosen. Its first year already saw King Frederik VIII contributing to its Golden Book, to be followed by other crowned heads and international celebrities such as Josephine Baker, Bob Hope and Audrey Hepburn. Its health club has very good facilities, while its Brasserie on the Square is a gourmet's delight.

Category II
(upper price
range)

⋆Ascot
Studiestræde 61; tel. 33 12 60 00, fax 33 14 60 40; 150 r
The Ascot's decorative reliefs hark back to the building in its heyday when designed as a pump room by leading architect Martin Nyrop in 1902. What was once the social meeting place of Copenhagen's bourgeoisie is now a comfortable well furnished hotel.

⋆Admiral
Toldbodgade 24–28; tel. 33 11 82 82, fax 33 32 55 42; 366 r
Eminently comfortable rambling hotel in a former 18th c. granary which still retains the original wooden beams. Beautifully appointed rooms with a view of the harbour and only a few paces from Amalienborg Palace.

⋆Kong Frederik
Vester Voldgade 25; tel. 33 12 59 02, fax 33 93 59 01; 110 r
Green box trees stand out against the venerable white façade of the building which traces its origins back to the 14th c. With its relaxed atmosphere it provides a haven of quiet, amidst its English antiques, in the bustling heart of the city. Since it is unclear which of Denmark's King Frederiks it was named after in 1898 you can admire portraits of all nine of them – a typically endearing Danish solution. The Queen's Pub, resplendent with polished wood, mirrors and brass, harks back to the good old days, and its visitors' book contains entries by King Gustav of Sweden, Desmond Tutu, Ella Fitzgerald, Sting and many others.

⋆71 Nyhavn Romantikhotel
Nyhavn 71; tel. 33 11 85 85, fax 33 93 15 85; 82 r
This lovingly restored 19th c. warehouse has a wonderfully romantic view over Nyhavn's waterfront with its old wooden ships, intimate bars and top fish restaurants; Pakhuskælderen is the hotel's own gourmet restaurant.

⋆Phoenix
Bredgade 37; tel. 33 95 95 00, fax 33 33 98 33; 212 r
The first Hotel Phoenix opened its doors in the financial district near Amalienborg Palace more than 150 years ago. The present upmarket hotel, re-opened in 1991, appears almost austere from the outside but inside abounds in fine antiques. The best of Danish cuisine is to be had in the Gyldensteen Restaurant – already a feast for the eye with its stucco and rich brocades – and in the Von Plessen gourmet rendezvous.

Radisson SAS Scandinavia
Amager Boulevard 70; tel. 33 96 50 00, fax 33 96 55 00; 542 r
Despite its size – this is Copenhagen's largest hotel – this stylish hotel

Hotel 71 Nyhavn has a romantic setting on Copenhagen's waterfront

The Hotel Phoenix, only a stone's throw from Amalienborg Palace, has two first-class restaurants

complex boasts all the trappings of luxury, from smart suites to indoor swimming pool, health club and the Copenhagen Casino.

Category III
(medium range)

★Alexandra
H.C. Andersen Boulevard 8; tel. 33 14 22 00, fax 33 14 02 84; 63 r
The late 19th c. building became a hotel in 1910. A pleasant old hotel, with 63 eminently comfortable rooms, the Alexandra boasts good service and good facilities, including underground parking and a no-smoking floor, and serves Danish specialities made in-house at its breakfast buffet.

Astoria
Banegårdspladsen 4; tel. 33 14 14 19, fax 33 14 08 02; 94 r
Eyecatching art deco building by the central station; modern comfort in the rooms.

Christian IV
Dr. Tværgade 45; tel. 33 32 10 44, fax 33 32 07 06; 42 r
Tastefully furnished hotel close by the King's Garden; try for a room off the green atrium.

Park
Jarmers Plads 3; tel. 33 13 30 00, fax 33 14 30 33; 61 r
In the west of the city, only 10 minutes from the Town Hall. Airy, generously appointed rooms; stylish breakfast room complete with chandeliers.

Category IV
(budget)

Ansgar Missionshotellet
Colbjørnsgade 29; tel. 33 21 21 98, fax 31 21 61 91; 87 r
Light, bright rooms with cheery wooden furniture.

Bertrams
Vesterbrogade 107; tel. 33 25 04 05, fax 33 25 04 02; 45 r
Welcoming establishment in Vesterbro with pleasant atmosphere; about 20 minutes from the main station.

Cab Inn Scandinavia
Vodroffsvej 57; tel. 35 36 11 11, fax 35 36 11 14; 201 r
Cabin-like rooms but with all mod cons; 15 minutes on foot from the centre.

★Ibsens
Vendersgade 23; tel. 31 13 19 13, fax 33 13 19 16; 50 r
Pleasant central hotel refurbished in 1997; individually styled rooms, some with four-posters.

Information

In the United Kingdom

Danish Tourist Board
55 Sloane Street
London SW1X 9SY
tel. (0171) 259 59 59, fax (0171) 259 59 55

In the United States

Danish Tourist Board
655 Third Avenue, 18th Floor
New York, NY 10017
tel. (212) 885 97 00, fax (212) 885 97 26

In Copenhagen

Wonderful Copenhagen Tourist Information
Bernstorffsgade 1, 1577 Copenhagen V
tel. 33 11 13 25, fax 33 93 49 69
(Mon.–Fri. 9am–5pm, Sat. 10am–2pm)
24-hour service: tel. 38 38 30 25
Hotel bookings: tel. 33 25 38 44, fax 33 12 40 45
Guided tours: tel. 33 25 38 22, fax 33 93 49 69

Tourist
information

Use It (Huset)
Rådhusstræde 13
1466 Copenhagen K
tel. 33 15 65 18, fax 33 15 75 18
Information for young people on cheap places to stay, where to eat,
what's on, etc.
(July–mid-Sep.: daily 9am–7pm, mid-Sep.–June: Mon.–Fri. 10am–4pm)

Youth Information
Centre

Information on fairs and conferences is available all year round from:
Wonderful Copenhagen Convention & Visitors Bureau
tel. 33 25 74 00, fax 33 25 74 10

Fairs,
conferences

Language

English is widely understood in Denmark, so that visitors are unlikely to
have any difficulty in getting about even if they know no Danish. It is
worthwhile, however, learning a few words of Danish – phrases of the
"Please" and "thank you" variety – and to carry a small dictionary or
phrase-book.

Danish is a Germanic language, and is not difficult to read if you have
some knowledge of German or Dutch; but spoken Danish is difficult,
mainly because of the frequent use of a glottal stop and a tendency
(shared with English) to "swallow" part of the word.

The pronunciation of some letters differs from English: d after a vowel
is softened to the sound of the in "the", or may be mute; g is hard, as in
"go", at the beginning of a syllable, but at other times is like the ch in
"loch" or is mute; j is like y in "yes"; r is a soft sound, not trilled; v before
a consonant or at the end of a word becomes the vowel u; the vowel y
is pronounced like the French u in "lune"; ej is like the vowel sound in
"high"; æ is like a in "take"; ø is like eu in French "deux"; and å has the
vowel sound of "awe". It should be remembered, when consulting a dictionary or telephone directory, for example, that the letters æ, ø and å
come at the end of the alphabet.

K.I.S.S., Nørregade 20; tel. 33 11 44 77
Studieskolen, Antonigade 6, tel. 33 14 40 22

Language schools

English	Danish	
		Some important words and expressions
America	Amerika, de forenede Stater	
an American	en Amerikaner	
England	England	
an Englishman	en Englaender	
Denmark	Danmark	
Danish	dansk	
do you speak ...	taler De ...	
I do not understand	jeg forstår ikke	
yes	ja, jo	
no	nej	
please	værsågod	

Language

English	Danish
(yes) thank you	(ja) tak
thank you very much	mange tak
no thank you	nej tak
excuse me	undskyld mig
I beg your pardon	omforladelse
good morning	god morgen
good day	god dag
good evening	god aften
good night	god nat
good-bye	farvel
gentleman	herre
lady, woman	dame, kvinde
young lady, miss	frøken
where is ...?	hvor er ...?
road, street	gaden
the road to ...	gaden vehen til ...
square (in town, etc)	plads
church	kirken
museum	museet
when?	hvornår
open	åbnet
town hall	rådhuset
post office	posthuset
police station	politistation
bank	bank
railway station	banegården, stationen
hotel	hotel
overnight (stay)	overnatning
I would like a room	jeg vil gerne have et værelse
with one bed (single room)	enkelt værelse
with two beds (double room)	doubbelt værelse
with bath	med bad
without bath	uden bad
the key	nøglen
toilet	toilettet
doctor	læge
(on/to the) right	til højre
(on/to the) left	til venstre
straight ahead	lige ud
above	oplpe, ovenpå
below	nede
old	gammel
new	ny
how much is it?	hvad koster?
dear (expensive)	dyr

	English	Danish
Traffic signs	Stop!	Stop!
	Customs	Told
	Caution!	Pas på!
	Slow!	Langsom!
	One-way street	Ensrettet
	No thoroughfare!	Ingen indkørsel!
	No through road!	
	Roadworks	Vejabejde
Geographical terms	mountain	bjerg
	peak	høj
	mountain ridge	ås
	hill	bakke

English	Danish
valley	dal
river	elv
small river	å
waterfall	foss
waterway	sund
inshore waters	vand
beach, flat stretch of coast	strand
steep rocky bank	klint
island	ø
wood, forest	skov
moor	mose
marsh, swamp	sump, kær
town, city	by
church	kirke
tower	tårn
castle, palace, mansion	slot
garden, park	have
country road	landevej
road	vej
(market) place	torv, plads
bridge	bro
railway	jernbane
ferry	færge

See Food and Drink

Gastronomic expressions

Libraries

In 1997/98 the Royal Library (Christians Brygge 8, entrance from courtyard of Christiansborg Palace) took over its modern extension built on Christians Brygge to house its vast stock of books. The Royal Library serves both as Denmark's national library and book museum. Its venerable reading room is particularly interesting.
Open: reading room and reference catalogue Mon.–Fri. 10am–7pm, Sat. 11am–6pm; exhibitions Mon.–Fri. 10am–4pm

★Det Kongelige Bibliotek

The Central Library at Krystalgade 15 has a large stock of foreign-language books, magazines and newspapers.
Open: Mon.–Fri. 10am–7pm, Sat. 10am–2pm

Hovedbibliotek

Fiolstræde 1, Open Mon.–Fri. 10am–7pm, Closed Sat./Sun.
Amager branch: Njalsgade 80, Open: Mon.–Fri. 10am–5pm, Sat. 11am–3pm

University library

Lost Property

Copenhagen Police, Slotsherrensvej 113
tel. 38 74 88 22
Open Mon.–Thu. 9am–5.30pm, Fri. 9am–2pm

Lost property office

Enquiries about lost luggage should be directed to the relevant airline or Copenhagen Air Services: tel. 32 47 47 25
Open daily 8am–9pm

On planes

Lyshøjgårdsvej 80; tel. 36 45 45 45
Open daily 7am–9.30pm

On buses

Lyshøjgårdsvej 80, Valby; tel. 38 77 88 22
Open Mon.–Wed., Fri. 9am–4pm, Thu. 9am–6pm

On trains

Markets

Flea markets

The only reminder of the old fish market that used to be on Gammel Strand is the "Fiskerkone", the monument to Copenhagen's fishwives (see A to Z, Gammel Strand). Nowadays they have been replaced by the bargain-hunters who come to browse through the stalls of the flea market that is held here on Fridays and Saturdays in summer (see Antiques). Flea markets also take place between 8am and 4pm on Saturdays from May to September behind Frederiksberg Town Hall, on Nørrebros Runddel and on Israel Plads.

The Salvation Army's Freisens-Hær market (Hørhusvej 5) is open Tuesday to Thursday from 1 to 5pm, Friday from 1 to 6pm and Saturday from 9am to 1pm.

Media

Newspapers & periodicals

English-language newspapers and periodicals are on sale at many city-centre news-stands, in the big hotels and at Central Station. Other English-language publications include the Tourist Board's Copenhagen This Week. The oldest Danish newspaper is the right-wing Berlingske Tidende which was founded in 1749 and has a circulation of around 150,000, with twice that on Sundays. The liberal daily Politiken has a circulation of around 160,000 during the week and 200,000 on Sunday. The papers with the largest circulation are the tabloids Ekstrablader (260,000) and its competitor B.T. (190,000).

Radio and TV

Danish radio has three channels. The news in English is broadcast at 8.30am Monday to Friday on Channel 3. Films on TV are shown in their original language with Danish sub-titles.

Medical Assistance

See Health Care

Motoring

Driving in Denmark

Road network

Denmark has a well-maintained and relatively uncrowded network of motorways (motorvej) and A-numbered main roads (hovedvej).

Rule of the road

Drive on the right, pass on the left.

Speed limits

Speed limits are 110kph/66mph on motorways, 80kph/48mph on other roads (70kph/43mph for cars with trailers; 80kph/50mph for coaches), and 50kph/30mph in built-up areas.
Any kind of speeding, however minor, can result in a large on-the-spot fine.

Seat belts, crash helmets

Driver and passengers must wear seat belts at all times, and motor cyclists and their passengers must wear crash helmets.

Warning triangle

Vehicles must be equipped with a warning triangle.

Priority

At junctions a row of broken white triangles on the carriageway means that traffic on the road ahead has priority. At roundabouts vehicles already on the roundabout have priority.

Cars and motorbikes must drive on dipped headlights at all times, and drivers should make sure that these dip to the right – you can be fined for using headlights that dip to the left or for not driving on dipped lights.

Lights

The maximum permitted blood alcohol level is 5 milligrammes per millilitre.

Drinking and driving

Denmark has two breakdown and towing services:
FALCK: tel. 70 10 20 30
DAHU: tel. 31 31 21 44
Both operate round the clock and charge for their services.

Breakdown

Forenede Danske Motorejere (FDM)
Firskovvej 32, 2800 Lynby
tel. 45 93 08 00
Open Mon.–Fri. 9am–5pm, Sat. 10–12am
The FDM can give technical, legal and tourist advice but does not operate a breakdown service.

Motoring organisation

Car Rental

To hire a car in Denmark you must be at least 20 years old (25 in some cases) and be able to produce a valid driving licence.

Car rental firms in Copenhagen include:

Kampmannsgade 1; tel. 33 15 22 99
Airport: tel. 32 51 22 99

Avis

Gammel Kongevej 13; tel. 33 14 01 11
Airport: tel. 32 50 30 90

Europcar/
Interrent

Ved Vesterport 3; tel. 33 17 90 00
Airport: 32 50 30 40

Hertz

Parking in Copenhagen

There are various car parks in and around the city but in the centre itself, with its one-way streets and pedestrian precincts, it is easier to get about on foot. Keep strictly to the parking and no parking rules – otherwise you risk getting a heavy fine or having your car towed away.
Parking signs with the wording "P-shive pådbudt" mean you must display a parking disc on which you have entered the time you arrived. These discs are available from police stations, post offices, banks and filling stations.
Signs worded "P" and "ZONE" denote pay and display parking where you pay for your ticket at the nearest machine and then display it on the dashboard or windscreen.

Car parks

"Parkering forbudt" means No Parking.
"Stopforbud" means No Stopping.

No Parking,
No Stopping

The inner city multi-storey car parks are usually open from 6 or 8am to 8pm or midnight. Some are closed Saturday afternoons and Sundays. Illum (Købmagergade) and Magasin du Nord (Bremerholm) also offer multi-storey parking during business hours at their department stores.

Multi-storey
car parks

Inner-city multi-stories include:
City Auto Parkering, Jernbanegade 1

Industriens Hus, H.C.Andersens Boulevard 18
Langebro Garage, Puggårdsgarde 21
Q8, Landgreven
Q8 Service, Nyropsgade 8
Q8, Nyropsgade 42
Statoil City Parkering, Israels Plads 1
Statoil Service Center, Dronningens Tværgade 4

Museums

Copenhagen Card   The Copenhagen Card (see Public Transport) provides free entrance to most of the city's museums as well as unlimited travel by public transport, and comes complete with a guide which includes information on almost one hundred museums and sights.

Museums in and around Copenhagen

Afstobningssamlingen (Royal Collection of Casts)
Vestindisk Pakhus, Toldbodgade 40
Bus: 284; open Wed.–Thur. 10am–4pm, Sat., Sun. 1pm–4pm
About 2000 antique plaster casts tracing the history of sculpture.

Amager Museum
See A to Z, Amager

Amalienborg, Royal Apartments
See A to Z, Amalienborg Palace

Aquarium
See A to Z, Akvarium

Arbejdermuseet (Danish Workers' Museum)
Rømersgade 22
Buses: 5, 7, 14, 16, 17, 24, 43, 84; S-train: Nørreport
Open: Nov.–June Tue.–Fri. 11am–4pm, Sat., Sun. 11am–5pm; July–Oct. daily 11am–4pm
Europe's first museum to tell the cultural history of the working classes was opened in 1983 as a tribute to Danish labour and class struggles since 1870. Using a series of tableaux it vividly depicts life as lived by the Danish working class.

Arken
See A to Z, Arken

Arkitekturcentret Gammel Dok
See A to Z, Christianshavn

Bakkehusmuseet
Rahbeks Allé 23
Buses: 6, 18, 27, 28
Open: Wed., Thu., Sat., Sun. 11am–3pm
Museum of literary and cultural history chronicling Denmark's Golden Age from 1780 to 1850.

Burmeister & Wain Museum
See A to Z, Christianshavn, B & W Museet

Carlsberg Museum
See A to Z, Carlsberg Brewery

Copenhagen City Museum
See A to Z, Københavns Bymuseum

Craft Museum
See Håndværksmuseet

Customs Museum
See Told-Scat Museum

Dansk Jagt- og Skovbrugsmuseum (Hunting & Forestry Museum)
Folehavevej 15–17, Hørsholm
Open: Feb.–Nov. Tue.–Fri., Sun. 10am–4pm, Sat. 12–4pm
Hunting tools from the Stone Age to the present.

Danske Filmmuseum (Danish Film Museum)
Filmhuset, Gothersgade 55
Open: Tue.–Fri. 9.30am–7pm, Sat., Sun. 11.30–7pm
Denmark's official film archive.

Davids Samling (Davids Collection)
See A to Z, C.L.Davids Samling

Dragør Museum
See A to Z, Amager

Dukketeatermuseet (Puppet Theatre Museum)
See A to Z, Dukketeatermuseet, Priors Papirteater

Experimentarium
See A to Z, Experimentarium

Erotica Museum
See A to Z, Købmagergade

Film Museum
See Danske Filmmuseum

Fredensborg Slot
See A to C, Fredensborg Slot

Frederiksborg Museum
See A to Z, Frederiksborg Slot

Frihedsmuseet (Museum of the Resistance)
See A to Z, Frihedsmuseet

Frilandsmuseet (Open Air Museum)
See A to Z, Frilandsmuseet

Gammel Dok (Architecture Centre)
See A to Z, Christianshavn

Geologisk Museum (Geological Museum)
Øster Voldgade 5–7
Buses: 10, 24, 43, 85, 384; S-train: Nørreport
Open: Tue.–Sun. 1–4pm
Besides minerals, fossils and meteorites there are exhibitions on the
geology of Denmark, Greenland and the Faroe Islands.

Georg Jensen Museum
See A to Z, Amagertorv

Gilleleje Museum
See Excursions, Gilleleje

Glyptotek
See A to Z, Ny Carlsberg Glyptotek

Guinness World of Records Museum
Østergade 16
Buses: 1, 6, 9, 10, 31, 7E, 15E, 17E
Open: daily 10am–8pm
Thousands of oddities and records from the Guinness Book of Records.

Hirschsprungske Samling (Hirschsprung Collection)
See A to Z, Hirschsprungske Samling

Holmegaard Glassworks
Fensmark near Næstved, 80km/50 miles south-west of Copenhagen
Train to Næstved then bus to Fensmark
Glassworks open: Mon.–Thu. 9.30am–12, 12.30–1.20, Fri. 9.30–12
(23.3.–20.10), Sat., Sun. 11am–3pm; closed for three weeks in July.
Glass museum open: Mon.–Fri. 10am–4pm, Sat., Sun. 11am–4pm

HT Museum
Islevdalvej 119, Rødovre
Buses: 12,125,148
Open: Wed., Sun. 10am–4pm
Old trams and buses from 1880 onwards.

Hunting & Forestry Museum
See Dansk Jagt og Skovbrugsmuseum

Kalvebod Brygge, Kaijplads 110
Open: June–Aug. daily 10am–8pm, Sep., Oct. daily 11am–6pm, end
Oct.–April Sat., Sun. 11am–6pm
Russian submarine from the Seventies.

Karen Blixen Museet
See A to Z, Karen Blixen Museet

Kastrupgårdsamlingen (Kastrupgård collections)
Kastrupvej 399, Kastrup
Buses: 9, 32
Open: April–Dec. Tue.–Sun. 2–5pm, Wed. also 7–9pm
Museum of modern Danish and foreign graphic design, temporary exhibitions and permanent display.

Knud Rasmussens Hus
Knud Rasmussens Vej 9, Hundested
Train to Hundested
Open: mid-Feb.–mid-April Tue.–Sun. 11am–2.30pm; mid-April–end Oct.
Tue.–Sun. 11am–4pm, end Oct.–mid-Dec. Mon.–Sun. 11am-2.30pm
The home of Knud Rasmussen, Danish explorer of Greenland, has exhibitions of Greenland costume and Inuit tools and implements.

Københavns Bymuseum (Copenhagen City Museum)
See A to Z, Københavns Bymuseum

Køge Museum
See Excursions, Køge

Køge Skitsesamling
See Excursions, Køge

Kongelige Stalde og Kareter (Royal Stables and Coaches)
See A to Z, Christiansborg Slot

Kronborg Slot
See A to Z, Kronborg Slot

Kunstindustrimuseet (Museum of Decorative Arts)
See A to Z, Kunstindustrimuseet

W.Ø. Larsen's Pipe Museum
See A to Z, Amagertorv

Lejre Forsøgscenter (Lejre Research Centre)
See A to Z, Lejre Forsogscenter

Livgårdens historiske Samling (Lifeguards' historical collection)
Gothersgade 100
Buses: 7, 14, 16, 17, 43; S train: Nørreport
Open: May–Sep. Tue., Sun. 11am–3pm; Oct.–April Sun. 11am–3pm
The collection recounting the history of the Royal Life Guard since 1658
is housed in the 200-year old barracks of Rosenborg Palace.

Louisiana
See A to Z, Louisiana

Marienlyst Slot (Marienlyst Palace)
See Excursions, Helsingor

Medicinsk-Historisk Museum
(Museum of Medical History)
Bredgade 62
Buses: 1, 6, 9
Guided tours: Wed.–Fri., Sun. 11 and 1pm
History of popular medicine since the Middle Ages.

Mindelunden i Ryvangen
(memorial to Danish resistance fighters 1940–1945)
See A to Z, Mindelunden

Mølsteds Museet
See A to Z, Amager

Musikhistorisk Museum
See A to Z, Musikhistorisk Museum

Nationalhistoriske Museum på Frederiksborg Slot
(National Historical Museum at Frederiksborg Palace)
See A to Z, Frederiksborg Slot

Nationalmuseet (National Museum)
See A to Z, Nationalmuseet

Nivågårds Malerisamling (Nivågård Collection)
Gl. Strandvej, Nivå; train to Nivå
Open: Tue.–Fri. 12–4pm, Sat., Sun. 12–5pm
Collection of Dutch and Italian Renaissance paintings and works from
Denmark's Golden Age (1800–1850).

Ny Carlsberg Glyptotek
See A to Z, Ny Carlsberg Glyptotek

Festal Hall in the Ny Carlsberg Glyptotek

Ordrupgårdsamlingen: a Matisse ...

Gaugin's "Mademoiselle Goupil"

Ole Roemer's Museum
Kroppedals Allé 3, Taastrup; bus: 133 from Taastrup
Open: Mon.–Thu. 9am–4pm, Fri. 9am–3pm, Sat., Sun. 2–5pm
Museum devoted to Danish astronomer Ole Roemer (1644–1710).

Ordrupgårdsamlingen
Vilvordevej 110, Charlottenlund
S-train: Klambenborg/Lyngby then bus 388
Open: Tue.–Sun. 1–5pm
Collection of French Impressionists and Danish art from the same
period.

Øresund Udstilling
Strandpark 9, Kastrup
Buses: 9, 250s, 36
Exhibition on the new bridge/tunnel between Copenhagen and Malmö
(information: tel. 32 50 55 22)

Orlogsmuseet (Danish Naval Museum)
See A to Z, Christianshavn

Palæsamlingerne (Palæ Collections)
Stændertorvet, Roskilde
Train to Roskilde
Open: 15.5–15.9 daily 11am–4pm; 16.9–14.5 Sat., Sun. 1–3pm
18th and 19th c. paintings and furniture

Pipe Museum
See A to Z, Amagertorv, Larsen's Pipe Museum

Politihistorisk Museum (Police Museum)
Fælledvej 20. Bus: 3
Open: Tue., Thu. 10am–4pm and 1st Sun. in the month 11am–3pm
Famous criminal cases and history of the Danish police.

Post & Tele Museum
Valkendorfsgade 9
New post and telecommunications museum; information: tel. 33 32 30 63

Ravhuset (Amber Museum)
See A to Z, Kongens Nytorv, Ravhuset

Ripley's Believe It Or Not Museum
Rådhuspladsen 57
Buses: 1, 2, 6, 8, 14, 16, 19, 27, 28, 29, 30, 32, 33
Open: 1.6–31.8 daily 10am–10pm; 1.9–31.5 10am–8pm
Exciting, exotic and amusing curios and rarities

Roskilde Museum
Sct. Olsgade 18, Roskilde
Train to Roskilde
Open: daily 11am–4pm
Local history museum.

Rosenborg Slot
See A to Z, Rosenborg Slot

Royal Naval Museum
See A to Z, Christinashavn, Orlogsmuseet

Museums

Søllerød Museum (Vedbæk Finds)
Attemosevej 170, Holte
Bus: 195 from Holte
Open: Tue.–Sun. 11am–4pm
Local prehistoric archaeological finds.

Sommers Veteranbil Museum (Vintage Car Museum)
Nærum Hovedgade 1, Nærum
Bus: 195 from Holte
Open: Mon.–Fri. 9am–5pm, Sat. 9am–1pm, Sun. 11am–3pm
Vintage and veteran cars (1908–1960) plus hundreds of model cars, planes and ships.

Sophienholm
Nybrovej 401, Lyngby
S-train to Lyngby then bus 191
Open: Tue.–Sun. 11am–5pm (Thu. 11am–9pm)
Temporary art exhibitions in a famous rural location.

Søren Kierkegaard Samling
See A to Z, Købrnhavns Bymuseum

Statens Museum for Kunst (State Art Museum)
See A to Z, Statens Museum for Kunst (re-opening Nov. 1998)

Storm P. Museet
See A to Z, Storm P. Museet

Teatermuseet (Theatre Museum)
See A to Z, Christiansborg Slot

Rudolf Tegners Museum
Museumsvej 19, Dronningmølle
S-train: Hillerød then bus 306
Open: March–Oct. Tue.–Sun. 9.30am–5pm
Park and hilltop museum showing the works of painter and sculptor Rudolf Tegner (1873–1950).

Tekniske Museum (Danish Technical Museum)
See Excursions, Helsingør

Telefonmuseet (Telephone Museum)
Svanemøllevej 112A, Hellerup
Bus: 1. Open: summer only, Tue., Wed. 10am–4pm, Sun. 1–4pm
Development of the telephone from 1876 to the present.

Thorvaldsens Museum
See A to Z, Thorvaldsens Museum

Tøjhusmuseet (Armory Collection of Militaria)
See A to Z, Tøjhusmuseet

Louis Tussaud's Wax Museum
See A to Z, Tussaud's Wax Museum

Vikingeskibshallen (Hall of Viking Ships)
See A to Z, Roskilde, Vikingeskibshallen

Willumsen Museum
See Excursions, Frederikssund

Zoologisk Museum (Zoological Museum)
See A to Z, Zoologisk Museum

Music

The Danish Radio Symphony Orchestra, which regularly tours abroad during the year, is Denmark's leading philharmonic orchestra. Its concerts are mostly on Tuesdays, Thursdays or Sundays in the Radio Concert Hall (Julius Thomsens Plads) and Tivoli Concert Hall or Homens Kirke. The famous Danish Radio Choir composed of 75 professional singers performs on its own or with the Radio Symphony Orchestra. Tickets and programmes are available from Danish Radio (Danmarks Radio-butikkken, Rosenoms Allé 34; tel. 35 20 30 40).

Tivoli Concert Hall (Tietgensgade) has a regular concert programme of foreign and Danish orchestras; tickets are available from Tivoli Ticket Centre, Versterbrogade 3; tel. 33 15 10 12 (Mon.–Fri. 11am–5pm) – but book early for concerts with celebrity star performers. Almost every week you can find a good concert in one of Copenhagen's churches, often showcasing young talent. The chamber music evenings in Old Fellow-Palæt (Bredgade 28; tel. 33 14 82 24) also enjoy a large following. Student concerts are regularly held in the Royal Music Conservatoire at Niels Brocksgade 1. The Louisiana Museum for modern art in Humlebæk is often a venue for other excellent concerts as well. The Danish Tourist Board (see Information) lists all these various concerts in their twice-yearly Coming Events publication.

Concerts (margin)

Det Kongelige Theater (Royal Theatre)
Kongens Nytorv 9
Buses: 1, 6, 7, 9, 10, 17, 28, 29, 31, 41

Opera/ballet (margin)

Theatre box office: open Mon.–Sat. 1–8pm
Booking by phone: tel. 33 69 69 69
Tickets also available from ticket offices (see entry). Half-price tickets for the same day: kiosk (see Ticket Offices). For programme details check in what's on in the local press or in Copenhagen this week and Coming Events.

The Royal Theatre's "Gamle" and "Nye Scene" – old and new stages – are venues for drama, opera and dance. The ballet repertoire includes works by the legendary Danish dancer and choreographer Auguste Bournonville (1805–1879) who was the Director of the Danish Royal Ballet for most of the time from 1830 to 1877. His versions of the classics include Les Sylphides (1836), Napoli (1842) and Et Folkesagne (1854), for which the most recent sets were designed by Queen Margarethe II. The more avant-garde era began with the gifted choreographer Harald Lander whose reign between 1932 and 1951 set the ballet school on its new course. The opera company has a wide-ranging repertoire, from Mozart and Verdi to Carl Nielsen and Kurt Weill. Since demand for the Royal Theatre's two stages has long since outstripped their capacity performances are also staged at alternative venues such as the "Turbinehallerne", a former power station at Adelgade 10, and "Baron Bolten" in Boltens Gård.

Popular venues for musicals include the Betty Nansen Teater, Frederiksberg Alle 57, Nørrebro Teater, Ravnsborggade 3, and Det Ny Teater, Gl. Kongevej.

Musicals (margin)

Copenhagen is famous for its annual jazz festival in July when local bands and the international greats come together to play in the many bars or outdoors in Copenhagen's squares. Traditional and modern jazz can also be heard live all year round in many of the city's cafés and jazz clubs. Several of the most popular of these are listed in the Nightlife section.

Jazz, Rock and Pop (margin)

Festivals

Venue Festival (last weekend in January)
Underground rock, especially in small music pubs.

Carnival (Whitsun)
Parades and open air concerts in Fælled park near Sortedams Sø, in Kongens Have and the city centre.

Roskilde Festival (extended last weekend in July)
Denmark's biggest rock festival at a large open-air site south of Roskilde, with a maximum attendance of 80,000. Tickets from BilletNet (see Ticket Offices) and Roskilde Posthus (Jernbanegade, DK-4000 Roskilde; information: tel. 33 15 62 64, fax 33 15 62 70).

Copenhagen Jazz Festival (early July)
Jam sessions by the very best – indoor and outdoor venues, and in the streets.

Glyptotekets Sommerkoncerter (mid August–early Sep.)
Classical concerts in the Ny Carlsberg Glyptotek

Golden Days in Copenhagen (September)
Plays, ballet, concerts and organised tours focussing on the Golden Age from 1780 to 1850.

Amager Music Festival (Sep.)
Church music on Amager

Ticket Offices

See entry

Newspapers

See Media

Nightlife

Copenhagen by night has something for everybody, from casino, pubs, clubs and discos to jazz cafés, live music bars and of course cinemas, theatres, and concerts (see Cinemas, Theatres, Music) plus, on Wednesdays, Saturdays and Sundays, Tivoli closes at 11.45 with a giant fireworks display. Many of the bars and clubs are open until 2am and later, and the streets around Nyhavn, Gammel Torv and the city centre, and in Frederiksberggade are thronged on summer nights with Copenhageners and visitors out for a night on the town.

Casino

SAS Scandinavia Hotel
Amager Boulevard 70
Open daily 2pm–4am; tel. 33 11 51 15
Stylish casino with black jack, baccarat and French roulette

Discos
(selection)

Blue Note
Studiestræde 31
Open Mon.–Sat. 11pm–5am
Favourite of the gay scene

★Annabel's
Lille Kongensgade 16
Open Mon.–Sun. 10pm–6am; tel. 33 11 00 57
Trendy disco for the smart set – no jeans!

New Fellini Night Club (SAS Royal Hotel)
Hammerichsgade 1; tel. 33 93 32 39
Open Mon.–Sat. 10pm–5am
Masterly mix of sound and light

Q House of Dance
Axeltorv 5
Open Sun–Thu. 11pm–5am, Fri., Sat. 11pm–7am
tel. 33 11 46 79
Very latest chart-toppers

Tordenskjold
Kongens Nytorv 19
Open daily 10pm–5am; tel. 33 12 43 56
Popular meeting place

Woodstock
Vestergade 12
Open Wed., Thu. 9pm–5am, Fri., Sat. 10pm–5am
tel. 33 11 20 71
Music of the Fifties and Sixties

★Bananarepublikken
Nørrebrogade 13
Open Sun.–Wed. 11pm–2am, Thu.–Sat.11pm–4am
tel. 35 36 08 30
Multi-music club from acid jazz to funk, salsa and tango

Jazz, blues, rock
and pop
(selection)

★Copenhagen Jazz House
Niels Hemmingsens Gade 10
Open Tue.–Sat. 4pm–5am; tel. 33 15 26 00
An absolute must for jazz fans, with everything from bebop to modern
jazz

Finn Zieglers Hjørne
Vodroffsvej 24
Open Mon.–Tue. 10pm–6am, Wed.–Sat. 10pm–2am; tel. 31 24 54 54
Intimate nightspot with good live music, especially mainstream jazz

★La Fontaine
Kompagnistræde 11
Open daily 8pm–6am; tel. 33 11 60 98
Spot-on jam sessions by established pros and up and coming talents

★Jazzhus Slukefter
Tivoli
Open May–Sep. daily 8pm–2am; tel. 33 14 30 74
New Orleans jazz and Dixieland

Mojo
Løngangsstræde 21c
Open daily 8pm–5am; tel. 33 11 64 53
Every variation on blues

★Momo
Griffenfeldtsgade 20, Nørrebro
Fri., Sat. live music from 9pm; tel. 31 35 80 00
The place for salsa

★De Tre Musketerer
Nikolaj Plads 25
Open Mon.–Sat. 8pm–2am; tel. 33 12 50 67
Famous jazz spot

*Pumpehuset
Studiestræde 52
Open concert days from 8pm; tel. 33 93 19 60
Insider spot with rock, pop and jazz in old pump house

Rust
Guldbergsgade 8, Nørrebro
Open daily 12 noon–2am, Wed. to 3am, Thu.–Sat. to 5am
tel. 31 37 65 33
Rock club for under thirties

Stengade 30
Stengade 18
Open Sun.–Wed. 9pm–2am, Thu. 9pm–4am, Fri., Sat. 10pm–5am
tel. 35 39 09 20
Hard rock and hip hop

Night clubs | Waterloo
Gammel Kongevej 7
tel. 31 22 39 46
Chic boîte with striptease

Wonder Bar
Studiestræde 69
Open daily 9pm–5am; tel. 33 11 17 66
Famous night club with striptease

Opening Times

Banks | See Currency

Post offices | See Post

Shops | Shops are normally open Monday to Thursday 9am–7pm (or 5.30pm in some cases), Fridays 9am–7pm – or 8pm for large department stores. On Saturdays some shops shut at 2, others at 5. Some shops close all day Monday or Tuesday.
In the summer several city-centre stores stay open on Saturday and Sunday afternoons. There are also special opening times during the pre-Christmas period.
Bakers are open on Sundays, as are smørrebrød shops, florists, kiosks and souvenir shops.
Central Station has a supermarket which stays open until midnight every night including Sundays.

Parking

See Motoring

Parks

Amaliehaven (Amalie Gardens)
Between Amalienborg Palace and Langelinie
Buses: 1,6,9,10
A stroll through Copenhagen's newest park, the Amalie gardens, opens
up a very pleasant route along the harbour from Amalienborg Palace to
Langelinie. The gardens are a feast of public art with sculptures and fea-
tures in tiling, granite, marble and bronze.

Botanisk Have (Botanical Gardens)
See A to Z, Botanisk Have

Frederiksberg Have
See A to Z, Frederiksberg Have

Kongens Have
See A to Z, Rosenborg Slot

Rosenhaven (Rose Garden)
Valbyparken, Hammelstrupvej
Bus 3; open daily 9am–7pm
Over 12,000 varieties of roses are in bloom here in June, July and August.

Police

Polititorvet
tel. 33 14 14 48

Police
headquarters

Freephone 112

Emergency

Post

Tietgensgade 35–39
Open Mon.–Fri. 10am–6pm, Sat. 9am–1pm
Poste restante will be sent here if not addressed elsewhere.

Main post
office

Open Mon.–Fri. 8am–10pm, Sat. 9am–4pm, Sun. 10am–5pm

Central station
post office

Postage for postcards and letters up to 20g within Denmark, Scandinavia
and the European Union is 3·75dkr; for elsewhere abroad it is 5.25dkr.

Postage

Telegrams can be sent from any post office or telecom centre.

Telegrams

Inside Central Station: telegram, telex and fax facilities
Open Mon.–Fri. 8am–10pm, Sat., Sun. 9am–9pm

Telecom Centre

Programme of Events

See Events

Public Holidays

January 1st
Maundy Thursday

Good Friday
Easter Monday
Day of Prayer (4th Friday after Easter)
Ascension
Whit Monday
June 5th (Constitution Day: from midday)
December 24th–26th

Public Transport

Buses/S-trains

Copenhagen has a good bus network. Buses start running at 5am on workdays and 6am on Sundays; the last buses are usually around half past midnight, but some services run through the night to 4.30am. The S-train network runs between the city centre and suburbs at between 10 and 20 minute intervals.
Information: Infozentrum, HT Terminal, Rådhuspladsen; tel. 36 45 45 45

Combined
HT bus and
train ticket

Most of Copenhagen's attractions can be reached using the combined HT bus and train ticket. You can buy this on the bus or at any station and you pay according to the number of zones that you plan to travel through. The ticket has to be time-stamped by the driver or in the ticket machine on the station platform.
Copenhagen S-train map: see opposite

Copenhagen
Card

The Copenhagen Card entitles holders to unlimited travel by bus and train throughout the Copenhagen area, plus 25–50% reductions on crossings to Sweden, and free entry to over 60 museums and attractions in and around the city and in North Zealand. The cards can be for periods of 24, 48 or 72 hours and, in 1998, cost 140, 255 and 320 dkr respectively, with half-price for children aged 5 to 11. With the card is a free guide containing a city map and information on nearly a hundred museums and other sights. Copenhagen Cards are obtainable from hotels and travel agents, tourist offices (see Information) and the Central Station. For more information contact Wonderful Copenhagen Convention and Visitors Bureau; tel. 33 25 74 00, fax 33 25 74 10.
Ticket coupons (rabatkort) are another way of getting cheaper travel and can, for example, entitle the holder to 10 rides of an hour each within two zones.

Children

Children under 7 travel free, and from 7 to 14 qualify for half-fare.

Rail Travel

Central Station

Hovedbanegården, Copenhagen's Central Station, is in the city centre just west of Tivoli. Trains leave every hour for all of Denmark's larger towns. Local trains run twice an hour to Helsingør and four to six times an hour to Roskilde. Between 6am and 9pm InterCity and expresses (lyntog) run every hour on the hour to Funen and Jutland. Seat reservations are necessary for all connections beyond the "Great Belt" (Store Bælt).

Information: tel. 33 14 17 01

Restaurants

Culinary delights

Copenhagen can satisfy the taste-buds of every type of consumer – from snacks in trendy cafés to dining out in top-class restaurants on the very

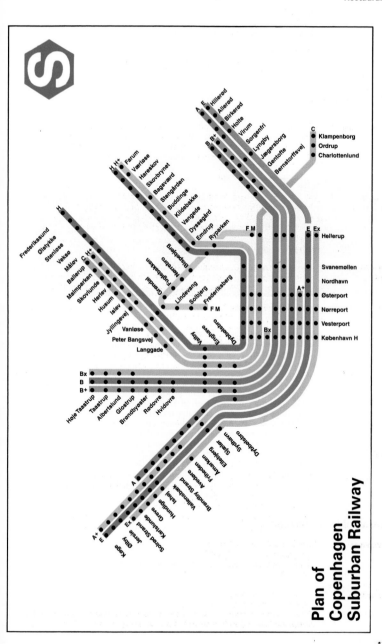

Plan of
Copenhagen
Suburban Railway

Central Station

best of gourmet cuisine. There are plenty of ethnic restaurants too, to suit the more exotically inclined. Some prices may seem high but bear in mind that they include 15% service charge and 25% MOMS, the Danish version of VAT.

Frokost,
Smørrebrød
and Koldt Bord

For a typically Danish meal try a frokost (see Food and Drink) of smørrebrød, Denmark's famous open sandwiches, or sample a koldt bord, a buffet (literally cold table) of all kinds of dishes, both hot and cold. Copenhagen's oldest and probably most famous smørrebrød restaurant is Ida Davidsen at 70 Store Kongensgade, now run by the fifth generation of Davidsens and still serving over 150 delicious variations of open sandwich – the length of its menu actually earned it a place in the Guinness Book of Records back in the Sixties. Another highly recommended establishment is the Værtshus Snaren at 2 Kompagnistræde with irresistible smørrebrød and a friendly atmosphere, while Kongens Kælder at 87 Gothersgade offers seafood and cheese specialities among the toppings on the bread of your choice.

Restaurants (a selection)

Categories

Category A – from 200 dkr
Category B – from 100 dkr
These categories are based on the average price of an à la carte meal plus VAT.

Category A

★St Gertruds Kloster
Hauser Plads 32; tel. 33 14 66 30
This gourmet establishment, with a wine list to match, promises the most exquisite food in a candle-lit medieval crypt.

Enjoying a beer in the Nyhavn

⋆Kong Hans
Vingårdsstræde 6; tel. 33 11 68 68
In another vaulted setting, this time the former wine cellar of King Hans
(1455–1513), you can dine in Denmark's first restaurant to have a
Michelin star, earned by the haute cuisine conjured up by its Alsace-born
chef Daniel Letz.

⋆Kommandanten
Ny Adelgade 7; tel. 33 12 09 90
The enchanting decor of this top restaurant, in the fine 17th c. former
abode of the city Commandant, was designed by Tage Andersen whose
museum-like florist's shop is directly opposite (see Shopping, Florists).

⋆Krogs Fiskerestaurant
Gammelstrand 38; tel. 33 15 89 15
Top place for fish. In summer you can also dine al fresco in front of this
imposing town-house (1798) overlooking the Canal and Christiansborg
Palace (p. 000).

A Hereford Beefstouw   Category B
Vesterbrograde 3; tel. 33 12 74 41
Juicy steaks and crisp salads.

⋆Café Victor
Ny Østergade 8; tel. 33 13 36 13
Stylish eating out for connoisseurs; awarded Danish Art Prize in 1993.

⋆Cap Horn
Nyhavn 21; tel. 38 28 50 42
Right on Nyhavn's waterfront with a view of the old museum ships, Cap
Horn's fish soup is a must, with breast of duck to follow (p. 155).

Cap Horn

★Den Gyldne Fortun
Fiskekælderen, Ved Stranden 18; tel. 33 12 20 11
Golden good fortune awaits lovers of seafood at this quayside Christianborg restaurant which specialises in a great variety of fish and shellfish.

Els
Store Strandstræde 3; tel. 33 14 13 41
An excellent restaurant, with its original mid-19th c. decor, the "Els" is only a few steps from Kongens Nytorv.

★Gammel Mønt
Gammel Mønt 41; tel. 33 15 10 60
Karen Rømer and Claus Christensen specialise in fabulous fish menus and delicious wild boar with hazelnut and honey sauce.

★Gråbrødre Torv 21
Gråbrødretorv 21; tel. 33 11 47 07
Extremely welcoming late 19th c. tavern in country house mode; try the smoked salmon on spinach and Bornholm chicken breast in thyme sauce.

★Philippe
Gråbrødretorv 2; tel. 33 32 92 92
Reminiscent of a Parisian bistro; Morten Sørensen cooks up a storm à la Française with moules marinières, breast of guinea fowl and truffle sauce.

Riz Raz
Kompagniestræde 20; tel. 33 15 05 75
Fine Mediterranean cuisine with lamb, feta, olives and fresh salads; very good service.

★Skipperkroen
Nyhavn 27; tel. 33 11 99 06
The smart restaurant of the "Sailors Inn" – with excellent fish dishes and a good wine list – spreads over two houses on the Nyhavn waterfront.

★Spiseloppen
Loppebyningen, Christiania,
Christianshavn; tel. 31 57 95 58
Amidst much greenery and modern art this friendly "dining hall" offers delicious food with a particular flair; try the vegetable gratin, or venison in red wine with thyme and rosemary.

Peder Oxe
Gråbrødretorv 11; tel. 33 11 00 77
Crisp salads and great smørrebrød, a lively place where everything on the menu is a real treat.

★Bali, Lille Kongensgade 4; tel. 33 11 08 08 (try Indonesian rijsttafel)
Bejing, Frederiksberggade 28; tel. 33 11 12 05 (top delicacy from the Middle Kingdom: Peking duck)
El Greco, Skindergade 20; tel. 33 32 93 44 (cheery taverna with large Greek buffet)
★Era Ora, Torvegade 62; tel. 32 54 06 93 (best of Italian cuisine)
India Palace, H.C. Andersen Boulevard 13; tel. 33 91 04 08 (try the curry Madras)
Sala Thai, Vesterbrogade 107; 31 23 03 50 (exceptional Thai delicacies)

Foreign and ethnic cuisine

Shopping and Souvenirs

Danish design, this great love of combining form and function, makes shopping in Copenhagen a real experience for very many of its visitors. Every item, from furniture to kitchen utensil, is marked by the quality, craftsmanship and elegant simplicity that are the key attributes of Denmark's timeless modern design (see Danish Design, p. 000). Shopping is one of the great pleasures of Copenhagen, even though Danish VAT (MOMS) at 25% means that many buys are not exactly on the cheap side.
To get an idea of the range of what is on offer start by looking around one of the big department stores such as Illum, Magasin du Nord, or Illums Bolighus, famous as a centre for the very latest in Scandinavian design. Copenhagen's main shopping area is centred in and around around the pedestrianised streets of Strøget and Købmagergade. Popular items on visitors' shopping lists include china from the Royal Porcelain Factory and Bing & Grøndahl, silverware by Georg Jensen and hand-blown glass from the Holmegaard glassworks, as displayed in the suitably elegant setting of Royal Copenhagen at Amagertorv 6. There is also a large selection of stores selling antiques (see entry), toys, delightful children's things, hand-made pipes, and warm sweaters. Delicacies to look out for in the food line include gravd laks, pâté, bacon, cheese and genuine Danish pastries. While alcoholic specialities such as aquavit are relatively expensive amber can be quite cheap compared with elsewhere.

Shopper's Paradise

VAT refunds on items costing over 600 dkr can be claimed by for foreign visitors. Shops taking part in this scheme display Tax-Free Shopping stickers. For further information call Global Refund Denmark: tel. 32 52 55 66.

Tax-free shopping

Specialist shops (a selection)

Ravhuset (amber specialist with three branches):
Kongens Nytorv 2 (amber museum with museum shop)

Amber

179

Shopping and Souvenirs

Frederiksberggade 34 (at the start of Strøget)
Langeliniekaj (on Langelinie)

Antiquarian bookshops	Busck Antikvariat, Fiolstræde 24 Frederiksberg Antikvariat, Gammel Kongevej 120 Harcks Einar Antikvariat, Fiolstræde 34
Antiques	See entry
Children's wear	Natoli, Grønnegade 35 (delightful children's things by Tintin etc.) Créatex Jeunesse (colourful clothing for kids)
Confectionery	★Sømod's Bolcher, Nørregade 24 and 36 (bonbon factory opened in 1891; you can watch the bonbons being made and then take away with you a big bag of the sweeties of your choice)
Craftwork	Håndarbejdets Fremme, Fredericiagade 21 (a treasure trove of handicrafts)
Delicatessen	J.Chr.Andersen's Eftefolger, Kobmagergade 32 (Danish cheese, connoisseur salads and fresh fruit) ★Fiskehuset, Hojbro Plads 19 (lobster, salmon and caviare – bliss for fish and sushi fans) ★Ole Jensen APS, CZAR, Kobmagergade 32 (cheese, cheese and more cheese)
Department stores	★Illum, Østergade 52 (legendary department store with international stock on six floors under a wonderful glass dome; also has the Louisiana museum shop, and antiques market on the third floor. Babychanging facilities in the Ladies on the 4th floor.) ★Magasin du Nord, Kongens Nytorv 13 (one of Scandinavia's biggest department stores with grand late-19th c. façade dating from the former Hotel du grand Nord, converted into a department store in 1893; famous international names as well as Danish top design; good book department.)
Duvets	Ofelia, Strøg-Arkaden, Amagertorv 3 (snug duvets of every kind)
Fashion for Him and Her	Strøget is full of boutiques selling everything from designer collections to way-out fun fashions and the very latest ready-to-wear. The cheaper stores are in the side streets off Strøget and Købmagergade. You can find modern modes in ancient settings in the Latin Quarter around the University, in Fiolstræde, Krystalgade and Rosengården, and there are more cheap fashion stores to be found in Vesterbrogade west of Central Station. Stores selling designer labels include:
Fashion stores	Bacher & Schilder, Stavangergade 6 (classics by Gant, Cottonfield, René Lezard and Peak Peformance) Carli Gry's Hus, Købmagergade 38 (young outfits with a classic slant) ★Birger Christensen, Østergade 44 (only finest fabrics by Hermes) Bison Bee-Q, Østergade 26 (chic outfits for him and her) Gucci, Østergade 46 (the name says it all) H & M, several branches including Amagertorv 23 (swinging fashion at affordable prices) ★Kaufmann, Nygade 2–4 (smart gents outfitters with Savannah, GB and other top designers) ★Monsoon, Amagertorv 16 (sumptuous British fashion in silk and velvet; romantic headgear and fabulous evening wear) ★Mads Nørgaard, Amagertorv 1 (young men's fashions) Peak Performance, Ny Østergade 10 (young chic) Red/Green, Bremerholm 1 (pricey and smart for him and her) Sand, Østergade 40 (top boutique with tradition)

★Maria Sander, Ny Adelgade 6 (elegance for that very special evening)
★Stresensee, Designer's Stock Sales, Ny Østergade 13 (factory sales of
in designers at up to 30–50% reductions)
★Sweater Market, Frederiksberggade 15 (warm sweaters and cardigans
in Scandinavian designs)

★Tage Andersen, Ny Adelgade 12 (museum-like florist with wonderful   Florists
flower arrangements and the exotic wrought-iron art made famous by
Tage Andersen)

Fog & Co., Klareboderne 16 (tasteful furnishings)   Furniture
★Illums Bolighus, Amagertorv 10 (Copenhagen's finest design store and
a Mecca for high quality furniture, textiles and handicrafts)
Toybox, Kompagnistræde 8 (Jan Egeberg supplies hand-made furniture
modelled on Disney and other cartoon characters)

C.E. Fritzsche, Komagnistræde 12 (Denmark's oldest glass dealer,   Glass
founded in 1788, Royal Warrant-holder C.E. Fritzsche is still owned by
the original family.)
Hinz/Kjær Design, Østergade 24C (modern glass from Gilleleje/North
Zealand with lovely vases and glasses)
★Holmegaard Glas, Amagertorv 10 (hand-blown glass from near
Næstved, see p. 000)

Bang & Olufsen, Østergade 3–5 (the very latest in stereo equipment from   Hi-Fi
the prestigious pioneer that quite literally set the tone for the best in hi-   equipment
fi design)

Inuit, Kompagnistræde 21 (gallery of Inuit art)   Inuit art

*Undoubtedly Copenhagen's finest store for high-quality furniture: Illum Boligus in the
heart of the city*

Shopping and Souvenirs

Jazz	Jazz Kælderen, Gråbrødre Torv 5 (everything about jazz; good CD selection)
Jewellery and silverware	English Silver House, Pilestræde 4 (fine candelabra and cutlery) ★Georg Jensen, Amagertorv 4 (masterpieces by the famous silversmith from the Twenties and Thirties, plus modern silver design; be sure to visit the adjacent Jensen Museum with exhibits from 1904 to 1940) Museums-Kopi Smykker, Grønnegade 6 (hand-made gold, silver and bronze copies of jewellery finds from the Bronze Age to the Vikings)
Lamps	Diser 37, Kompagnistræde 37 (stylish Thirties lamps) Housewarming, Lars Bjørnsstræde 5 (old lamps in elegant setting)
Leather	Bally, Østergade 55 (the name synonymous with quality) Borgen Bags, Sct. Peders Stræde 25 (fine bags and shoes) Le Pied Skoubogade 1 and Sværtegade 7 (way-out footwear fashion) Lædersmeden, Vestergade 15 (every variation on leather) ★Neye, Vimmelskaftet 28 (smart leather goods) Royal Skin, Frederiksberggade 10B (fine leather jackets and trousers) Skin Galleriet, Amagertorv 31 (way-out leather jackets and bags)
Pipes and tobacco	Paul Olsen's Tobaksblanderi, Gammel Mønt 4 (Royal Warrant-holder with exceptional blends of tobacco) ★W.O. Larsen, Amagertorv 9 (a must for pipesmokers; visit the little tobacco museum, see p. 000)
Porcelain	Artium, Vesterbrogade 1 (Scandinavian design centre with good selection of tasteful gifts) ★Royal Copenhagen, Amagertorv 6 (from Flora Danica's grand tableware to hand-painted porcelain figures, only the very best from Royal Copenhagen and by Bing & Grøndahl)

Over 400 years of tobacco history can be seen in a little museum in W.O. Larsen's pipe and tobacco shop

⋆Rosenthal Studio, Frederiksberggade 21 (masterpieces by Bjørn Wiinblad and other Rosenthal artists)

Helly-Hansen Shoppen, Nørregade 45 (top-of-the-market sailing wear and gear)

Sailing outfitters

See Leather

Shoes

Englebasserne, Vestergade 14 (everything a child could want)

Toys

Sightseeing and Organised Tours

Baedeker suggestions for sightseeing:
see Introduction Section, Sightseeing.

Baedeker suggestions

City Tour
General tour of the city: from early May to late September at least once a day. Duration 1½ hours; English-speaking guide. Depart: City Hall Square. Tickets can be bought from travel agents, hotel receptionists, or Danish tourist offices (see Information).

Coach tours
Information:
tel. 31 54 06 06

Grand Tour of Copenhagen
Grand tour covering all the major sights: all year round at least once a day. Duration: 2½ hours; English-speaking guide. Depart: City Hall Square. For ticket availability see above.

Open Top Tours – Hop-on, Hop-off
See Copenhagen from the open top of a double decker bus: daily from 9.30am to 5.30pm. Duration: approx. 1 hour, but you can hop on and hop off again when and where you like. Depart: City Hall Square. For further information contact your hotel receptionist or travel agent, or call tel. 31 55 44 22.

City and Harbour Tour
By coach and by motor boat starting from City Hall Square and ending at Gammel Strand and Strøget; pick-up from hotels possible.
From early May to mid-September at least once a day. Duration: 2½ hours.

Tour round the reception rooms at Christiansborg Palace and viewing the Crown Jewels at Rosenborg Palace.
From June to mid-September; Tue., Sat. 10am. Duration: 3 hours.

Vikingland Tour
Tour to Roskilde via the Viking Ship Museum and other Viking sites.
From early April to late October at least once a week. Depart: 9am City Hall Square.
Duration: 6 hours.

Individually packaged tours for Copenhagen and North Zealand, by car, boat, bicycle, on foot or by public transport.
Duration: 1 to 10 hours. Information: Ibis Excursion; tel. 39 62 41 62

See entry

Boat Trips

Christiania Tour
Guided walk through Christiania "free state"; every Sat., Sun. at 3pm; meet at entrance to Princessgade

Guided walks

Medieval Nightwatch
Evening walk round medieval Copenhagen; from May to Sep., Thu.–Sat. 9–10pm; meet in Gråbrødretorv. (No tours on July 2, 3, 4, 9 and 10)

Views from towers	A good way to get an overall view of the city is to climb one of the several towers which are open to the public. Copenhagen's highest point is the top of the Town Hall tower (113m/370ft) and the rather strenuous ascent is rewarded with views as far as Sweden (guided tours from 1.6 to 30.9, Mon.–Fri. 10, 12am, 2pm, Sat. 12am). Another good view is to be had from the top of the 87m/285ft high tower of the Vor Frelser Church in Christianshavn. Not so high, but worth trying if only because it is the only tower with a lift, are the viewing tower (43.5m/143ft) at the Zoo, plus there is also the Round Tower (Rundetårn) with a panoramic view from the Old Observatory.

Souvenirs

See Shopping and Souvenirs

Sport

Angling	Fishing trips on the Øresund – usually lasting 5 to 7 hours – can be arranged with a number of boat operators, including the following:

M/S Antares/M/S Arresø
Helsingør (Elsinore) harbour; tel. 30 22 36 30

M/S Hanne Berit
Rungsted harbour; tel. 30 22 36 30

M/S Kastrup
Kastrup industrial port; tel. 32 50 54 38

A fishing licence, obtainable from post offices and angling shops, is required for fishing in inland waters and offshore fishing. For further details contact the national angling association: Danmarks Sportsfisker-forbund, Worsæsgade 1, 7100 Vejle; tel. 75 82 06 99. |
| Cycling | See Bicycles |
| Football | Football is very popular with the Danes and at weekends during the season Copenhagen's main stadium at Idrætspark is the venue for league games and internationals. |
| Golf | Københavns Golf Klub
Dyrehavn 2, Lyngby; tel. 39 63 04 83
S-train to Klampenborg then bus 388 |
| Squash | Copenhagen Squash Club
Vestersøhus, Vester Sogade 58; tel. 33 11 86 38 |
| Swimming | Outdoor pools
Amager-Helgoland Søbadeanstalt, Øresundsvej (1.6.–31.8.)
Bavnehøj Friluftsbad, Enghavbevej 90 (15.5.–31.8.)
Bellahøj Friluftsbad, Bellahøjvej 1–3 (15.5.–31.8.)
Emdrup svømmebad, Bredelandsvej 20 (15.5.–31.8., otherwise indoors)
Sundby svømmebad, Sundbyvestervej (15.5.–31.8., otherwise indoors)
Vestbad, Nykær 26, Rodovre

Indoor pools
Frankrigsgades svømmehal, Frankrigsgade 35
Frederiksberg svømmehal, Helgesvej 29 |

For information about opening times contact the Tourist Information Board (see Information).

Beaches
See entry

B93
Gunnar Nu Hansens Plads; tel. 35 38 80 93
Buses: 1,6,14

Københavns Boldklub
Peter Bangsvej; tel. 38 71 41 50
Bus: 2

Tennis

Swimming Pools

See Sport, Swimming

Taxis

Taxis that are available for hire have an illuminated "Fri" sign on the windscreen. Most drivers understand English – and the fare includes the tip!

"Fri"

For taxis call: Københavns Taxa; tel. 31 35 35 35
For minibuses/disabled access: tel. 31 39 35 35

Numbers
to call

Telephone

Calls can be made from public phones in telephone boxes and post offices. These take 1, 5, 10 and 20 dkr coins or phonecards – an international call costs at least 5 dkr. Phonecards are available from DSB kiosks and post offices.

Public
telephones

National: tel 118
International: tel. 113

Directory
enquiries

To Denmark: 00 45 (NB Denmark has no area codes)
From Denmark
to UK: 00 44 then area code minus 0 followed by subscriber's number
to Canada, USA: 00 1 then area code etc.

International
dialling codes

Theatres

However attractive a visit to the theatre in Copenhagen may seem, most foreign visitors *will* have to contend with the language barrier. The exceptions are Tivoli's Commedia dell'Arte and the Mermaid Theatre. Tickets are relatively cheap and often are available at half-price on the day of the performance.

Mermaid Theatre
Vestergade 27; tel. 33 16 14 45

Shows in
English

See Music

Det Kongelige
Teater

See Music

Opera, Ballet

See Ticket Shops below

Ticket sales

Ticket Shops

Ticket shops,
box offices

ARTE, Hvidkildevej 64; tel. 38 88 22 22
Open 10am–4pm
Billet-Net, Hvidkildevej 64; tel. 38 88 70 22
Café-Teatret, Skindergade 3; tel. 33 12 58 14
Open Mon.–Fri.2–6pm, Sat. 12–4pm
Circus Building, Jernbanegade 8; tel. 33 93 37 28
Open 12–5pm
Dansescenen, Østerfaelledtorv 34; tel. 35 43 58 58
Open: Mon.–Fri. 12–5pm
DR-butikken, Rosenørns Alle 34; tel. 35 20 30 40
Open Mon.–Fri. 10am–4pm, Sat. 10am–1pm
Engstrøm + Sødring, Bordergade 17; tel. 33 14 32 28
Open Mon.–Fri. 9am–5.30pm, Sat. 9am–1pm
M&M, Nygade 1; tel. 33 12 43 50
Open Mon.–Thu. 10am–6pm, Fri. 10am–7pm, Sat. 10am–5pm
Kanonhallen, Serridslevvej 2; tel. 35 38 66 11
Open Mon.–Fri. 2–6pm, Sat. 11am–2pm
Tivoli Concert Hall Ticket Centre, Vesterbrogade 3; tel. 33 15 10 12
Open Mon.–Fri. 11am–5pm

Time

Denmark observes Central European Time, i.e. one hour ahead of Greenwich Mean Time (six hours ahead of New York time). Danish Summer Time from the end of March to the end of October is two hours ahead of Greenwich Mean Time.

Tipping

Service is included in restaurant and hotel bills, and in taxi fares, so that as a rule tips are given only for exceptional services.

Tourist Card

See Public Transport, Copenhagen Card

Tourist Information

See Information

Traffic Regulations

See Motoring

Travel Documents

Passports

All visitors from EU countries with a passport can stay up to three months without a visa. Children not entered on a parent's passport must have one of their own.

Motorists must carry their national driving licence and car registration papers. Vehicles must have a national identity sticker.

Vehicle papers

It is also wise to have the additional insurance cover of a Green Card. This is not compulsory but can save a lot of time if anything goes wrong.

When to Go

Copenhagen enjoys much the same climate as most of northern Europe. Thus the winters are not too cold, summer is seldom too hot, autumn is long and mild, and spring takes time to warm up. Come prepared for some rain although it is not likely to last for very long. Evenings can be quite chilly, even in summer, so pack something warm to be on the safe side.

Climate

Copenhagen is at its brilliant best in summer, which is also when many of its major events take place, including the big rock festival in Roskilde. The down side of all this activity is crowded restaurants and fully booked hotels. You may well choose to avoid the peak holiday period and aim instead for May, June or early September. After all, Tivoli is open from late April to mid-September and September is the month of Copenhagen's Golden Days festival. Another good time to visit is in the weeks before Christmas when the city is ablaze with lights and Tivoli opens up again for the festive season.

High season

Youth Hostels (danhostel)

Danish youth hostels offer budget overnight accommodation. There is no age-limit but a valid youth hostel card is necessary. This is obtainable from home or from the Danish Youth Hostels headquarters: Vesterbrogade 39, DK-1620 Copenhagen V; tel. 31 31 36 12. It is also possible to get an international guest card for one year or a visitor's card for one night.

Youth hostel card

Copenhagen Danhostel Amager
Vejlands Alle 200, 2300 Copenhagen S; tel. 32 52 29 08, fax 32 52 27 08
528 beds; 4km/1½ miles from City Hall Square. Disabled access.

Youth hostels

Copenhagen Danhostel Bellahøj
Herbergvejen 8, 2700 Brønshøj; tel. 38 28 97 15, fax 38 89 02 10
250 beds; 5km/3 miles from City Hall Square

Lyngby-Tårbæk Vandrerhjem
Rådvad 1, 2800 Lyngby; tel. 45 80 03 07, fax 45 80 30 32
94 beds; 8km/5 miles from City Hall Square

Ajax Copenhagen
Bavnehoj Alle 30, 2450 Copenhagen SV; tel. 31 21 24 56
33 beds; 3km/2 miles from City Hall Square

Sleep-ins

City Public Hostel Vesterbro Ungdomsgård
Absalonsgade 8, 1658 Copenhagen V; tel. 31 31 20 70, fax 31 23 51 75
202 beds; 1km/½ mile from City Hall Square.

See also Information, Youth Information Centre

Information

Index

Imprint

122 illustrations, 15 maps and plans, 1 large map at end of book

Original German text: Dr Madeleine Reincke, Dr Gerhard Eckert and Isolde Maier
Editorial work: Baedeker-Redaktion (Dr Madeleine Reincke)
General direction: Reiner Eisenschmid, Baedeker Ostfildern
Cartography: Franz Huber, Munich; Hallwag AG Bern (large map)

English translation: Alec Court, Margaret Court, Brenda Ferris, Bruce Clark, David Cocking, Crispin Warren

Source of illustrations: Baedeker-Archiv (10); Blixen Museet (1); Cabos/Reincke (98); Historia-Photo (1); IFA Bilderdienst (1); Søren Jensen (1); Helga Lade Fotoagentur (2); Louisiana Museum (2); Ullstein Bilderdienst (4); ZEFA (1)

Front cover: Powerstock/Zefa. Back cover: AA Photo Library (D. Forss)

4th English edition 1999
Reprinted 2000 (×2), 2001, 2002

Published by AA Publishing, a trading name of Automobile Association Developments Limited, whose registered office is Millstream, Maidenhead Road, Windsor, Berkshire SL4 5GD. Registered number 1878835.

Distributed in the United States by:
Fodor's Travel Publications, Inc.
201 East 50th Street
New York, NY 10022

Licensed user: Mairs Geographischer Verlag GmbH & Co., Ostfildern

Typeset by Fakenham Photosetting Limited, Fakenham
Printed in Italy by G. Canale & C. S.p.A., Turin

ISBN 0 7495 1984 3